FINANCE AGAIN

More than one billion people around the world live in poverty; most of them live in developing countries. The idea that these people might improve their living standards by becoming micro-entrepreneurs – and that financial institutions should support their initiative with small loans – has found many supporters over the last decade.

Finance against Poverty examines this theory and reviews the practical results in seven countries. Volume 1 offers an in-depth analysis of the theory and practice of microfinance, as well as policy recommendations for practitioners in the field. Volume 2 presents the empirical evidence from seven developing countries: Bangladesh, Bolivia, India, Indonesia, Kenya, Malawi and Sri Lanka.

Both volumes provide a wealth of information and research on the impacts of savings and credit on productivity, employment, poverty levels and sociopolitical relations. With its detailed assessment of both the benefits and the limitations of financial intervention, *Finance against Poverty* is the most comprehensive study of microfinance to date. It is essential reading for all those interested in development, poverty-reduction, social welfare and finance.

David Hulme is Professor of Development Studies and Director of the Institute for Development Policy and Management at the University of Manchester. **Paul Mosley** is Professor of Economics and Director of the International Development Centre at Reading University.

FINANCE AGAINST POVERTY

Volume 1

David Hulme and Paul Mosley

London and New York

First published 1996
by Routledge
11 New Fetter Lane, London EC4P 4EE

Simultaneously published in the USA and Canada
by Routledge
29 West 35th Street, New York, NY 10001

Routledge is an International Thomson Publishing company.

© 1996 David Hulme and Paul Mosley

Typeset in Garamond by
J&L Composition Ltd, Filey, North Yorkshire

Printed and bound in Great Britain by
TJ Press (Padstow) Ltd, Padstow, Cornwall

British Library Cataloguing in Publication Data
A catalogue record for this book is available from the British Library.

Library of Congress Cataloging in Publication Data
A catalogue record for this book has been requested.

ISBN 0–415–09544–1 (hbk)
ISBN 0–415–12429–8 (pbk)

CONTENTS

FIGURES

FIGURES

TABLES

ABBREVIATIONS

ACCU	Asian Council of Credit Unions
ADAB	Association of Development Agencies in Bangladesh
ADB	Asian Development Bank
ADD	Agricultural Development Division (Malawi)
ADMARC	Agricultural Development Marketing Corporation (Malawi)
AO	Area office
ARDRS	Agricultural and Rural Debt Relief Scheme (India)
B	Boliviano (monetary unit of Bolivia)
BAAC	Bank for Agriculture and Agricultural Co-operation (Thailand)
BAB	Banco Agricola Boliviano
BAMIN	Banco Minero Boliviano
BancoSol	Banco Solidario (Bolivia)
BANEST	Banco del Estado (Bolivia)
BB	Bangladesh Bank
BBD	Bank Bumi Daya (Indonesia)
BBS	Bangladesh Bureau of Statistics
BI	Bank Indonesia
BIDS	Bangladesh Institute of Development Studies
BIMAS	Bimbangan Massal (Indonesia)
BKB	Bangladesh Krishi Bank
BKD	Bank Kredit Desa (Indonesia)
BKK	Badan Kredit Kecamatan (Indonesia)
BNP	Bangladesh Nationalist Party
BPD	Bank Pembangunan Daerah (Indonesia)
BPR	Bank Perkreditan Rakyat (Indonesia)
BRAC	Bangladesh Rural Advancement Committee
BRDB	Bangladesh Rural Development Board
BRI	Bank Rakyat Indonesia
BSBL	Bangladesh Sambaya Co-operative Bank
BUD	Bank Rakyat Indonesia Unit Desa

CB	Co-operative Bank (India)
CCA	Canadian Co-operative Association
CIDA	Canadian International Development Agency
CIGP	Credit-based income-generating project
CMA	Credit and Marketing Assistant (Malawi)
COP	Client Orientation Programme (Kenya)
CRB	Co-operative Rural Bank (Sri Lanka)
CRCS	Comprehensive Rural Credit Scheme (Sri Lanka)
DFI	Development finance institution
DTW	Deep tubewell
DU	District Union (Sri Lanka)
DYD	Directorate of Youth Development (Bangladesh)
EPA	Extension Planning Area (Malawi)
FAO	Food and Agricultural Organisation
FTCCS	Federation of Thrift and Credit Co-operative Societies (Sri Lanka)
GA	Group Animator (Bangladesh)
GB	Grameen Bank
GDP	Gross domestic product
GNP	Gross national product
GS	*Gram Shebok/Shebika* (local village worker, Bangladesh)
GTF	Group Trust Fund (Bangladesh)
GTZ	(German technical assistance agency)
HAT	Hadiah Angsuran Tepat Waktu (Indonesia)
HRM	Human resource management
HYV	High-yielding variety
IDA	International Development Association
IDSS	International Development Support Services (Australia)
IFAD	International Fund for Agricultural Development
IFM	Informal financial market
IGVGD	Income Generation for Vulnerable Group Development (Bangladesh)
IIC	Interamerican Investment Corporation
ILO	International Labour Organisation
INDEBANK	Investment and Development Bank (Malawi)
INDEFUND	Investment and Development Fund (Malawi)
INE	Instituto Nacional de Estadistica (Bolivia)
IPTW	Insentif Pembayaran Tepat Waktu (Indonesia)
IRDP	Integrated Rural Development Programme (India)
ISP	Informal Sector Programme (Kenya)
JLBS	Joint Loan Board Scheme (Kenya)
JTF	*Janasaviya* Trust Fund
KCB	Kenya Commercial Bank
KIE-ISP	Kenya Industrial Estates–Informal Sector Programme

KIWA	Kikundi Cha Wanabiashara (Kenya)
KREP	Kenya Rural Enterprise Programme
KSh	Kenya shilling (monetary unit)
KUPEDES	Loan scheme for small rural enterprises operated by BRI, *q.v.* (Indonesia)
KURK	Kredit Usaha Raykat Kecil (Indonesia)
LDB	Land Development Bank (India)
LDC	Less-developed country
LLDP	Lilongwe Land Development Project (Malawi)
MHP	Million Houses Programme (Sri Lanka)
MK	Malawi kwacha (monetary unit)
MMF	Malawi Mudzi Fund
MPCS	Multi-Purpose Co-operative Society (Sri Lanka)
MRFC	Malawi Rural Finance Company
MUSCCO	Malawi Union of Savings and Credit Co-operatives
NABARD	National Bank for Agricultural and Rural Development (India)
NCB	Nationalised commercial bank
NCRCS	New Comprehensive Rural Credit Scheme (Sri Lanka)
NFPE	Non-Formal Primary Education Programme (Bangladesh)
NGO	Non-governmental organisation
NHDA	National Housing Development Authority (Sri Lanka)
NORAD	Norwegian International Development Authority
NRDP	National Rural Development Programme (Malawi)
ODA	Overseas Development Administration (UK)
OP	Outreach Programme (Bangladesh)
OTEP	Oral Rehydration Therapy Extension Programme (Bangladesh)
PL	Poverty line
PNN	Praja Naya Niyamaka (Sri Lanka)
PO	Programme organiser
PRIDE	Promotion of Rural Initiatives and Development of Enterprises (Kenya)
PRODEM	Fundación para la Promoción y Desarollo de la Micro Empresa (Bolivia)
PTCCS	Primary Thrift and Credit Co-operative Society (Sri Lanka)
R	Rupee (Indian movetary unit)
R&D	Research and development
RBI	Reserve Bank of India
RCP	Rural Credit Project (Bangladesh)
RCTP	Rural Credit and Training Programme (Bangladesh)
RDP	Rural Development Programme (Bangladesh)/Rural Development Project (Malawi)
RDRS	Rangpur and Dinajpur Rural Services (Bangladesh)

REP	Rural Enterprise Programme (Sri Lanka)
ROSCA	Rotating Savings and Credit Association
Rp	Rupiah (Indonesian monetary unit)
RRB	Regional Rural Bank (India)
RRDB	Regional Rural Development Bank (Sri Lanka)
SACA	Smallholder Agricultural Credit Administration (Malawi)
SANASA	Federation of Thrift and Credit Co-operative Societies (Sri Lanka)
SAP	Structural adjustment programme
SDI	Subsidy Dependence Index
SDR	Special Drawing Rights
SEDOM	Small Enterprise Development Organisation of Malawi
SEFCO	Small Enterprise Finance Company (Kenya)
SIDA	Swedish International Development Authority
SIMPEDES	Savings scheme organised by BRI, *q.v* (Indonesia)
SLFP	Sri Lanka Freedom Party
SMI	Small and medium industries
SUSENAS	National social survey office (Indonesia)
T&V	Training and visit extension
TABANAS	Tabungan Nasional (Indonesia)
TCCS	Thrift and Credit Co-operative Society (Sri Lanka)
Tk	Taka (monetary unit of Bangladesh)
TRDEP	Thana Resource Development and Employment Programme (Bangladesh)
UNDP	United Nations Development Programme
UNP	United National Party (Sri Lanka)
UNRISD	United Nations Research Institute for Social Development
USAID	United States Agency for International Development
VO	Village Organisation (Bangladesh)
WOCCU	World Council of Credit Unions

PREFACE

This book originates in our teaching at the Institute for Development Policy and Management at the University of Manchester in the late 1980s. This was a time of still unresolved conflict between two tendencies in developing countries: the emergence of a huge range of creative solutions to the problem of how to lend to poor people, all of them involving interference with the market mechanism, and the universal pressure from international financial institutions to remove all interferences of this kind, including interventions in financial markets. Many of the developing-country practitioners whom we taught at the time put their finger on the key questions arising out of such controversy: Who is right? When and where is intervention at the bottom end of the financial market justified? Of what kind: direct intervention, subsidy, regulation or what? Will an attempt to make such interventions cost-effective jeopardise their impact on poverty, and vice versa? The literature of that time, which for the most part consisted more of polemic and counter-polemic than of empirical investigation, did not answer these questions, and so all we could do was to pass on to our practitioner colleagues the flavour of the debate, in the hope that it might stimulate them to work out solutions that might at least have validity within their local working environment.

This felt unsatisfactory. Huge amounts of money were being thrown by national governments, international financial institutions and non-governmental organisations (NGOs) at credit-based solutions to rural poverty (particularly in the wake of the World Bank's 1990 initiative to put poverty reduction at the head of its development priorities); and yet those responsible for such transfers had, and in many cases continue to have, only the haziest of ideas of what they achieved, and how their intervention could be designed to improve matters. The studies of the Grameen Bank and other micro-enterprise finance institutions that were beginning to emerge tended to look at their chosen institution alone, and often to idealise it, so that it was extremely hard to form an impression from these studies of which of the new ideas might work in which environment. In an attempt to fill the gap, we approached the Overseas Development Administration's ESCOR fund in late 1990 for a study of 'effective financial institutions for lending to the poor' in five countries: Bangladesh, Sri Lanka, Indonesia, Malawi and Zimbabwe. The intention at that stage was to study only 'exemplary' institutions. A grant of £116,000 was awarded to us the following year, and we are most grateful to the ODA for making our field research possible.

The research project which was eventually carried out is slightly more extensive than that for which the ODA originally made provision. Early in the proceedings Zimbabwe was replaced by Kenya, in part because the 1992 drought made Zimbabwe a difficult environment for research. The case-studies of Bolivia and India were added when invitations to do consultancy work in each of those countries made it possible to include two further fascinating experiments in microfinance to our portfolio. But by 1993 it was quite clear that we were dealing, not with a set of 'exemplary' institutions, but rather with a very wide range of competence and in particular of ability to adapt to adverse circumstance. We feel that the existence of this broad spectrum of achievement within our sample has enormously enriched the findings, and we would like to be able to boast that we planned the outcome deliberately. But in truth, we cannot. It was one of those lucky accidents which defines the shape of an enterprise. As readers will discover, many of the institutions we study have themselves had their shape determined less by design than by accidents, some of them lucky and some less so.

This book is the joint work of an economist (Mosley) and a human geographer-cum-sociologist (Hulme) and we both feel that our collaboration across disciplines has improved the final product. The argument is sequential through all the chapters, and in general we take joint responsibility for everything. There is one exception. Chapter 2 is the product of Paul Mosley's belief that it is important to set out the relationship between lenders and borrowers in a formal way so as to generate hypotheses about 'what works and why' which can then be tested. Mosley therefore takes full responsibility for what is written there. Readers who hate maths and diagrams, and also those more interested in the study's conclusions than in its premises, may wish to skip this chapter and go straight from pages 15 to 42.

We have been very fortunate in our collaborators. Early in our research we had the luck to discover that Lynn Bennett of the World Bank's Asia Technical Department, in association with her colleagues Michael Goldberg and Jacob Yaron, was pursuing research on problems similar to ours and, so far as Asia was concerned, in many of the same countries. We could not have wished for a more enthusiastic and sustaining colleague, both in treading the long and painful road of applied research with us and specifically in helping us plan (in conjunction with Carlos Cuevas) the March 1995 conference at which many of the results from both projects were presented. David Wright, of the Overseas Development Administration's (ODA) small-enterprise department, helped us secure supplementary finance for this conference, in conjunction with the Norwegian Agency for Development Aid (NORAD). The field research was excellently supervised by Richard Montgomery (now of the University of Wales, Swansea), Graeme Buckley (now working for CAFOD in El Salvador), and Deb Bhattacharya (Bangladesh Institute of Development Studies) in collaboration with the principal investigators. The country case-studies of Volume 2 bear the names of the individual authors, and could not have been carried out without the help of some fifty expert and enthusiastic helpers within the developing countries where we worked, who are named at the beginning of the relevant chapters. The staff, members and clients of all our case-study institutions gave generously of their time and wisdom. Their patience, hospitality, good humour and politeness (in not pointing out the foolishness of some of our enquiries) made the fieldwork possible and often made it great fun. Back in Manchester, Jayne Hindle and Pauline Whitehead facilitated work overseas by creating order out of the chaos of our logistical and administrative arrangements. The vast majority of the word-processing on the final draft was carried out by Melanie Waller and Debra Whitehead. Finally, Georgina Hulme, Helena Mosley and our respective children are to be thanked for putting up so often and with such good humour with the absence of a 'migrant worker' from their households. Without the support of all of these the book could not have existed, but responsibility for its errors rests with the authors alone.

DAVID HULME
Manchester

PAUL MOSLEY
Reading

1

WHY DEVELOPMENT FINANCE INSTITUTIONS EXIST

Market failure versus government failure

INTRODUCTION

Enigmatic though the development process is, two propositions about it have stood the test of time: capital investment is a key factor in determining economic growth and raising incomes; and capital markets in developing countries do not, in a state of nature, work well. One of the few trustworthy findings produced by the massive recent flood of research results on comparative economic growth has been 'a positive, robust correlation between growth and the share of investment in GDP' (Levine and Renelt 1992: 942); and yet it has proved extremely difficult, especially in recent years, for the poorer countries to finance that investment through the market.[1] A very large part of such investment that has taken place in the poorer countries has been financed by public-sector authorities, often heavily buttressed by international aid, and by multinational corporations, with small farms and businesses playing only an insignificant part. The further one proceeds down the income spectrum, the harder it becomes to finance investment by borrowing from private banks, and the enterprises of the poor – both in rural areas and in the shanty towns on the edge of the cities – generally have no access to them at all. This is more than a pity, since the potential for such 'micro-enterprise' – using that term to include small farmers – is colossal. This book documents that potential, and seeks to define how it can best be tapped. In particular, it uses our own case-study research to try and learn the necessary lessons from a number of promising experiments in lending to low-income households, and thereby to try and generalise concerning which institutional designs work and which do not.

It is now no mystery why the bottom end of the capital market fails in developing countries. Most institutions regard low-income households as 'too poor' to save, while potential lenders, faced with borrowers whom they do not personally know, who do not keep written accounts or 'business plans' and who want to borrow small and uneconomic sums, are exposed to very high risks every time they lend: this has been called the *screening* problem. Worse, they are unable to shield themselves against those risks

1

by means of the familiar expedients of banks in industrialised countries, since borrowers, by hypothesis, are too poor to offer collateral, the courts too weak to repossess any collateral which is offered, and insurance against the commonest hazards which afflict small producers in developing countries – for example, drought, livestock disease and breakdown of equipment – is generally unavailable: the so-called *enforcement* problem. The problems of inadequate information and difficulty in enforcing loan repayment reinforce one another, and it is not difficult to prove (for example, Akerlof 1970; Rothschild and Stiglitz 1976) that in such conditions markets for credit and insurance may simply not exist. In practice such markets often shrink to a small supply of short-term consumption loans, provided to known individuals only by kith and kin or monopolistic informal money-lenders: the financial landscape described seventy years ago in Darling's (1924) classic study of the Punjab is still abundantly evident in all the countries studied in this book.

Since the 1930s 'development finance institutions' (DFIs) have been sponsored, usually by national governments and agencies, to fill the gap. Some of these are sectoral in focus (for example, agricultural finance corporations or small enterprise development trusts), some orientated towards specific regions, some aimed simply at 'the rural poor'. Many of them have been unsuccessful, at least in a financial sense, and a famous table in the World Bank's *Agricultural Sector Policy Paper* (World Bank 1975: annex 12) suggests that in the mid-1970s over half of a sample of 44 development finance institutions known to the World Bank had arrears rates of more than 50 per cent, implying that they stood to lose half of their capital with each passing year.[2] A reaction against the influence of such institutions began in 1973, in the shape of USAID's *Spring Review of Agricultural Credit*; although firmly rooted now in a majority of international financial institutions around the world, the ideas of this counter-revolution are still popularly known as the 'Ohio School', in honour of a group of economists at Ohio State University who gave it its intellectual underpinning. Since much of this book offers a challenge to the views of the Ohio School, it is necessary to pause briefly at this point to examine the basis for their ideas and the influence which they have had.

THE GROWTH OF THE 'OHIO ORTHODOXY'

The best-known members of the Ohio School are Dale Adams, Carlos Cuevas, Gordon Donald, Claudio Gonzalez-Vega and J.D. von Pischke, the last of these based until recently in the World Bank rather than in academe and as such a crucial conduit for the transmission of the School's ideas into the Bank's operational practice. From the wide range of publications by these authors listed in the bibliography, the following consensus of guiding principles may be distilled:[3]

2

1 a belief that credit plays a facilitating and not a leading role in the process of economic development, and in consequence that financial services should be supplied to meet existing needs, and not in advance of demand. Sometimes this general principle is expanded, as in Adams and von Pischke's most recent paper (1992: 468), to allege that 'debt is not an effective tool for helping most poor people enhance their economic condition – be they operators of small farms or micro entrepreneurs, or poor women';[4]

2 a belief in the efficacy of informal financial institutions in developing countries (informal moneylenders, rotating savings and credit associations, and 'part-time' sources of credit such as suppliers, traders, friends and relatives) in meeting such needs; in particular, an insistence that their costs are likely to be lower and their working practices more flexible than the DFIs which have been set up to replace them;[5]

3 emphasis on the crucial importance of savings mobilisation as a necessary financial discipline for lending institutions, and as a means of enabling such institutions to get to know their market better;

4 scepticism concerning the ability of all credit institutions set up by government to escape the contamination of their portfolios by loan write-offs granted following leverage exerted on government officials or legislators by powerful borrowers;

5 opposition to the idea of 'targeting' loans on specific sectors, types of economic activity or socio-economic groups;

6 hostility to the idea of subsidy for DFIs in any form, an idea well captured by the title of one of the Ohio School's most famous publications, *Undermining Rural Development with Cheap Credit.*

Before we come to any serious appraisal of the Ohio School's work, it is important to stress its positive contribution. Its emphasis on the behaviour of financial markets as a whole rather than of individual institutions within those markets, on the practicalities of how voluntary savings are mobilised, and on the political threats to the viability of rural financial institutions, has been of major value for all students of rural financial systems. It is tempting to see the Ohio School's work as the rural finance component, and indeed the advance guard, of the 'counter-revolution' in development theory (Toye 1987) which dominated the policy debate in developing countries throughout the 1980s and which has provided the intellectual ammunition for the World Bank's assault on structures of state intervention in developing countries during that period. And indeed, the Ohio School echoes not only the general preference for the market over state action given voice by writers such as Bauer, Little and Krueger, but also much of their methodological approach, including the assumption that within public-sector institutions 'rent-seeking' behaviour would dominate any attempt to outdo the performance of the private sector, and a general aversion from statistical evidence, in particular evidence to support their claim that 'informal' sources of credit offer a cheaper and more efficient service than DFIs.[6] However, the work of the Ohio School is very much more of a critique than a policy manifesto, and is pervaded by a deep ambiguity concerning what the role of government in rural financial markets should be. What may be called the hardline strand within the School insists that any DFI which is unable to make profits should be closed:

> If DFIs were to charge market rates for their services, many would soon lose their customers. Where other institutions offer competing services and the existing DFIs are financially and institutionally weak, the best course is to close the DFIs or merge them with sounder institutions. There is no reason to close DFIs that can mobilise their own funds and are profitable at market interest rates – although it might be sensible to merge them with commercial banks, which thereby would gain expertise in long-term financing.
>
> (World Bank 1989a: 106)

By contrast, a number of Ohio School writings, including Gonzalez-Vega's long essay on Indonesia (1992) and von Pischke's chapter on the Grameen Bank of Bangladesh (1991: ch. 10) go out of their way to offer generous praise to specific donor- or state-subsidised DFIs. This ambiguity forces us to ask how proposition 4 above should be interpreted, since if it is taken as an iron law of the perversion of state-sponsored DFIs by their clients' political leverage, as it is for example in von Pischke's 1980 essay, then the argument for state intervention in financial markets collapses. If, on the other hand, client leverage is only taken as a possibility, against which institutional defences may exist, then a role for intervention remains.

CRITIQUE

The difficulties with the Ohio School approach, however, go much deeper than ambivalence concerning the proper role of the state in financial markets, crucial though this is. The fundamental problem is the School's assumption (usually implicit rather than overt) that informal financial markets in developing countries are characterised by perfect competition and that those producers who can use credit productively are able to reap the advantages of such competition. It is a cliché that such informal markets, if they exist, are in fact often monopolistic; but they often do not exist. If (to fix ideas) a Malawian smallholder with two acres of maize, needing to borrow about half his average annual income for the previous five years in order to buy a 'green revolution package' of fertiliser, hybrid seed and a water pump, is unable to borrow that money from the state through a farmers' club, his alternative is often not to borrow it from a competitive network of informal moneylenders, but not to borrow at all

(Chipeta and Mkandawire 1992; Chapter 4 below). The same applies to most other poor African or Asian farmers and micro-entrepreneurs. The reason for this, to recapitulate, is (a) the scarcity of investment funds in Malawi; and (b) the presence of risks of non-repayment against which the lender cannot insure, neither by gathering more information about the borrower's motives and projected cash-flow (since the borrower cannot plausibly supply these), nor by taking collateral (since the borrower is too poor to supply it), nor by buying insurance (since that, for the same reasons, is not available for the risks in question). In such a situation, it is disingenuous to propose 'the closure of existing DFIs', hoping that the private sector will take up the slack, since that is the last thing which the private sector, anxious to limit its own risks, is likely to volunteer to do. As our field research in seven countries demonstrates, the private sector is very reluctant to invest in creating the knowledge that will push forward the frontier of financial intermediation.

An implication of the existence of hidden information (about borrowers' motivation and competence) is that those who cause such information to be revealed confer an external benefit on those who subsequently trade in the market. 'Pioneer institutions' which lend to those who have not previously borrowed encounter a very substantial risk of lending to bad borrowers, but in the course of what is often a bitter experience they are able to screen out some good from some bad borrowers. In this way they reduce the risks confronted by subsequent lenders. In some cases such as KREP and BancoSol (Vol. 2, Chapters 5 and 10) they are able to offer explicit help and advice to these successor institutions; or indeed to predecessors, such as NGOs in the same country not run on business lines. This external benefit is seldom paid for or 'internalised' (for example, a borrower who is able to demonstrate a good payment record or has received training from one bank thereby does a favour to any other bank with which he or she does business,[7] but the second bank pays nothing for the favour). Henderson and Khambata (1985) have demonstrated that there is a case for paying a subsidy equal in value to these externalities, which would equate the interest rate borrowers actually pay to that which would bring the rate of investment to its socially optimal level. This case is only valid during the period when a lending institution's lending costs are falling sharply, during which period the benefit generated by financing additional good projects (that is, with social marginal benefit in excess of social marginal costs) is likely to outweigh the costs incurred by taking on new projects which are not socially beneficial. This case for protection of 'infant financial institutions' is simply ignored by the Ohio School, which has used opposition to all credit subsidy of whatever kind as a litmus test to screen out believers in the true faith from unbelievers rather than referring the question to the test either of logical coherence or of empirical validation.

5

The evidence presented by the Ohio School against DFIs is, in fact, of two kinds. The first is related to the financial performance of development finance institutions and in particular their arrears rates, as in the case of the table from the World Bank Agricultural Credit Sector Policy paper cited earlier; and this evidence is very dismal. Adams *et al.* (1984: 1) describe the results of DFI-sponsored rural development programmes as 'disappointing'. Von Pischke (1980: 83) argues that they 'provide services of low quality'. The World Bank in its 1989 review of financial systems in developing countries goes further, insisting that 'many [DFIs] in many developing countries are insolvent, and some have actually failed. Bank insolvency is nothing new, but the scale of the problem – the number of insolvent institutions, the size of their losses and the number of countries affected – is without precedent' (World Bank 1989a: 3); and its employee S. Thillairajah (1994) describes state-financed African DFIs as having 'a 100% failure rate'. The second line of attack consists of *a priori* micro-economic analysis used to demonstrate that if the price of credit (that is, the interest rate) is capped, the aggregate quantity of credit offered is less than if the interest rate is allowed to rise to its equilibrium value.[8] Both of these ways of argument, however, beg the fundamental question, which is not the financial profitability of particular institutions, financial systems or the aggregate quantity of credit which they produce, but the benefit derived from the resources committed to them. Data on the social productivity of credit projects from sources other than the World Bank are very scarce, but the Bank's data from its annual *Reviews of Project Performance Audit Results* suggest that *ex post* social rates of return on credit projects which it evaluated over the twenty years 1960–80 – nearly all of them channelled through DFIs – is 28.1 per cent, higher than the rates of return achieved by most companies in the private sector and higher than the rate of return achieved by the Bank over the period mentioned in other natural resources related sectors (Table 1.1). Rates of return on credit projects are particularly high in India,[9] and in many cases high on projects within the Integrated

Table 1.1 World Bank: *ex post* rates of return on natural resource projects, 1980–4

Type of project	Estimated ex post rate of return (%)
Rural credit	28.1
Irrigation	17.7
Tree crops and estates	12.4
Livestock	10.8
Area-based projects	10.6
Other agriculture and rural development projects	16.3
Weighted average	18.4

Source: World Bank (1993a: 171)

Rural Development Programme (IRDP) which is now routinely stigmatised as an example of how not to do poverty-focused rural credit. Recent work within the World Bank (1993a: ix) has pointed to the undue pessimism generated by Ohio School criticisms and argues that agricultural credit and rural finance projects 'are basically satisfactory, especially when measured against the original objectives and giving more weight to production than repayments'. Clearly something very strange is going on: how can specialised farm credit institutions be so productive and so 'disappointing' at the same time? It all depends, of course, on the measuring-rod which is used, and until the critics and the criticised are using the same yardstick little reconciliation can be expected. But the reluctance of the Ohio School to subject their judgements on the efficacy of DFIs – and some of their operating procedures, such as subsidy – to the test of quantitative with-and-without comparisons has resulted in a situation where those judgements are accepted or rejected on the basis of prior faith or lack of it rather than on the basis of whether they are consistent with the available data.

Broadly similar observations apply to the question of the poverty impact of DFIs: namely that such impact is an urgent consideration for both the sponsors and the beneficiaries of development finance institutions, but that it is ignored by the Ohio School, except for the invariable assertion that any interest rate subsidy that is offered will be captured by the rich rather than the poor. This claim is not often put to the test, but a careful study of Costa Rica by Vogel (in Adams *et al.* 1984: 133–45) demonstrates, fairly convincingly, that 'approximately 80 per cent of bank agricultural credit and hence about 80 per cent of the subsidy went to the large farmers who received the largest 10 per cent of the loans'.

A preliminary balance-sheet on the Ohio School's work, then, would applaud its general equilibrium approach, its emphasis on savings mobilisation and on the politics of lending, but would convict it of idealising the 'informal financial sector', of ignoring externalities, and of failing to produce data concerning the social rate of return and the poverty impact of the institutions they are concerned to expose. It will be the concern of this study to fill in a part of the data gap mentioned for particular institutions and to do so in a way which takes due note of what is valuable in the Ohio School's approach. However, the financial landscape has changed over the last fifteen years in a way which makes the use of the global term 'development finance institution' of questionable value. So-called 'innovative' financial institutions have sprung up in every part of the developing world offering extremely varied solutions to both the screening and the enforcement problems. These institutions, in their turn, have come to be idealised, and it is a matter of major concern for the poor of the Third World and for those seeking to assist them whether they genuinely offer a new way forward, or whether, as two stalwarts of the Ohio School contend, they constitute the same approach and the same problems '*déjà vu*' (Adams and von Pischke 1992) as the old DFIs: a leopard which has indeed not changed its spots. We now discuss what is new about the 'innovative' institutions.

THE WAY FORWARD?

As noted in our first section, any organisation seeking to provide financial services to significant numbers of poor people needs to adopt approaches that make it attractive for the poor to make savings and that make effective lending feasible (from both borrower and lender perspectives). While savings have commonly been neglected by development finance institutions, credit activities have faced severe difficulties. With regard to the latter, three particular problems must be overcome: first, how to ensure that large numbers of poor borrowers can *access* loans; second, how to provide a mechanism for *screening out* bad borrowers (in terms of character and/or projects) in the absence of written records and business plans; third, how to give borrowers who cannot offer collateral an *incentive to repay* or, failing this, compel them to repay on time.

Each of these problems, however, can be tackled in different ways by mechanisms which are often complementary. The access problem can be overcome either directly, by excluding borrowers who are 'too rich' to be eligible, or indirectly by charging market-related interest rates (which do not encourage elite capture of loans); by providing loans so small that only the poor will want them; or by adopting requirements to which the wealthy will not agree (for example, compulsory attendance at weekly meetings, contributions of physical labour). The screening problem can be tackled by abandoning direct interest rate subsidies, so that borrowers take loans on the basis of prospective returns and not simply to capture subsidies; by providing loans for 'fail-safe' technical packages, fertiliser or milch cow rearing, that 'cannot go wrong'; by using borrower groups to screen for both character and proposed loan use; or by using local power structures so that senior local officials have to approve loan applications. The 'incentive to repay' problem can be approached by the use of either sticks (intensive loan monitoring and supervision, either directly by the lender or indirectly through joint liability groups) or carrots (offering progressively larger loans for good borrowers or rewards to borrowers, bank staff, even local officials, for achieving repayment targets). If all else fails, compulsory savings schemes can be developed alongside the credit operations which will partially insure the lender against default. Table 1.2 gives an indication of the 'technologies' which have been used in recent years as a means of dealing with these problems, and of institutions in which they have been tried out in the countries covered by our study.

As Chapters 3, 4 and 5 in this volume will demonstrate, many innovative

Table 1.2 Design innovations in microcredit

	Bolivia	Indonesia		India	Bangladesh		Sri Lanka		Kenya		Malawi	
	BancoSol	BPD[a] institutions	BRI[b] unit desas	RRBs[c]	Grameen	BRAC[d]	TRDEP[e]	SANASA[f]	KREP[g]	KIE-ISP[h]	SACA[i]	MMF[j]
Access methods												
Maximum income/assets	✓			✓	✓	✓	✓					✓
Small loan size	✓			✓	✓	✓	✓					✓
Screening techniques												
Market interest rates	✓	✓	✓		?	?		✓	✓			
Self-selected groups	✓				✓	✓		✓	✓		✓	
Character reference		✓	?				✓	✓	✓		✓	✓
Incentives to repay												
Intensive supervision		✓	✓		✓	✓	✓	✓	✓			✓
Peer group monitoring	✓				✓	✓	✓			✓	✓	✓
Borrower incentives (e.g. rebates)		✓	✓				✓	✓	✓			
Agency staff incentives		✓	✓		✓	✓	✓		✓			
Progressive lending	✓	✓	✓		✓	✓	✓	✓	✓			✓
Compulsory savings	✓	✓	✓		✓	✓	✓	✓	✓		✓	✓

Notes
[a] BPD = Bank Pembangunan Daerah (provincial development bank)
[b] BRI = Bank Rakyat Indonesia
[c] RRBs = Regional Rural Banks
[d] BRAC = Bangladesh Rural Advancement Committee
[e] TRDEP = Thana Resource Development and Employment Programme
[f] SANASA = Federation of Thrift and Credit Co-operative Societies (Sinhalese acronym)
[g] KREP = Kenya Rural Enterprise Programme
[h] KIE-ISP = Kenya Industrial Estates Informal Sector Programme
[i] SACA = Smallholder Agricultural Credit Administration
[j] MMF = Malawi Mudzi Fund

financial institutions have indeed shown promise in reconciling productive and redistributive impact with financial sustainability. These and other institutions have given rise in recent years to an enthusiastic literature celebrating the achievements of almost all 'new wave' microfinance schemes and especially those sponsored by NGOs – for example, ILO (1984), IFAD (1985), Devereux and Pares (1987), Panos Institute (1989), Remenyi (1991) and most recently Otero and Rhyne (1994). The message of this literature has been that if certain simple principles of design are observed, financial interventions sponsored by external agents of change can be a powerful instrument for combating innate imperfections in developing-country capital markets and for bringing about technical change in both agriculture and industry. As Remenyi argues, implicitly refuting the approach of the Ohio School,

> At this time it is difficult to assemble accurate and comprehensive data on the economic and financial impact of NGO credit-based income-generation projects of the poor. [None the less] some general observations suggested by the data are worth highlighting:
>
> 1   Where there are project-level statistics on the impact of small loans on the income of borrowers they are overwhelmingly positive and appear to be very significant;
> 2   The few internal-rate-of-return studies done and reported indicated that CIGPs (credit-based income-generating projects) may be the most profitable way in which society can invest its scarce development funds. Diminishing returns have not yet set in this field of development assistance;
> 3   If on-time repayment rates are any sort of indicator of programme effectiveness, then these data also confirm that banking on and with the poor is a very good thing to do for development generally and the alleviation of poverty in particular;
> 4   The typical successful CIGP examined in this study required an investment well below $1,000 per sustained wage-paying position created (one-tenth of the ratio in the formal sector);
> 5   The impact of CIGPs on the livelihood and prospects of the poor is dramatic rather than marginal. The reasons for this are likely to reflect two factors: the serious underinvestment in the micro-enterprises of the poor in most Third World countries; and when one is living at the margin of survival earning around $1 a day, an increase in earning capacity of 50 cents a day represents a substantial improvement in cash flow and the capacity to act on the range of economic choices available for investment, saving and consumption.
>
> (Remenyi 1991: 105–6)

Such a vision is appealing as it promises a developmental 'dream ticket' combining the efficiency objectives of the new right with the welfare concerns of those who are to the left of centre. But this may be dangerous optimism; and at the very least it lacks the support of a proper empirical data-base. For there is no such thing as a free lunch: each of the burglar-proofing devices in Table 1.2 has its costs, in terms of resources committed to administration of one kind or another intended to push incentives into the right channels, and they are by no means all watertight: witness the fact that several of the schemes examined by our research (and very many other experimental microcredit schemes) have failed some or all of the tests of financial viability, productive impact and poverty impact. The crucial questions for policy, therefore, are (a) which of the innovations listed in Table 1.2, and in which environment, has benefits that exceed its costs, and whether a design can be produced which is robust in the sense that it is likely to pass all three tests under many different environments; and (b) what forms of aid and technical assistance are most likely to foster the creation of effective microfinance institutions? These are the questions which our research seeks to answer.

ORIGINS, SCOPE AND METHOD OF THE RESEARCH PROJECT

The essence of our research method is very simple: we examine as wide a range of design options as possible, assess their results in terms of financial, technical and redistributive criteria, and seek to isolate the truly crucial design features of the successful schemes. The range of schemes examined is listed in Table 1.3. Each of these is the subject of a separate essay[10] in Volume 2 of this book. The current volume serves only to generalise and theorise across the results of the country case-studies.

Information on the performance of specific schemes was obtained partly from the schemes' financial archives, partly from a pre-coded questionnaire, and partly from structured but not pre-coded interviews with borrowers, lenders and other key informants. Interviews were carried out by locally recruited enumerators in whatever local language was appropriate, but an English 'ideal type' of the standard pre-coded questionnaire is reproduced as the appendix to Volume 2. Evaluations of project impact, such as these studies, are notoriously subject to the bias of ascribing to the project (here, the finance scheme under examination) benefits which in fact arise from non-project sources. To guard against this bias we generally measure project benefit in terms not only of change over time, but also in terms of the difference between the material welfare of borrowers and that of a 'control group' of non-borrowers, selected to be as similar as possible to the borrower group except for the characteristic of not having received a loan from a case-study institution; wherever possible we selected as a

Table 1.3 Institutions to be studied

	Bolivia	Indonesia		India		Bangladesh		Sri Lanka	Kenya		Malawi	
Name	BancoSol	BKKs and KURKs	BRI unit desas	Regional Rural Banks	Grameen Bank	BRAC	TRDEP	Thrift and Credit Co-operative Societies	KREP Juhudi Programme	KIE Informal Sector Programme	Smallholder Agricultural Credit Administration	Mudzi Fund
Type	NGO (until 1992, now commercial bank)	Village units established by regional development banks	Branches of state-financed agricultural bank	Banks jointly owned by 'sponsor' bank; State government and government of India	Statutory financial institution (80% member owned, 20% government owned)	NGO	Branch of central government	Co-operative	NGO	Parastatal	Branch of central government	Trust fund (with board members mainly from public service)
Design features real interest rate (%) (1992)	28	52	22	3	15	15	15	11	20	11	7	8
group or individual loans	G	I	I	I	G	G	G	G	G	I	G	G
loan collection method	Fortnightly on bank premises	Weekly at mobile bank offices	Mainly on bank premises	Annually, post-harvest	Weekly at group meeting place	Weekly at group meeting place	Weekly at group meeting place	Monthly at co-operative HQ	Weekly at group meeting place	Monthly at borrower's premises	Annually post-harvest	Weekly at group meeting place
Incentives to repay	Loan size dependent on prompt repayment of previous loan ('progressive lending')	Progressive lending; profit-related pay for bank and local government staff and bonus for prompt repayment	Progressive lending; bonus for prompt repayment	Threat of legal action	Progressive lending	Progressive lending	Progressive lending (but lending ceases after 4 loans)	Access to future loans, loss of compulsory savings, guarantors lose savings	Progressive lending	Collateral required	None	Progressive lending

Savings/insurance arrangements	Political environment	No. of borrowers (1992)	% female borrowers	Loan size (1992, US$)	Borrower eligibility	Restrictions on purpose of loan
Compulsory 10% deposit and voluntary savings	No government influence on interest rate or loan policy	50,000	74	322	Any person over 18 willing to form a group	Any pre-existing business
Compulsory 10% deposit and voluntary savings		700,000	55	38	No restrictions	Any productive purpose
Voluntary savings	Banks (but not statutory bodies) still subject to some residual guidance on interest rates	1.8m	24	600	No restrictions	Any productive purpose
None	Controlled interest rates on small loans; periodic union and State government amnesties; IRDP lending decisions taken by government	1.2m	—	99	Income <Rs11,000 p.a.; assets <1 ha land	Any productive purpose
Compulsory savings of Tk1 per week, 5% of loans in 'Group Fund' and 5% into 'Emergency Fund'	Minimal government influence on lending policies	1.4m	94	80	<½ acre land and other criteria	Any productive purpose
Compulsory savings of Tk2 per week, 5% of loans in 'VO Fund', 4% in 'Savings Fund' and 1% life insurance	No direct government influence on policies	650,000	75	75	<½ acre land and other criteria	Any productive purpose
Compulsory savings of Tk1 per week only	Policies determined by government	25,000	29	75	<½ acre land	Any productive purpose
Voluntary savings available and compulsory saving for borrowers	Co-operatives able to set own interest rates and lending policies with limited government oversight	700,000	50	50	<½ acre land	No restrictions: production or consumption
Compulsory 20% deposit and voluntary savings	No direct government influence on NGO lending policies	1,177	51	347	Assets of less than US$5,000	Any productive purpose
None	Policies determined by state-appointed board	1,717	23	799	Must be licensed, complete a business plan and have collateral	Any productive purpose KIE-ISP judges viable
None	Government-controlled interest rates and lending policies	400,062	28	69	<10 ha land	Only for seed and fertiliser
Compulsory savings of 20 tambala per week and 5% of loan in 'Group Fund'	No direct government control on policies, but much influence	223	82	52	<1 ha land	Any productive purpose

control group people who had been approved for, but who had not yet received, a loan from the credit institution under scrutiny.

It is right to begin our investigation with a sense of humility, even astonishment, at the achievements of microfinance institutions so far, high though the failure rate has been. Nature, as we argued earlier, both exposes the poor to the highest levels of risk and makes it difficult for them to insure themselves against those risks. This is what makes credit markets imperfect, and if there were any easy or straightforward way around the problem it would have been found and exploited long ago. The chapters which follow seek to determine which routes through the minefield offer promise in different environments. Chapter 2 illustrates the problem of 'intrinsic imperfection' in credit and insurance markets, and puts forward hypotheses as to what design features are likely to be able to attack that imperfection without distorting incentives or imposing excessive costs. Chapters 3, 4 and 5 test these hypotheses: they assess the effectiveness of the selected case-study institutions in terms of financial performance, technical impact and poverty impact, and seek to infer what contributions different design features make to performance. Chapter 6 examines the issue of state intervention, explicitly confronting the Ohio School's advice to avoid subsidies and its charge that micro-enterprise credit schemes are condemned to be subverted by political pressure from borrowers and politicians. Chapter 7 examines the management processes of successful case-study institutions: it demonstrates the ability of non-governmental organisations (NGOs), parastatals and government agencies to adopt private-sector management techniques; analyses how mobile banking systems can be administered; examines the issue of group versus individual approaches to credit; and identifies the different managerial demands that occur as institutions evolve. All of this leads up to the fundamental question of whether poverty alleviation and financial performance are in conflict (as common sense suggests) or mutually supportive (as some recent experiments suggest) and our findings on this issue are set out in Chapter 8. Chapter 9 concludes, and identifies some unanswered questions requiring further examination at country level in the case-studies of Volume 2.

NOTES

1 Gross investment rates in the twenty poorest countries listed in the World Bank's 1993 *World Development Report* averaged 12 per cent in 1991, by contrast with 28 per cent for developing countries as a whole, and 21 per cent for industrialised countries.

2 Such a consequence would, of course, only come to pass if no arrears were repaid. Major difficulties in the interpretation of arrears rate data are caused by differences in measurement between institutions, which are discussed in Chapter 3 below.

3 This list only includes propositions on which a consensus between Ohio School authors can be identified. On many issues there are differences of interpretation within the Ohio School, in particular the appropriate role of state institutions within credit markets.

4 Note the use of the word 'debt' in place of 'credit' in this quotation: a characteristic Ohio School usage, designed to shock the reader into removing the rose-tinted spectacles through which one is assumed to view DFIs.

5 See for example the introduction to Part v of von Pischke *et al.* (1983: 228):

> Moneylenders supply services desired by their clients without the costly apparatus of buildings, papers and staff, and they do this at low cost to borrowers because of proximity, their quick response to requests and the flexibility they permit in repayment. There is no doubt about the broad access of low-income rural people to such credit, nor do cultural gaps separate lenders from clients. Informal lenders are often better judges of creditworthiness among their neighbours, and better at collecting debts from them, than are institutional lenders – certainly better than many government-owned banks.

6 The Ohio School has produced a great deal of quantitative work; for example, the essays by Vogel, Cuevas and Graham, and Gonzalez-Vega in Adams *et al.* (1984): but this only documents the high costs and high arrears of existing DFIs, and says nothing about the relative costs of, or poor people's access to, credit from informal moneylenders.

7 The 'favour' consists partly of a reduced level of default associated with the transaction, and partly of lower unit administrative costs associated with the same transaction. For formal analysis, see Henderson and Khambata (1985: 360–3), also Chapter 2 below.

8 Partial-equilibrium analysis of this type assumes that 'cheap institutional credit' consists of a restriction on the maximum legal interest rate rather than, say, an x per cent subsidy on each dollar of credit offered, or other form of state support. It also ignores, of course, (a) the external effects discussed in the previous paragraph; (b) knock-on effects in other markets from that under analysis (e.g. effects on the supply and price of credit in informal markets); (c) effects working through the demand side such as the effect of cheaper credit on the consumption of borrowers and in particular on their use of new technology. But the operationally important question is not whether it is possible to construct a more complete model of the effect of intervention in the credit market, but what effect such intervention has in the real world. The number of available empirical tests of this question are still surprisingly few, hence the focus on this issue in Chapters 3 to 5 of this book.

9 For analysis, see Lipton and Toye (1990: ch. 5). For more detail on IRDP-financed projects, see Vol. 2, Chapter 14.

10 With the exception of the Grameen Bank, which has been extensively studied by other researchers (Fuglesang and Chandler 1986, 1993; Hossain 1984, 1988; Khandkar *et al.* 1993; Schuler and Hashemi 1994; Yaron 1991).

2

WHY CREDIT MARKETS FAIL THE POOR

WHY CREDIT MARKETS FAIL THE POOR

We say that the credit market *fails* if poor people – whether farmers or micro-entrepreneurs – are unable to borrow for socially beneficial projects, that is, projects with an excess of social benefits over social costs. This can happen for any of four reasons:

1 no lender is willing (or legally permitted) to pass on the extra costs associated with lending to unknown customers in small quantities;
2 no insurer is willing to compensate for borrowers' and lenders' risk-aversion (and for the presumed absence of collateral) by offering insurance against non-repayment due to natural hazards;
3 even if 1 and 2 are untrue, potential borrowers are unwilling to borrow because of risk-aversion although the expected value of their profits outweighs the expected cost of their investment, including interest and insurance payments;
4 social and private values of cost and benefit diverge because of externalities or otherwise, so that some projects which are socially profitable do not survive scrutiny on the basis of private costs and returns.

Figure 2.1 illustrates. CD and EF represent the expected profitability (marginal efficiency) of capital for groups of farmers or micro-entrepreneurs who are, respectively, risk-neutral and risk-averse. AB is the cost curve associated with lending to small-scale entrepreneurs, taking into account the additional cost of administration and insurance when dealing with the latter group. All potential borrowers with projects in region OG will invest, all borrowers with projects in region DH will not, and those in region GH will either invest or not according to risk-aversion and size of business. In Figure 2.1, all those in region GG' fail to invest even though loan and insurance markets (by hypothesis) exist and their investments, if carried out, would have been profitable. This is case 3 above.

We now consider the role of collateral and insurance. A lender who raises

16

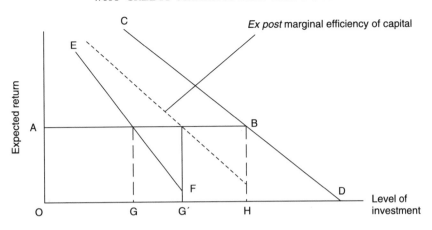

Figure 2.1 Risk, cost of capital and market failure

the value of the collateral requirement from zero to some positive amount raises the expected return E to himself:

$$E(X) = rX(1 - \pi) + (C - X - rX)\pi \qquad [2.1]$$

where π is the probability of failure of the project and C the value of the collateral to the lender, r the rate of interest paid by the borrower and X the value of the loan. As collateral is increased from zero, the second term (the lender's pay-off if the project fails) increases progressively since only the difference between the collateral and the loan amount plus interest is lost. If (as is true for most of the borrowers examined in this book) the borrower is too poor to offer collateral, the alternative is for the lender to add an insurance premium to the interest rate r, either in the form of a compulsory savings requirement or by requiring the borrower to subscribe to a private insurance scheme; in this event, the insurance scheme pays out an indemnity (in place of collateral C) if the project fails. A risk-averse lender, by raising the collateral (or insurance) requirement to levels larger than the loan size, can cause the expected return to exceed the rate of interest, a technique which can be used to circumvent the effect of interest rate ceilings.

All this is easier said than done. In practice, insurance markets may simply fail to exist for the riskiest (generally the poorest) borrowers. On only one of the thirteen schemes considered in Volume 2 (India Regional Rural Banks) did borrowers have automatic access to an insurance scheme external to the lender, and only four others (Indonesia KUPEDES and BKK, Bangladesh Grameen Bank and Kenya KREP) had a scheme of insurance against project failure out of savings compulsorily deposited by borrowers. At the high-risk end of the market it is common for insurance markets to fail to exist because of the potential insurers' inability to gauge the size of the risks to which they are subject, compounded by 'adverse selection', that is, the tendency of bad risks to demand insurance and of good risks not to demand it. A vicious circle can easily develop in which the insurer's miscalculation of the true risk first time round leads it not to raise the insurance premium to a 'realistic' level, but simply to withdraw from any attempt to insure what it perceives as the higher-risk individuals,[1] with the consequence that for some would-be purchasers of insurance (poor borrowers, in the case of Figure 2.1) the cost of borrowing-plus-insurance becomes, not just a higher level than AB, but infinity: a service which they cannot buy at any price. In such a case they will drop out of the market for loanable funds and not invest. This is case 2 of market failure above.

A third problem is that lenders cannot normally know borrowers' intentions about paying back loans. A utility-maximising borrower, using the notation of equation [2.1], will default if the utility of his or her wealth, less loss of future earnings from default (D) and of collateral if any is taken (C), exceeds the utility of that wealth when the loan amount plus interest is repaid, that is:

$$U(W - D - C) < U(W - X - rX) \qquad [2.1']$$

Utility costs of default will be higher, as Binswanger and Sillers (1983: 16) note,

> the lower the mobility of borrowers, the easier it is to trace them and attach their assets, and the more easily information about their default can be transmitted to other potential lenders.

Thus each lender must logically make a personal judgement on each potential borrower whether [2.1'] is positive or negative for the lender, and if it is negative, refuse to lend at any price. Inability to take collateral (C = 0) and legal restrictions on the interest rate which lenders can charge ($r < \bar{r}$) clearly increases the likelihood that a lender's judgement on a borrower's creditworthiness will be adverse. Even though a collateral-poor borrower may be willing to pay a higher interest rate to cover the higher risk inflicted, a lender may still refuse to lend; indeed, since the utility gain for the borrower from default increases with the interest rate charged, the expected utility for the lender may go down as the interest rate increases (Stiglitz and Weiss 1981). This is case 1 of market failure above.

Lastly, lenders may fail to lend for some projects because they are socially beneficial but not privately profitable. Two important reasons where this may occur are: a discrepancy between market prices and scarcity prices (or 'shadow prices'); and secondly, the inability of lenders to recapture the financial value of benefits which they confer (by means of, for example, training, research or the provision of information about borrowers) to other lenders. This is case 4 of market failure above, and is examined in Chapter 3.

For these reasons – externalities, risk aversion among borrowers, inability of insurers to combat adverse selection, and inability of lenders to combat moral hazards – 'good' but poor borrowers in the Third World may be unable to borrow. As noted in Chapter 1, the first wave of attempts to compensate for this market failure were not very successful. We now consider, initially at an abstract level, whether the kinds of defences erected against these problems by the 'second wave' and listed in Table 1.2 above, have any better hope of filling the gap.

FINANCIAL SUSTAINABILITY: THE REQUIREMENTS FOR 'BREAK-EVEN'

We begin this section from tautologies, by defining the requirements for break-even in a financial institution. The picture is broadened in pp. 23–32 by focusing on the design choices listed in Table 1.1, including loan supervision method, use of savings or insurance schemes, and group versus individual lending. Up to this point the focus is purely on financial viability and sustainability. On pp. 32–7 we examine the extent to which such viability is in conflict with the reduction of poverty. The way forward, by reducing the discussion to a set of hypotheses which can be subjected to empirical testing in a variety of institutional environments, is indicated on pp. 37–40.

The break-even condition for any financial institution over a period of time is simply that net income must be at least equal to total expenditure. In other words:

$$\left[\begin{array}{l}\text{income from} \\ \text{loan portfolio}\end{array} + \begin{array}{l}\text{other} \\ \text{income}\end{array}\right] \geq \left[\begin{array}{l}\text{cost of borrowing} \\ \text{(principal and interest)}\end{array} + \begin{array}{l}\text{other} \\ \text{expenditures}\end{array}\right]$$

In symbols:

$$(\alpha_j + r) \Sigma (1 - p_j) X_j + Y \geq \Sigma (\beta_j + i + a_j) X_j + Z \qquad [2.2]$$

where:

X_j = size of each loan
i = interest rate paid per unit of principal on borrowing and savings deposits
a_j = administrative cost per unit of principal
r = lending interest rate
p_j = expected default rate on loan j, i.e. expected losses due to non-repayment of principal and interest on loan j
α_j, β_j = share of principal of each loan that has to be paid back per time period to the lender (α) or by the lender (β)

Y = 'non-loan' income (consultancy fees, capital appreciation, etc.)

Z = 'non-loan' expenditure (training, outreach work, etc.)

Let us express the default rate (p), the level of administrative cost (a) and the share of principal that has to be repaid per time period (α, β) as averages for the entire loan portfolio, for example:

$$a = \frac{\sum_{j=1}^{n} a_j X_j}{\sum_{j=1}^{n} X_j} \, , p = \frac{\sum_{j=1}^{n} p_j X_j}{\sum_{j=1}^{n} X_j} \qquad [2.2']$$

If these definitions are substituted back into [2.2] we have

$$(\alpha + r)(1 - p) \geq \beta + i + a + (Z - Y)$$

$$[2.2'']$$

or

$$r(1 - p) = \beta - \alpha(1 - p) + i + a + (Z - Y)$$

or

$$r^* = \frac{(\beta - \alpha) + i + a + \alpha p + (Z - Y)}{1 - p} \qquad [2.3]$$

which expresses the break-even condition [2.2] in the form of an interest rate.

To simplify, we may assume that the share of principal that has to be paid back by borrower and lender each period is the same ($\beta = \alpha$), as are 'non-loan' income and expenditure ($Z = Y$). If this is the case, the break-even formula [2.3] reduces to

$$r^* = \frac{i + a + \alpha p}{1 - p} \qquad [2.3']$$

Let us now examine the implications of this formula for the design of LDC financial institutions. If we take typical values of the parameters of equation [2.3'] for developing countries, the borrowing rate i is unlikely to be less than 10 per cent (unless the borrowing institution is receiving subsidy from central government or international aid) and administrative costs will be at least 5 per cent.[2] In other words, even if default rates are zero, the institution will need to charge an interest rate of 15 per cent, simply to break even, and more than this to the extent that it wishes to create a surplus for reinvestment. In practice, default rates at the beginning of an experimental programme of lending to small farmers or businessmen are very seldom zero; the World Bank's Sector Policy paper (World Bank 1975: annex 12) gives an average of 38 per cent. If this value of the default rate is substituted into [2.3], then (taking $\alpha = 1$) this gives a break-even interest rate of

$$\frac{0.10 + 0.05 + 0.38}{1 - 0.38} \simeq 85\%$$

In practice, interest rates actually charged in developing countries are frequently prevented from rising to such levels by legally imposed maxima,[3] which appear to abort the chances of financial success of such schemes. A common policy recommendation in face of this problem is to remove all interest rate ceilings, and to allow financial institutions to charge whatever rate will enable them to cover costs. However, even before we come to the question of whether such an approach assists the poor, we note that it begs two major questions. The first is that if this policy is followed, it may not be easy for a pioneer banking institution to pursue a strategy of bringing new borrowers into the market, expanding loans to them and thereby lowering costs, because the level at which interest rates are set may deter those new borrowers from borrowing in the first place. Worse, following the argument of Stiglitz and Weiss (1981), a high interest rate will be harder to repay, and may actually exacerbate the rate of default. The second is that, given the imperfection of the capital market, there is a divergence between private and social benefits associated with being a pioneer lender.

These points are illustrated by Figure 2.2. When a new financial institution begins its operations, it is venturing out amongst new borrowers all of whom (by hypothesis) are poor. In consequence, few of them can offer collateral or the kind of business plan which would enable the lender to make a reliable assessment of the expected rate of return. Because of these two facts the institution will need to begin by offering small loans with a high administrative cost per dollar lent (hence a will be high) and it will be unable to distinguish reliably between good and bad borrowers (hence p will be high). At the outset, therefore, the break-even interest rate

$$r^* = \frac{(\beta - \alpha) + i + a + \alpha p + (Z - Y)}{1 - p} \qquad [2.3]$$

will be high, possibly as high as 80–90 per cent if administrative costs (a) are abnormally high at the start of operations or if heavy bills for training and outreach work exceed receipts from non-loan sources ($Z - Y$). At such a rate, the demand for loans will be restricted: the institution's only hope of survival is if still higher rates are being charged by traditional moneylenders, thereby allowing the new institution to compete for part of

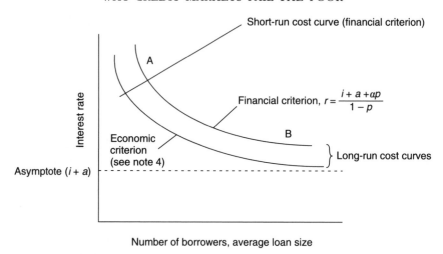

Figure 2.2 Relationship of financial and economic 'break-even' interest rate to loan size

their market, or if those moneylenders for whatever reason are unwilling to finance the type of lending propositions which the institution is willing to take on.

However, if the new institution is able to negotiate the knife-edge in which its break-even rate is barely competitive, it may be able to increase its average loan size, in which event two things will happen. In the first place, administrative cost per donor disbursed, a, will decline; in the second place the probability of default p also will decline as the lending institution learns through experience to screen out the good from the bad borrowers; in the limit, if loan recovery can be pushed up to 100 per cent, the break-even interest rate falls to the sum of borrowing and administrative costs, as in Figure 2.1. A new bank may therefore be tempted to widen its market at the outset by charging an interest rate below the 'break-even' rate, and gamble that it can recoup current losses out of future profits; in the interim, of course, it requires a subsidy until such time as it reaches break-even.

The benefits from a reduction in a and p, if they materialise, are not confined to the institution making the loans. The ability of pioneer lending institutions to identify, and sometimes to train, good borrowers through their market research activities lowers the operating costs of those borrowers themselves and the institutions which subsequently lend to them. In other words, they confer an externality by venturing into a capital market made imperfect by the presence of risk and by providing information which will enable other lenders to screen new borrowers more effectively, and by reducing the variance to which lenders' returns are subject. In consequence the 'shadow price' of loanable funds to new borrowers, or the interest rate which it is economically optimal to charge them, falls short of the 'financial break-even interest rate' (r^* in [2.3]) by the extent of the externality.[4] This was case 4 of market failure above. In Figure 2.2 we illustrate both the economic and financial break-even interest rates.

POSSIBLE TECHNIQUES FOR RISK REDUCTION

It is appropriate to see the movement down the long-run cost curve (the transition from point A to point B in Figure 2.2) as a knife-edge, which very many infant financial institutions in developing countries fail to negotiate successfully.[5] The high mortality rate is due to a number of factors, which include:

1 inability to make an accurate and realistic estimate of p, with the result that the interest rate is set too low;
2 investment of bank resources in administrative activities which do not lower the default rate but simply add to the bank's overheads;
3 political interferences in the bank's loan portfolio, staffing policy or interest rate policy;

and less spectacularly:

4 retreat by the bank from the 'frontier' of poor borrowers previously excluded from the credit market into the safer pastures of lending to rich borrowers with collateral, so that it ceases to fulfil its function of extending the credit market downwards, and becomes a conventional credit institution.

How can a pioneer institution avoid falling off the knife-edge? It will be useful to think, following Hoff and Stiglitz (1990) of direct and indirect methods by which it may seek to protect itself. *Direct* methods are those by which the lender expands resources directly (in the form of administrative expenditure, a) on screening, enforcement or insurance and hopes to gain a more than proportionate reward in the form of a lower default rate. *Indirect* methods are those by which the lender provides borrowers with an *incentive* to take actions which provide information about the riskiness of lending to them and/or which reduce the risk of default. Both direct and indirect methods have been heavily used in practice (see Tables 1.2 and 1.3), but we do not yet know which of them can be considered effective.

Direct methods

Intensive loan collection and 'incentives to repay'

It is untypical for poor farmers and entrepreneurs in developing countries to keep bank accounts, and in consequence the payment of loan instalments by them is a *discretionary* and not an *automatic* process: typically the borrower pays a cash sum to the lender at regular intervals – say once a year – on the lender's premises. This circumstance gives considerable bargaining power to the borrower,[6] and it is in the lender's interests to devise a strategy to counteract this. The most obvious such strategy is *intensive loan collection*: for example, the practice followed by the Grameen Bank (p. 27 below) of collecting loan repayments at a specific time each week at or near the borrower's premises, thereby reducing the borrower's transactions costs and increasing the pressure to repay. Logically identical is the *incentive to repay*, where the bank remits a part of the interest payment due from the borrowers who repay on time. In each case the bank's costs are *increased* by this kind of arrangement, and the key operational question for the bank is whether the additional costs, whether of supervisory labour required to monitor a scheme of this type or of discounts for prompt repayment, bring about a more than proportionate reduction in default rates, and thereby improve its cash flow. To formalise this question, let us split administrative cost (a in equation [2.2]) into three components:

$$a = a_1 + a_2 + a_3 \qquad\qquad [2.4]$$

where a_1 = supervisory expenditure (or costs or repayment incentive)

a_2 = expenditure on loan insurance (to be discussed in the following section)

a_3 = all other administrative costs (e.g., training, maintenance of buildings, other overheads).

What we require is that profitability be improved by increases in a_1, that is, if $\beta = \alpha$ and $Z = Y$,

$$\frac{\partial \pi}{\partial a_1} = \frac{\partial}{\partial a_1} (r \Sigma (1 - p_j) X_j - \Sigma(i + a_j) X_j) \geq 0$$

Using [2.2'] and [2.4] this becomes

$$\frac{\partial}{\partial a_1} ((1 - p(a_1)) r) - [i + a_1 + a_2 + a_3] \geq 0$$

i.e.
$$-r \frac{\partial p}{\partial a_1} - 1 \geq 0$$

24

i.e.
$$-r\frac{\partial p}{\partial a_1} \geq 1$$

i.e.
$$\frac{-\partial p}{\partial a_1} \geq \frac{1}{r} \qquad\qquad [2.5]$$

in other words, the 'effectiveness' of supervisory expenditure – the derivative of default with respect to it – must exceed a critical value which will be higher, the higher is the interest rate. Is this condition satisfied? The empirical evidence suggests that it may be. The data in Table 2.1 for the mid-1980s suggest that as supervisory expenditure rises, default rates fall more than in proportion.

The cost analysis in Chapter 3 will tend to confirm this relationship. Indeed, if the values of a and p reported for the Grameen Bank (12 per cent and 2 per cent respectively) are fed into equation [2.3'], then if $i = 8$ per cent we reach a break-even interest rate $r*$ of 24 per cent – very similar to the rate the Grameen Bank actually charged – by contrast with a break-even interest rate of 81 per cent for the average of 42 schemes reported by the World Bank. The derivative of p with respect to a (the slope of the curve implied by the data in Table 2.1) is approximately 32, well in excess of $\frac{1}{r}$, which, even if r is set at its most 'unfavourable' values encountered anywhere in our sample of institutions (0.05), is still only 20. As the interest rate rises, the condition for supervisory expenditure to be 'effective' becomes less stringent. Thus the condition for 'effective' administrative expenditure set by equation [2.5] appears to be well satisfied on the evidence of these preliminary calculations. For incentives to repay, we present evidence in Chapters 3 and 11 which suggests that these too earn their keep in the context of Indonesia, the only environment in which they have so far been seriously tried. The effectiveness of administrative expenditure cannot, however, be expected to be as high as this in organisations which lack the charismatic leadership and the thoroughness of outreach of the Grameen Bank.

Table 2.1 Administrative expenditure and arrears rates for a range of developing-country schemes

	Administrative expenditure (a) as % of portfolio	Arrears rate (p) as % of portfolio
BancoSol, Bolivia (1988–92)	28.0	0.6
BKKs, Indonesia (1988–92)	18.0	2.1
Grameen Bank, Bangladesh (1986)	12.3	4.5
Small Farmers' Development Programme, Nepal (1986)	7.6	11.7
Average of 42 small-farmer and small-business schemes for different developing countries (1975)	4.7	39.0

Sources: Mosley and Dahal (1987); Table 3.2 below; World Bank (1975: annexes 12 and 13)

Savings schemes and loan insurance

A second method of combating the moral hazard inherent in lending without collateral consists of requiring the borrower to contribute a specified amount each month to a compulsory savings scheme, the proceeds of which can be used to insure against certain named events which may cause the borrower's project to fail and the borrower to default. Examples of such events are (in the case of agricultural projects) drought, the death of livestock, or storm damage, and (in the case of small business projects) mechanical breakdown, the bankruptcy of a major supplier or client, or major illness. To the extent that the propensity to default on loans is caused by unexpected ill-fortune of this type, insurance against such events will also lower the default rate p, and save bank officials the costs of demoralisation, threatening letters, and so on, associated with high and rising default rates. As in the case of supervision expenditure, the point at issue is whether it will do so to such an extent that this benefit overrides the increased cost, that is, the insurance premium. By an analogous argument to that used to derive [2.5] it can be demonstrated that the condition which must be satisfied for this to be the case is

$$\frac{-\partial p}{\partial a_2} > \frac{1}{r} \qquad [2.5']$$

where a_2 is the amount of compulsory saving used as an insurance premium; again, the desirability of committing resources to compulsory savings schemes depends on their leverages on the default rate and the interest rate.

A number of writers, for example von Pischke (1991) and Yaron (1991), have argued the desirability of introducing voluntary savings schemes for agricultural and micro-enterprise borrowers, whether or not savings are compulsorily used as insurance against loan default. The arguments used include:

1 Savings in the form of a bank deposit increase both the size and the liquidity of the saver's net worth, and this provides an effective insurance to the saver against insolvency and consequent default (Remenyi 1991: 111). In other words, savings provide a partial, but administratively cheap, form of loan insurance.

2 The existence of savings deposits provides a lender with free information by distinguishing those potential borrowers who are most likely to repay. In other words, savings act as a screening device. (The argument here is in terms of reduced administrative cost of screening rather than lower probability of default; but the implications of the two lines of approach are identical.)

3 The existence of a savings scheme lowers the probability of default

because borrowers will feel more obligated to repay loans if they feel that the money they are borrowing belongs to their neighbours and colleagues rather than to an impersonal institution (von Pischke 1991: 311).

Again, the criterion for the success of such an investment is [2.5'], but the device of using a savings scheme only in lieu of an insurance scheme transfers some transactions costs from the lender to the borrower and reduces the level of a_2 below what it is with a full insurance scheme.[7] Against this, of course, factors 1 to 3 on their own provide the lender with less protection against default than a formal insurance scheme offers.

Indirect methods

Group lending and other peer-monitoring devices

The third strategy which a lender may use to move the 'break-even interest rate' constraint is to set up a structure by which the job of monitoring and encouraging prompt loan repayment is partly delegated to borrowers rather than being done by the lender alone: that is, *indirect reduction of risks.* Financial incentives to repay (such as half a per cent off the interest rate for on-time payers), the involvement of members of the local administration in the screening process, and indeed public exposure of defaulters, come into this category, but by far the most important indirect strategy the lender can use is to lend to *groups* of borrowers rather than to individuals. The logic of doing this is firstly that administrative costs (a) are reduced for the borrower (since ten loans of $100 will cost him more to make than one loan of $1,000 to a ten-person group); and secondly, that the probability of default (p) is reduced as a consequence of peer pressure to repay loans being exerted *on one another* by group members over and above the lender's pressures in the same direction. This peer pressure arises because (we may assume) no members of the group can receive credit as long as any member of it is in default on a loan, and it helps, as it is often expressed, to substitute for collateral. Very many group schemes now exist in every continent of the Third World; a number of them are reviewed by Remenyi (1991).

Two problems with the group concept will immediately be apparent. The first is that considerations of minimising administrative cost – or at any rate the lender's administrative cost – favour large groups, whereas considerations of minimising default favour small groups which will stand a better chance of effectively monitoring one another's behaviour – and of being genuinely like-minded individuals in similar material circumstances, who will have *pro tanto* less temptation to exploit one another.

This points the way to the second problem. Groups do indeed generate the positive effect of peer monitoring, but they also, potentially, generate the perverse effect that group members who are tempted to default may

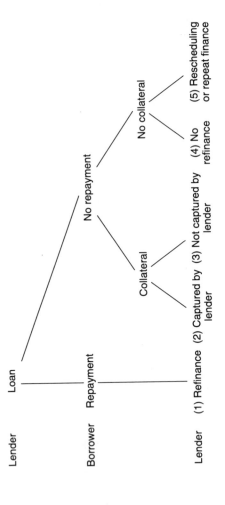

Game 1: Individual credit

Game 2: Group credit with automatic penalties

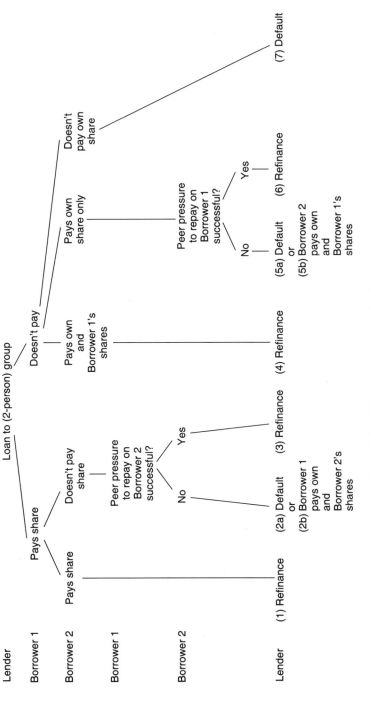

Figure 2.3 Individual and group lending as games

ask another group member to pay on their behalf in addition to their own share (possibly pleading poverty or misfortune), an option which is not available with individual lending schemes. The decision between group and individual lending schemes depends, then, first of all on the relative level of administrative costs under each scheme and, secondly, on whether the peer-monitoring advantage of group schemes dominates or is dominated by the within-group exploitation effect.

Both of these issues are clarified by regarding the act of lending as a *game*: a two-person game involving borrower and lender only in the case of individual credit, and a multi-person game in the case of group credit. The game is *non-zero-sum*: that is, both parties (all parties in the group lending case) gain more from playing the game according to the rules (disbursement on time, and repayment on time) than not playing it at all. But the borrower (only) gains even more from playing the game against the rules (that is, taking the loan and not repaying) *if, that is, the lender is unable to devise effective sanctions against this behaviour*. If lending is to an individual the possible threats are repossession of collateral (if there is any) and refusal of further credit; if it is to a group we may add the possibility of a social penalty on defaulters, which may take either a material or, more normally, an intangible form such as ostracism and loss of social standing.

Figure 2.3 clarifies the moves which each party may make in either game, making the simplifying assumption that in the group credit case there are only two players in the group. There are five possible outcomes in the individual credit case and nine in the group credit case. To make a comparison between the two we need to assign pay-offs to each outcome. Taking the individual credit case first, let us assume for simplicity that the recipient is limited to two strategies once an initial loan has been

		Lender	
		Relend	Not relend
Borrower	Repay	(case 1) *l,b*	(cases 3 & 5) $-\lambda, b+\beta$
	Not repay		(cases 2 & 4) 0,0

Figure 2.4a Pay-offs in the simplest individual-credit case

30

made (to repay it or not) and that the donor is likewise restricted to two responses (to relend or not to relend).

Let the pay-off to each party in the event of breakdown of negotiations (no repayment, no follow-on loan) be zero. If both parties behave in the orthodox manner (borrower repays, lender relends) the short-term cash-flows of both parties benefit the lender to the extent of l and the borrower to an extent b. We call this the *co-operative outcome*. But if the borrower fails to repay and the lender (for example, under political pressure, or in hope of future repayment) forgives this, then the borrower is better off than under the co-operative outcome to an amount β, whereas the lender is at least as badly off as under the co-operative outcome and (we would argue) worse off than this to an amount λ, because his exposure to a demonstrably untrustworthy borrower has increased. In other words, we have a classic situation of *prisoners' dilemma*, as shown in Figure 2.4a: co-operation is better for both parties than conflict, but for one of the parties exploitation is better still. The prisoners' dilemma is one-sided, because if the borrower repays, the lender has no motive to refuse refinance.

The obvious counter-strategy for the donor is the threat never to implement the strategy *Relend* if the borrower implements *Not repay*: but if this punishment strategy is to be credible it imposes obvious costs, in particular of loan supervision, as discussed under 1 above. The alternative strategy of group lending enables those costs to be shared with members of the borrower group, *and invites them to take countervailing action*.

To examine the forces at work consider, in the first instance, Figure 2.4b,

Borrower 1

		Overpay	Pay	Underpay
	Overpay			(case 5b) $b_1 + \beta_1, b_2 - \beta_2$
ᵔrrower 2	Pay		(case 1) b_1, b_2	if $r > s$: $0, -\beta_2$ (case 5a) if $s > r$: b_1, b_2 (case 6)
	Underpay	(case 2b) $b_1 - \beta_1, b_2 + \beta_2$	if $r > s$: $-\beta_1, 0$ (case 2a) if $s > r$: b_1, b_2 (case 3)	(case 7) $0,0$

Figure 2.4b Pay-offs in the group-credit case (case 2: Lender imposes automatic penalty)

which represents only the game between the two borrowers within the group, and assumes that if all or part of a group loan is outstanding, the lender invokes his threat never to relend. The group is sustainable *either* if both borrowers pay their share on time (case 1 of the 'game tree') *or* if exploitative behaviour on the part of one borrower is compensated by altruistic behaviour on the part of the other borrower (cases 2b and 5b). It collapses if neither borrower pays (case 7) or if only one does (cases 2a and 5a). What is missing from this story is, of course, the social penalty imposed on defaulting group members by those who do not default. As an initial simplifying assumption let us assume that this social penalty is fixed at a level s and is unrelated to the borrower's capacity to repay. Under this assumption, if the social penalty exceeds the value of the financial penalty r imposed by repaying the loan instalment due, then peer pressure will be effective, and we shall have cases 3 and 6; if it does not, peer pressure will fail, and we are back with cases 2a and 5a.

If social pressures to repay within the group are strong enough, then group lending will be a more effective means of securing group repayment than individual lending for two reasons: (a) if some group members threaten to default, peer pressure will discourage them from doing so; (b) if this fails to work, richer group members may bail them out. Strategy (b), however, may come unstuck. We shall wish to consider the hypothesis that *social pressures to repay are stronger, the more homogeneous the level of income and wealth within the group*; in the limiting case, where all group members have equal income, 'free riding' has no rationale, and (b) should not arise. There are also, as we saw, some administrative economies to be derived from the provision of group credit. Hence we can say with some confidence that group credit will move the break-even locus (2) downwards so long as group sanctions are effective and the pathological cases (2b) and (5b), in which group members unsuccessfully gamble that others will pay their share, are avoided. Under what conditions will group sanctions be effective? We take up this question in more detail in Chapter 7, where we shall wish in particular to consider the hypothesis: the smaller the group, the tighter are intra-group linkages, and the more effective will social penalties against non-repayment be.

CREDIT AND POVERTY IMPACT

We now expand the analytical framework to examine the circumstances under which variations in the conditions under which credit is made available to low-income farmers and businessmen will influence output and poverty. The key links in the chain are:

1 an *investment function*, linking the price of credit (the interest rate) to the quantity of productive investment that it makes possible;

2 an *employment function*, linking the amount of productive investment carried out to the number of employment and self-employment opportunities that it creates;

3 an *employment-poverty reduction linkage*.

We concern ourselves here only with the likely shape of the relationship, and with the influences which are likely to disturb them from outside.

The investment function

Other things being equal, the demand curve for productive investment will be downward-sloping as in Figure 2.1: the lower the rate of interest, the lower the rate of return that is required to realise a profit, and the larger the number of investments that will be profitable. Not all the investment financed by a 'pioneer' bank, of course, will be a net increment to the capital stock; some of it will consist of borrowers already within the capital market who switch to the new institution once it becomes able to offer them better terms. Hence the net investment function for the rural economy as a whole will be steeper (less responsive to the entry of the new bank) than that for the new bank alone. In the discussion which follows we assume that the function relating net new investment to the new bank's interest rate remains negatively sloped, but this is an empirical question which our research must resolve.

Figure 2.5 links up this idea with the discussion in the previous section. It

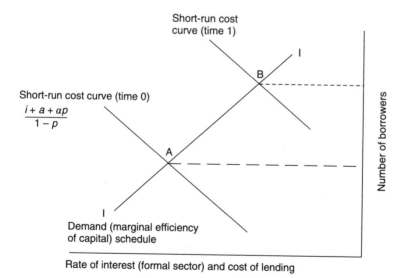

Figure 2.5 Demand for credit in relation to the break-even interest rate
Note: The long-run cost curve from figure 2.2 is not represented.

is simply the relationship between interest rate and supply of credit depicted in Figure 2.2 turned anti-clockwise through 90° with a demand curve for credit added from Figure 2.1. In the *short term* the cost curve of credit is upward-sloping: the more borrowers, the greater the recourse which is needed to informal, high-cost sources of credit. But if this cost curve shifts downwards over time, the lender can move from point A to point B on the demand curve, and becomes able to lend at a progressively lower 'break-even' interest rate. In this way a long-run cost curve which shifts downwards from A to B as the costs of administration and default fall over time, as in Figure 2.2, is generated. This long-run cost curve can be shifted downwards if the direct and indirect default reduction devices discussed above are successful.

The investment function I–I' is defined subjectively for each investor, as in Figure 2.1. It will be subject to shifts according to (at least) the level of market demand, the price of investment goods and government policies affecting the ability of investors to retain any profits they make.

The 'income creation' function

The next issue to be investigated is the rate at which new investment can reduce poverty; but there are two links in the chain, one from investment to the pattern of income change, and the second from the pattern of income change to poverty reduction. We look at each sequentially. The pattern of new income-earning opportunities which results from credit-financed investment will depend upon the rate of return to projects which are financed by credit, and their ability to generate new employment both directly and indirectly through production and consumption linkages. Again, it is *net* employment creation with which we are concerned, not simply the employment which is created by the new bank's loans: to the extent that this new employment causes others to lose their jobs, for example through the installation of a technology which displaces those in competing lines of business, the aggregate, or general-equilibrium, effect of the new bank on employment generation will be less than the firm-specific or partial-equilibrium effect. Again, this employment effect may in principle even be negative. The rate of return to credit-financed projects will depend fundamentally on demand for the output which they finance but can also be importantly influenced, as we shall illustrate, by investments in both social and physical infrastructure.

The labour-intensity of activities generated by credit is conventionally determined by the wage paid to labour relative to other factor prices. However, in an imperfect capital market, output prices and therefore, once again, final demand for the product or service invested in may also play a role.

Figure 2.6 illustrates our general argument. The left-hand half of the

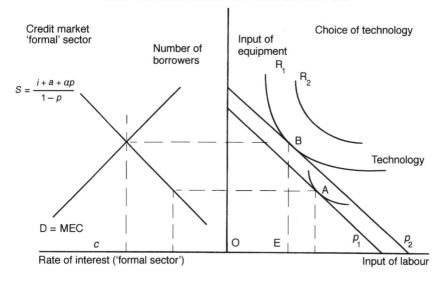

Figure 2.6 Interlinkage between credit market and choice of technology

diagram is identical to Figure 2.5, and the right-hand half is a standard choice-of-technology diagram. In general, the faster the growth of output (that is, the rate of expansion along the line OA) and the more labour-intensive the production technique (that is, the flatter the line OA in relation to the horizontal axis) the greater will be the number of new income-earning opportunities that can be created. For the moment, we assume that technology is given by the isoquants Q1, Q2 and so on. The rate of expansion along the line OA will be determined both by growth of demand and by 'transactions costs', including costs of transport, electricity, training, and so on. However, growth of demand (and, indeed, the development of new credit institutions itself) may make possible the shift to an entirely new technology: for example, in agriculture, a combination of high yield varieties (HYVs), fertiliser and irrigation, which can only be envisaged once the financial constraint has been relaxed. This new technology can be represented by the isoquants R_1, R_2 and so on. Once it becomes financially accessible, it may become rational to switch to the more capital-intensive technique OB even without any change in relative factor prices; thus it is possible that the creation of a new financial institution may create new jobs but at the cost of an increase in overall capital-intensity. The more that credit is subsidised, the more likely is this outcome to occur.

Poverty reduction

The final question to be examined is how effectively the new incomes generated by credit programmes reduce poverty. Our emphasis is on *absolute poverty reduction*, that is, on the number of people below the poverty line whom the programme assists, and the extent to which it assists them. Thus if the employment increase brought about by the loan programme (taking note of any persons who directly or indirectly lose employment or income as a result of the loan) is ΔE, then the consequent reduction in poverty will be:

$$\Delta P \ \triangleq \ \frac{P}{NP} (w - w') \Delta E \qquad [2.6]$$

where P and NP are the proportion of poor and non-poor beneficiaries respectively, w is the wage rate and w' is the average income of poor beneficiaries before employment. As the objective of credit-based income-generating programmes is to reduce poverty, what is to stop the sponsoring authority from raising the P/NP ratio to one? There are three potential answers, administrative, economic and political.

The *administrative* problem is that the targeting on the poor of credit or any other input imposes costs of research (finding out who is eligible), communication with the eligible and monitoring to prevent access by the ineligible, which may if pushed too far outweigh the benefits of poverty reduction. Besley and Kanbur (1991) speculate that administrative costs as a proportion of revenues may rise exponentially as targeting is made more precise (for example, by the application of income and assets ceilings, see part 1 of Table 1.2), and the funding of a large number of World Bank projects, reported in Lipton (1988a: 49) as having extreme difficulty in reaching the ultra-poor bottom 10 per cent of the income distribution, suggests that the problem is indeed a serious one. However, to the extent that programme eligibility is 'self-targeted', that is to say, directed to the poor automatically by the giving out of small loans only, the problem falls away. Our study will investigate in some detail the extent to which this can be done.

The *economic* constraint on the targeting of benefits is that many of the indirect benefits of credit projects, transmitted through production or consumption linkages, may accrue to the non-poor. The beneficiaries of credit projects may spend their income on both consumption goods and production inputs provided by the non-poor rather than the poor, and the ratio in which they do so is an important influence on the effectiveness of targeting. This ratio is a purely economic choice, not an administrative decision; it is likely to be heavily influenced (Mosley 1987: 169–72) by the technology on which the loan is spent. Labour-intensive, locally made equipment is far more likely to generate effective linkages at the production level than are capital-intensive imports.

It is, finally, a commonplace that many targeted credit programmes for the poor fail for *political* reasons: because a group of non-poor individuals, possibly the village leadership, insists on becoming borrowers, on pain of wrecking the scheme if their wishes are not respected. There are even cases (Mosley 1987: 173; see also Vol. 2, Chapter 16) where non-poor borrowers have pushed poor borrowers out of group schemes designed for the poor. It may be that non-poor borrowers have a stronger incentive to penetrate schemes of this type if interest rates are subsidised, as argued by von Pischke (1980, 1991). Chapters 5 and 8 contain a detailed examination of such issues.

If targeting is successful, however, it may well, of itself, push up repayment rates. Although *within* programmes there seems to be a tendency for default rates to be greater among the very poor (Pulley 1989: 41 for the Indian IRDP; Mosley and Dahal 1985 for Nepal) there seems little doubt that *between* programmes the poor have higher repayment rates than the rich. For example, the Grameen Bank in Bangladesh, BancoSol in Bolivia, BKK in Indonesia, all of which are aimed at very poor borrowers, have higher repayment rates than any LDC commercial bank in those countries. There are various plausible reasons for this: (a) the poor, unlike the rich, lack the political leverage with which to pervert the process of loan collection; (b) the poor, unlike the rich, have no alternative sources of finance, hence it is more important for them to maintain repayment; and more speculatively (c) schemes targeted on the poor are more effective at reaching women borrowers, and they have a better repayment record than men.

This brings our analysis full circle, to the factors determining repayment rates and hence the 'break-even' interest rate. It is now time to assemble the component parts and examine the hypotheses which emerge from so doing.

THE COMPOSITE PICTURE: HYPOTHESES TO BE TESTED

Figure 2.7 brings together the five steps in our argument. These are:

Quadrant (b)

1 The 'break-even' rate of interest charged by an innovative financial institution is determined by cost of borrowing, administrative cost and probability of default. At a given level of loan size, it can potentially be shifted either by *direct* methods (loan supervision and savings/insurance schemes) or by *indirect* methods (group lending and other incentives to repay).

2 Net incremental investment will be negatively correlated with whatever interest rate is offered by the new institution, even if the effects on existing institutions are taken into account. The nature of the response will depend on business conditions and the price of capital goods.

Quadrant (c)

3 Incremental employment created by this new investment will depend on the growth of demand, relative factor prices, rate of return on projects

and transactional costs. This employment effect may on balance be either positive or negative when the effects on competing firms are taken into account (these two quadrants are identical with those in Figure 2.6).

Quadrant (d)
4 To the extent that any of those employed under (3) are below the poverty line, poverty will fall as a direct consequence of any new employment created. Various policy measures may be taken to raise the poor/non-poor ratio amongst such beneficiaries, but there are both political and economic obstacles to targeting the employment increase in this way.

In this way a decision by a 'pioneer' credit institution to lend an amount of money OC to new borrowers at an interest rate OD will generate investment OB, employment creation OE and poverty reduction OF. It may seem as though a virtuous spiral is in progress. But this result depends crucially on the slopes of the functions, the factors which may disturb them (the 'shift parameters') and the, so far unexplored, relationship between factors in quadrants (d) and (b).

There is one final issue to be brought into the picture. This is the relationship between the formal and informal parts of the credit market, of which the latter has so far been simply left off-stage. The simplest assumption would be that of simple substitution: as the 'quasi-formal' sector expands, so it takes away business from the informal sector which therefore contracts. Such has indeed been the explicit intention of many 'quasi-formal' programmes, including the entire co-operative movement in India.[8] However, reality may be more complex:

1 Moneylenders and 'quasi-formal' lenders may be serving different markets; in particular moneylenders may be unwilling to lend long term or to individuals from outside their village whom they do not know (see, for example, Udry 1990); hence 'quasi-formal' lenders may be tapping new markets and thus expanding the aggregate volume of credit available.
2 There may be income as well as substitution effects to take into account; for example, those who successfully borrow from 'quasi-formal' institutions may experience an increase in income, part of which is then used to borrow from moneylenders for specific purposes and thus expand their aggregate volume of business.

For these reasons we postulate a link not between *interest rates* prevailing in the formal and the informal markets, but between *conditions of access* prevailing in the formal and informal markets. This is done in quadrant (a) of Figure 2.7. If conditions in the informal market tighten (in other words, the possibility that a borrower with given characteristics will obtain credit from a moneylender diminishes) the demand for 'formal' sector

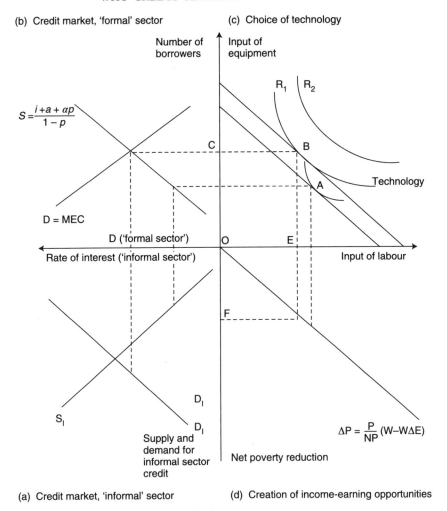

Figure 2.7 Interlinkage between credit market, choice of agricultural technology and income-earning opportunities

credit, that is, the marginal efficiency of capital schedule, moves outwards. By the same token, if conditions in the 'quasi-formal' credit market tighten, the demand curve for informal credit will shift in an outward, that is, in a south-westerly direction. The third and fourth quadrants of the figure remain unaltered.

From the above discussion we deduce the following propositions for empirical testing:

Relationship	Shift parameter	Examined in Chapter
1 Loan size → 'break-even' rate of interest (quadrant (b))	(1) Borrowing rate (2) Administrative cost	3
2 Administrative cost → 'break-even' rate of interest (quadrant (b)) (Subsidiary hypotheses: group size, group homogeneity → default rate)	Group credit insurance Savings schemes	3
3 Social penalty → default rate		7
4 Interest rate and terms net of access to credit → net investment rate (quadrant (b))	Price of capital goods Personal incomes	4
5 Investment rate → net employment generation and output growth (quadrant (c))	Relative factor prices Rate of return on capital	4
6 Employment generation → poverty (quadrant (d))	Wage rates, ratio of poor to non-poor beneficiaries, political pressures	5, 8
7 Supply of credit in formal sector → supply of credit in informal sector	Cost (including transactions cost) of acquiring credit	3

Note: The right-hand column lists the chapters of the book where tests of the propositions set out in the preceding argument may be found.

NOTES

1 This situation, is of course, not confined to the case of credit markets. In his famous article, Akerlof (1970) began with the case of buyers of used cars whose demand depends on both price and quality but who are unable to distinguish poor-quality cars ('lemons') from others. He then generalises from this case to sellers of insurance who are unable to distinguish bad risks from good risks within quite large categories (e.g. persons over 65 for life insurance, persons under 25 for motor insurance, non-landowners for crop insurance), as a consequence of which would-be buyers of such insurance are completely unable to exercise their preference in the market.

2 The average value given for 38 developing-country financial institutions by the World Bank Sector Policy Paper (1975) is 4.7 per cent.

3 In India, for example, the maximum interest rate which may be charged on agricultural loans below 10,000 rupees is 14 per cent.

4 Let $B = B(q)$ denote the expected future economic benefits from investment

financed by all those loans, or fractions of loans, that it is expected will be repaid. B is the willingness of these borrowers to repay principal plus interest and is related to the marginal efficiency of capital schedule, $R = R(q)$, as follows. $R(q)$ is the rate of return to projects in the interval q to $(q + \delta q)$, so that the willingness to repay principal plus interest in this interval is $(1 + R)\delta q = \delta B$. Hence $\delta B/\delta q = (1 + R)$. For any good borrower $R \geq r$, where r is the optimum interest rate, which we are to determine.

It is taken as given that economic benefits are generated only by those loans, or fractions of loans, that are repaid. There are two reasons for this: (a) those who default because the business failed evidently gain no economic benefit from that portion of the loan on which they have defaulted. In fact they may incur additional losses, which are not taken account of above; (b) those who default because of dishonesty may well invest the borrowings in activities that make a measurable addition to economic output; but given the damage done to lending activities if default rises to significant levels, there seems no good reason for including such additions in the benefit stream. The net expected benefits for any volume of lending Q are then $B(p, Q) - (1 + i + a)Q - (Q)$ where γ denotes the variance of profits $(R - C)$. Differentiating with respect to Q gives:

$$(1 + R)\left[(1 - p) - Q\frac{\partial p}{\partial Q}\right] - (1 + i + a) - Q\frac{\partial a}{\partial Q} - \frac{\partial \sigma}{\partial Q}$$

Setting this expression equal to zero gives the marginal conditions at which the rate of return to capital (on the marginal projects) should just equal the rate of interest. Hence putting $R = r$ and solving for r^* the 'break-even' interest rate gives

$$r^*(E) = \frac{(b - d) - (i + a + p(Z - Y) + Q(\partial a / \partial Q + \partial p / \partial Q) - \frac{\partial \sigma}{\partial Q}}{1 - p - Q(\partial p / \partial Q)}$$

$$[2.3'']$$

The term $Q(\partial p/\partial Q)$ (which is negative) reflects the marginal benefits from an increased expectation of financing good borrowers, the greater the volume of lending undertaken. The term $Q(\partial/\partial Q)$ (also negative) reflects corresponding reductions in administrative costs.

The economic optimum interest rate, $r^*(E)$ as defined by [2.3''] is contrasted with the financial break-even rate r^*, for levels of a and p which are expected to fall over time, in Figure 2.1.

5 For discussion of failures among rural financial institutions in LDCs, see in particular World Bank (1989a).

6 The lender's bargaining power is particularly weak if – as in the case we are considering – it is an impersonal bank, rather than a moneylender who knows the borrower and possibly has additional leverage over the borrower through acting as employer or landlord.

7 There are various halfway houses between the two schemes, including that commonly applied to the repayment of housing loans in industrial countries, in which monthly repayments of principal are made into a loan insurance fund which is expected eventually to cumulate to the total value of the loan.

8 'The whole object of [creating a structure of rural co-operatives] is to provide a positive institutional alternative to the moneylender himself, something which will compete with him, remove from the forefront and put him in his place' (Reserve Bank of India 1954: 2. 481–2).

3

FINANCIAL PERFORMANCE AND SUSTAINABILITY

The role of 'innovative credit institutions' in the capital market

INTRODUCTION

In the course of the analysis of Chapter 2 we made a distinction between two processes by which an 'innovative' credit institution might seek to make itself viable. It could seek to raise its profitability at a stroke by employing one of the range of devices described in that chapter (screening techniques, incentives to repay, and the laying-off of risks through insurance or equity participation); alternatively, it could seek to raise its profitability more gradually by progressively enlarging average loan size. There is a third approach, that of obtaining subsidy from a sponsor; although this should only be a short-term option and can easily be perverted into 'rent-seeking' (seeking subsidy to protect inefficiency rather than increase efficiency), it is an option which very few 'innovative' institutions have in practice been able to avoid, and for which we argued in Chapter 2 that a perfectly good theoretical case can in any case be made. In this chapter we examine the financial performance of our case-study institutions in relation to development finance institutions more generally, and the extent to which it was affected by the implementation of the three strategies described above.

FINANCIAL PERFORMANCE AND ITS DETERMINANTS

It is common to assess the performance of any commercial organisation, including development finance institutions, in terms of the profits it makes; and without profits, of course, no commercial organisation can sustain itself. However, if profits depend on external subsidy, they imply nothing about the efficiency of the organisation, or even about its sustainability, since the abolition of a subsidy can make an institution incapable of standing on its own feet. For these reasons, it is right to evaluate the financial performance of our selected institutions in terms of indicators which measure more accurately the organisation's financial efficiency. Table 3.1 offers two such alternative indicators in respect of our case-study

42

institutions: arrears rates, defined as the proportion of loans more than six months in arrears,[1] and the Subsidy Dependence Index devised in 1991 by Jacob Yaron.

The most important, and inspiring, message to emerge from Table 3.1 is that it is possible to lend profitably and with very low arrears to very poor people. Arrears rates in our thirteen innovative case-study institutions, over the five-year period 1988–92, average out at under 10 per cent by comparison with over 35 per cent for two large control samples of Third World development finance institutions reported by the World Bank. In all of our case-study institutions except Kenya Industrial Estates Informal Sector Programme and SANASA, average beneficiary income is below the poverty line for the country in question. The ability of these institutions to lend effectively beyond the 'frontier' of those who have collateral to offer, when those safely behind the frontier make much bigger losses lending to more prosperous people, is one of the most extraordinary achievements of development policy in our time. A low arrears rate appears to be a necessary, but not a sufficient, condition of achieving profitability: all the profitable schemes listed in the table had low arrears rates,[2] but Bolivia BancoSol and Bangladesh Grameen Bank, over the period under examination, had exceptionally low arrears (less than 5 per cent) and negative profitability, a circumstance caused by reluctance to raise interest rates to a level which would cover a surge in, respectively, the cost of raising funds and the cost of training and outreach activities.

The third row of the table calculates the level of Yaron's Subsidy Dependence Index (SDI) for all of the schemes. The SDI is a measure of the extent to which the lending interest rate would have to be raised in order to cover all operating costs if any subsidies the institution receives were stripped away.[3] It is positive for all the institutions studied here (that is, some subsidy is required) except the long-established BRI unit desas in Indonesia, and it is more than 100 per cent for all the non-Indonesian institutions (including the profitable Juhudi Fund in Kenya), implying that lending interest rates would have to be more than doubled for these institutions to meet all of the real resource costs which they impose on the economy out of current income.[4] For Bangladesh BRAC and the two Malawian schemes, SACA and the Mudzi Fund, the SDI rises to astronomical levels. In an imperfect capital market, as argued in Chapter 2, a subsidy can be justified if its benefits exceed its costs, either in terms of enabling an 'infant institution' to move down its cost curve or by offering external benefits to other institutions; we examine in the final section of this chapter the extent to which the subsidies revealed here earned their keep.

In Chapter 2 we pictured newly established DFIs as having a knife-edge to negotiate in their early years. If all goes well, then as the loan portfolio is built up some customers would reveal themselves as able to take larger loans, other customers would reveal themselves as uncreditworthy, and the

Table 3.1 Alternative measures of financial performance

	Bolivia BancoSol	BRI unit desas	Indonesia BKKs	KURKs	India* RRBs	Bangladesh GB	BRAC	TRDEP	Sri Lanka* Thrift and Credit Co-op Societies	Kenya Juhudi	KIE-ISP	Malawi* SACA*	Mudzi fund	Weighted average	Comparison I: 39 LDC schemes in World Bank (1975) Asia	Africa	L. Am.	Comparison II: 33 LDC schemes in Webster (1991) Asia	Africa	L. Am.
Profitability (1988–92 average; % of portfolio)	-3.4	3.5	5.6	0.9	-2.8[a]	-0.015	—	—	-5.5[a] / 17.0[b]	58.5	-9.1	6.2	-9.9	—	—	—	—	—	—	—
Arrears rate (1988–92 average)	0.6	3.0	2.1	13.7	42.0[a]	4.6	3.0	0	[41.0[a] / 4.0[b]]	8.9	20.2	27.8	43.4	—	40.2	40.1	42.1	30.5	44.7	8.3
Yaron SDI (%) (1988–92 average)	135	-9	32	—	[153.4[a] / 106.6[b]]	142.1	408.3†	199.4†	226.0	217.0		398	1884	—	—	—	—	—	—	—
Average beneficiary income 1992 ($p.a.)	360	296	125	119	150	150	107	—	143	267	445	197	78	—	—	—	—	—	—	—

Sources: Case studies in Volume 2, except Bangladesh GB which is from Khandkar (1993: table 6.6); 39 LDC schemes in Comparison I from World Bank (1975: annex 12); 33 LDC schemes in Comparison II from Webster (1991)

Notes
† 1988–91
[a] Overall average for entire organisation
[b] Case-study schemes sampled by this investigation
* Schemes with predominantly agricultural portfolio

resulting increase in average loan size and fall in default rate would bring costs down to the point where the lender was able to make a profit on a 'competitive' interest rate. If this strategy is to succeed, however, *either* loan default must be kept down during the early years (which ordinarily cannot be done without a heavy investment in loan-collection systems and other

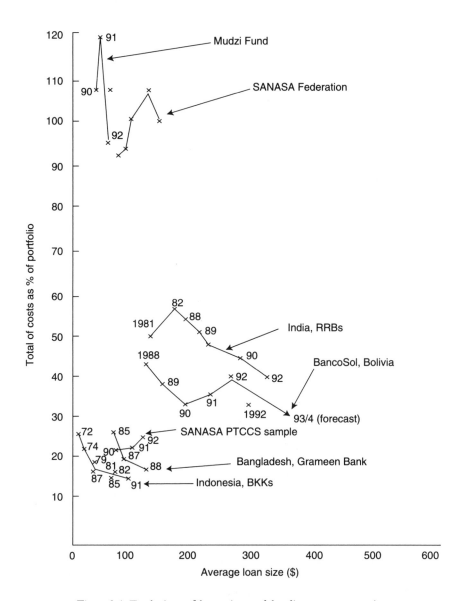

Figure 3.1 Evolution of loan size and lending costs over time

administrative infrastructure), *or* external subsidy must rescue the banking institution from the consequences of high default rates, *or* the same objective must be achieved through a rapid build-up of deposits. The last two, of course, are not strategies which can ordinarily be sustained over the long term if default rates continue at a high level.

In Figure 3.1, which charts the course of costs as a share of the total loan portfolio for our sample institutions, we can find examples of all of these scenarios:

- *Case 1* In Indonesia (BKKs and BRI unit desas), Malawi SACA until 1992, and Bangladesh Grameen Bank, the 'break-even interest rate' (total operating costs as a function of the overall loan portfolio) falls continuously over a period of ten years or more as loan size gradually expands. In all these cases, default rates were kept low (or, in the case of BRI unit desas, brought down from an initially high level) throughout the period of expansion of loan size.
- *Case 2* In Bolivia BancoSol, Kenya Juhudi Fund, and our sample group of Sri Lanka Thrift and Credit Co-operative Societies (not the entire SANASA Federation) we have what can be described as a probationary process of cost reduction. In each of these cases the level of costs does not fall without interruption as loan size increases, but rather is subject to an upward kink as external flows of concessional funds are partly phased out. In all these cases however, overdues have been kept well below 10 per cent so that the break-even interest rate is prevented from spiralling out of control. The level of costs, however, remains well above that prevailing in the Case 1 schemes.
- *Case 3* In India, Regional Rural Banks (RRBs), average loan size has been expanded over the years, but costs (that is, break-even interest rates) have scarcely fallen, on account of continuing high levels of overdues; but in absolute terms total cost levels are around those of Case 2 institutions. The RRBs have been successful in rapidly expanding savings deposits, and so rapid has this expansion been that no RRB has yet been forced to close, in spite of severe political constraints on the salaries which RRBs must pay and the interest rates which they are allowed to charge. Crisis has superficially been averted without the need for external subsidy; but there is substantial internal subsidy from the RRBs' sponsor banks, the Government of India standing behind them, and external aid donors standing behind the Indian Government.
- *Case 4* In the case of Malawi Mudzi Fund, loan size has not expanded nor has the break-even interest rate fallen below 100 per cent, which is well above that charged by the other institutions considered here, and indeed more than the amount charged by the moneylenders with whom the Mudzi Fund is attempting to compete. There are no

significant savings deposits available to the Fund as a financial reserve (or source of income), and so the Fund has to fall back on external subsidy to keep going, principally at present from IFAD. In the drought year of 1992–3 the Malawi SACA fund, after twenty years of highly creditable loan recovery performance, suddenly experienced a catastrophic fall in loan recoveries in the wake of a severe drought and the political fallout from democratisation; lacking internal financial reserves, it was therefore forced to abandon itself to a World Bank restructuring operation and in the course of one year plummeted from category 1 to category 4.

Why have some institutions, therefore, apparently fallen off the knife-edge of financial viability whereas others aiming at the same goal with the same resources have not? And is better performance in the financial sphere bought at the expense of lower impact on income, technology or poverty? The first of those questions is tackled in the remainder of this chapter, and the second in Chapters 4 and 5.

We begin by subdividing total costs (Table 3.2) into their component parts: the cost of borrowing, the cost of default and the cost of administration, with the last of these subdivided into four categories identified as functionally important in Chapter 2: costs of loan supervision, costs of loan insurance, costs of 'extraneous support' functions (including research, training and technical advice to other institutions) and other, residual costs. These are not standard accounting categories, and a considerable amount of juggling has been required to produce the standardised presentation in the table, details of which are presented in the end-notes. The table appears to indicate:

1 that default is overwhelmingly the most important component in the cost-structure, even on the basis of a simple listing of costs (in fact, as we saw in Chapter 2, default has even greater leverage than appears from the table, since if any borrower defaults, income from the good accounts has to cover losses of both interest and principal by the defaulter);

2 that there is no apparent connection (see Figure 3.2) between the interest rate actually charged and default rates. If true, and it is consistent with the evidence of Khalily and Meyer (1993) for Bangladesh, this has interesting implications, since one of the major arguments advanced by theorists for capital market failure is that high default rates might force banks to charge higher interest rates to cover their costs, and that this in turn might increase the rate of default, thereby bringing about a process of progressive withdrawal of both lenders and 'good' borrowers from the capital market (Stiglitz and Weiss 1981);[5]

3 that there is a significant inverse correlation between the level of administrative costs and the default rate. As shown in Figure 3.3, the

Table 3.2 Components of cost structure (all figures are percentages of total portfolio)

Average levels as percentage of portfolio, 1988–92 (per annum)

		Bolivia	Indonesia			India		Bangladesh		Sri Lanka	Kenya		Malawi	
Symbol	Meaning	BancoSol	BRI unit desas	BKKs	KURKs	RRBs	GB	BRAC	TRDEP	PTCCs	KREP Juhudi	KIE informal sector programme	SACA Farmers' Club	Mudzi Fund
i	Borrowing interest rate	8	11	3	—	9.7	3.5	0	0	1	0	0	0	0
a	Administrative costs of which:	28	12	18	—	8.1	12.3	40	100	17	33	27	11	722
a_1	Loan supervision costs	17	7	6	—	6	4.3	16	16	—	19	9	8	238
a_2	Insurance costs	4.5	—	6	6	—	6	5	5	—	3	—	—	1.5
a_3	Research, training and support of other institutions	4	1	1	—	—	2	2	2	—	9	6	—[a]	67
a_4	Other costs	3	4	5	—	2	1	14	77	—	2	12	3	415
p	Costs of default	1	3	2	14	42	5	3	—	4	9	20	28	43
$\left(\dfrac{i+a+p}{1-p}\right)$	Break-even interest rate[b]	37	27	24	—	45	22	52	100	23	36	34	53	1266

Sources: Vol. 2, Chapters 10–16.

Notes: [a] Ascribed to other Malawi Government operators.
[b] Assumes that α, the share of the principal that has to be paid back in the current time period, equals 1 (see pp. 19–20 above).

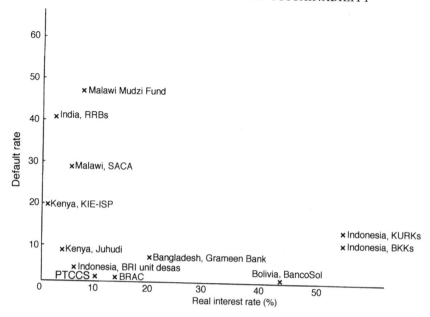

Figure 3.2 Real interest rates in relation to default rates

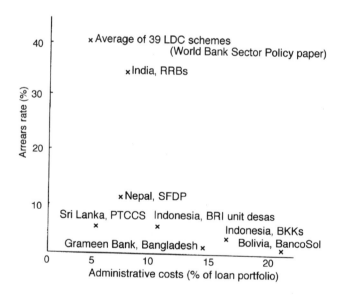

Figure 3.3 Administrative costs in relation to arrears rates, 1988–92 averages

Table 3.3 Banks lending to the poor: relationship between design features and performance

	Group A						Group B								
	Bolivia BancoSol	*BRI unit desas*	*BKKs*	*Indonesia KURKs*	*Gramen Bank*	*BRAC*	*Bangladesh TRDEP*	*Sri Lanka Thrift and Credit Co-operative Societies*	*Rural Enterprise Programme Jubudi Scheme*	*Kenya Industrial Estates Informal Sector Programme*	*India Regional Rural Banks*	*Malawi Smallholder Agricultural Credit Administration*	*Mudzi Fund*	*Sub-sample average, Group A*	*Sub-sample average, Group B*	*Student's t-statistics for difference between sample means[a]*
Type	NGO, now Commercial bank	Statutory body overseen by national agricultural bank	Village units established by regional development banks		Statutory financial institution (80% member owned, 20% government owned)	NGO	Branch of central government	Co-operative	NGO	Parastatal	Rural development bank jointly owned by 'sponsor bank', State Government and Government of India	Branch of central government	Trust fund overseen (with board members mainly from public service)			
Group (G) or individual (I) loans	G	I	I	I	G	G	G	G	G	I	I	G	G			
Design features: Political environment	No government influence	Banks subject to some residual guidance on interest rates	No government influence on lending policies of non-bank institutions		Minimal government influence on lending policies	No direct government influence on policies	Policies determined by government	Co-operatives free to set own interest rates and lending policies	No government influence on NGO lending policies	Government controlled interest rates on loans < Rs.10,000: periodic union and state government amnesties; IRDP lending decisions taken by government agents	Policies determined by state-appointed board	Government-controlled interest rates and lending policies	No direct government control but much influence			

Real interest rate % (1992)	45	6	60	60	15	15	15	11	9	−1	3	7	8	27.1	4.2	2.83**
Loan collection method	Fortnightly or monthly at bank branch	Monthly at bank branch	Weekly at village post in borrower's village	Weekly at village post or at borrower's door	Weekly at group meeting	Weekly at group meeting	Weekly at group meeting	Monthly at co-operative HQ	Weekly at group meeting	Monthly	Annually post-harvest	Annually post-harvest	Weekly at group meeting	45.2[b]	16.5[b]	2.14*
Savings/insurance arrangements	Compulsory 10% deposit + voluntary savings	Voluntary savings	Compulsory 10% deposit + voluntary savings	Compulsory 10% deposit + voluntary savings	Compulsory 25% contribution to 'emergency fund'			Voluntary savings available	Compulsory 20% deposit + voluntary savings	None	Statutory crop insurance scheme available in some states	None	Compulsory 5% deposit (often waived)[c]			
Insurance charge/portfolio % (a_2)	4.5	—	6.0	6.0	6.0	5.0	5.0	—	3.0	—	—	—	1.5[c]	4.43	0.37	3.67**
Incentives to repay	'Progressive lending'[d] (loan amount tied to repayment of previous loan)	'Progressive lending'[d] + borrower incentives to repay	'Progressive lending'[d] + borrower incentives to repay + profit-linked bonuses for local government staff		'Progressive lending'[d]	'Progressive lending'[d]		None	'Progressive lending'[d]	None	None	None	None			
(Value of dummy variable)[c]	1	2	3	3	1	1	1	0	1	0	0	0	0	1.44	0.0	4.36**
Financial performance indicators																
6-month arrears rate % (1992)	0.6	3.0	2.1	13.7	4.5	3.0	3.0	4.0	8.9	20.2	42.0	27.8	43.4	4.4	33.3	4.98**

Table 3.3 Continued

| | Group A | | | | | | | Group B | | | | | | Sub-sample average, Group A | Sub-sample average, Group B | Student's t-statistics for difference between sample means[a] |
	Bolivia BancoSol	BRI unit desas	BKKs	Indonesia KURKs	Gramen Bank	Bangladesh BRAC	TRDEP	Sri Lanka Thrift and Credit Co-operative Societies	Rural Enterprise Programme Jubudi Scheme	Kenya Industrial Estates Informal Sector Programme	India Regional Rural Banks	Malawi Smallholder Agricultural Credit Administration	Mudzi Fund			
Subsidy Dependence Index % (1988–92)	135	–9	32.0	34.5	142.1	408.3	199.4	226.0	217.0		106.0	398.0	1884.0	153.0	796.0	1.16
Impact/ effectiveness indicators																
1 Per cent of borrowers new to capital market	68		66	77		58	65	70	79	72	39	61	56	69.0	63.0	1.10
2 Beneficiary income as % of income of control sample	179.4	172.9	123.1		107.0		129.2	115.6	134.3	101.5	107.5	401.0	167.9	137.3	223.4	0.94
3 Indicators of poverty impact (a) Average beneficiary income 1992 ($)	360	296	125	119	(115)	107		143	217	445	87	197	78	185.2	217.5	0.37

| (b) % of borrower sample crossed poverty line in 1992 | 29.0 | 8.4 | 6.6 | 3.3 | | | | 33.0 | | | | | | | | |
| (c) % women borrowers | 75 | 24 | 55 | 72 | 94 | 68 | 38 | 53 | 51 | 23 | 9 | 28 | 82 | 58.8 | 35.5 | 1.34 |

Notes

[a] Student's T-statistic is defined as $\bar{x}_1 - \bar{x}_2$ where $\bar{x}_1$, $\bar{x}_2$ are

$$\sqrt{\frac{S_1^2}{n_1} + \frac{S_2^2}{n_2}}$$

Group A and Group B sample means, S_1, S_2 are Group A and Group B standard deviations, and n_1, n_2 are Group A and Group B sample sizes.

** denotes significance at 1 per cent level, * denotes significance at 5 per cent level.

[b] Intensity of loan collection methods proxied by dummy variable: weekly collection = 52, fortnightly collection = 26, monthly collection = 12, annual collection = 1.

[c] For details of implementation of Mudzi Fund savings scheme, see Vol. 2, Chapter 16.

[d] 'Progressive lending' is defined as loan amounts tied to repayment performance on previous loans.

[e] Incentives to repay represented by a dummy variable as follows: 0 = no incentive, 1 = progressive lending, 2 = progressive lending plus bonus for prompt repayment, 3 = as 2 plus incentives to staff and local officials.

relationship is a rectangular hyperbola,[6] with one or two egregious outliers such as (on the credit side) Indonesia BRI unit desas and our sample of Sri Lanka Thrift and Credit Co-operative Societies and (on the debit side), spectacularly, the Malawi Mudzi Fund.

WHICH DESIGN FEATURES MATTER?

Given the first and third of these findings, it is important now to try and make the analysis more precise, since self-evidently it is not the case that all increases in administrative spending will *ipso facto* lower the default rate. Table 3.3 splits the sample into two groups; 'financial successes' with repayment rates over 80 per cent and 'financial failures' with repayment rates under 80 per cent (and, in all cases, subsidy dependence over 100 per cent). For each scheme, we then examine the level of two particular categories of administrative expenditure: loan supervision expenditure (a_1 in our notation) and insurance costs (a_2 in our notation). We also specify the nature of the political environment surrounding lending decisions (as reflected, for example, in the level of the real interest rate) and the nature of any incentive to borrowers, or others, to maximise repayment. The results of the table are startling. All the successful schemes had all the following attributes: positive real interest rates, 'intensive' (that is, monthly or more frequent) loan collection, some provision for voluntary savings or insurance, incentives to repay. None of the unsuccessful schemes (India Regional Rural Banks, Malawi SACA and Mudzi Fund, and Kenya Industrial Estates ISP) had any of these attributes except positive real interest rates (and even here, interest rates are held down by legislative fiat in both India and Malawi). There is, therefore, a statistically significant difference in the incidence of each of these design attributes as between group A schemes (the 'successes') and group B schemes (the 'failures'). Furthermore, lower down in the table it appears that there is no significant difference in poverty impact as between the 'successes' and 'failures', suggesting that the improvement in financial performance which the design attributes offer is not bought any any obvious cost in terms of poverty reduction. It appears that we may have tracked down some of the necessary, if not the sufficient, conditions for success at the financial level. In order to widen the perspective and check on the possibility that some significant variables may have been left out, we now resort to regression analysis, widening the sample to include, in addition to our thirteen case-study institutions, another seventy or so from which summary data are available from World Bank surveys. The results are presented in Table 3.4, and are even more interesting for what is revealed as insignificant than for what is confirmed as important. In within-sample regressions, borrower's education emerges as a positive determinant of propensity to repay (significant in Bangladesh), and borrower's income and gender emerge as insignificant influences on repayment. In other words, better-educated borrowers repay loans slightly better than the less-educated. In the across-sample regressions, women repay better than men. This may well be due to the fact that women, and poorer borrowers in general, have fewer alternative sources of credit than richer borrowers, and provides an apparent rationale for the decision taken by a number of group-lending NGOs (including Grameen, BRAC and the Malawi Mudzi fund) to lend only to women henceforth.[7] Some measures of the borrower's environment, including rainfall and roads per square kilometre, emerge as significant determinants of propensity to fall into arrears in some regressions. The across-sample regressions, finally, confirm that, contrary to the arguments of some recent NGO-based work (see pp. 10–11), the organisation of borrowers in groups is neither necessary nor sufficient for success (witness the Malawian and Indonesian cases as examples, respectively, of unsuccessful group-based and successful individual-based schemes). Contrary to the arguments of the Ohio School, state sponsorship as such has neither a positive nor a negative role in determining financial success: many of the most successful schemes, including all the Indonesian ones, are state-sponsored, but so are some of the signal failures, such as India Regional Rural Banks and the Malawi Mudzi Fund. But as suggested by Table 3.3, intensive loan collection, the existence of savings and insurance facilities and the existence of incentives to repay all serve as significant 'shift parameters' exercising an upward influence on the repayment rate. These design features, indeed, can be seen as inputs into a production function whose output is financial sustainability, and the coefficients in Table 3.4 can be seen as first estimates of the 'marginal product' of these 'factors of production'. However, taking the metaphor further, there is no reason why they should enter the production function in fixed proportions: like physical building materials, all of them have a resource cost which will be different in different economic environments, and just as architectural styles vary from country to country to reflect local traditions and tastes, the productivity of each of them can be increased by tailoring them appropriately to the local cultural environment. The following section explores the available scope for locally specific variations in the architecture of micro-enterprise lending schemes.

PRINCIPLES OF DESIGN

The different design features identified as critical in Tables 3.3 and 3.4 have different operating modes and hence consume different factors of production. Intensive loan-collection systems use the labour of bank staff (and some capital goods, such as motor cycles) to reduce the cost which the borrower incurs in repaying loans, and mount a credible threat against default. Incentives to repay offer a carrot rather than a stick by increasing the benefits associated with loan repayment; their opportunity cost consists

Table 3.4 Determinants of arrears rates: results of regression analysis

I Cross-section regressions
Ordinary least squares analysis. Dependent variable: proportion of borrowers less than 6 months in arrears

| | | | | | | Regression coefficients on independent variables | | | | | Natural endowments | | |
| | | | | | | Design features: | | | | | | | |
Sample	Number of observations	Constant	Borrower's income/education	% female borrowers	Group organisation dummy variable	Loan collection method dummy variable	Savings/insurance dummy variable	Incentives to repay dummy variable	Government policy: Real interest rate	Km. roads per million persons	Average yearly rainfall	$\bar{r}^2$
This survey	46	43.8[a] (8.37)	[income] -0.00027 (0.06)	0.31[b] (2.03)	1.65 (0.37)	0.61[a] (3.36)	4.19[a] (2.73)	0.16 (0.46)	-0.00045 (0.008)	0.063[b] (2.14)		0.70

II Within-sample regressions
Ordinary least squares analysis (limited dependent variable). Dependent variable: level of repayment as a percentage of expected repayment

Bolivia												
BancoSol borrowers	35	124.7 (0.80)	0.0037 (0.26)	12.18 (0.25)					-0.25[b] (2.07)			0.08
Bangladesh												
Grameen Bank borrowers	383	1.43[b] (4.49)	[education] -1.61[a] (4.54)	-0.01 (0.59)						0.00 (1.66)		0.536

Sources
I Cross-section regressions: Table 3.3 for schemes studied in Vol. 2; Webster (1989) for other schemes; also World Bank, *World Development Report 1994*: appendix tables 12 and 32 for data in last two columns.
II Within-sample regressions: Vol. 2, Chapters 10 and 11; also Khandkar *et al.* (1993). In the Bolivia BancoSol regression, the independent variables are dummies (0–4 according to highest educational level, and 0 = male and 1 = female)

Notes
[a] Denotes significance at 1 per cent level.
[b] Denotes significance at 5 per cent level.

mainly of the capital locked up in the provision of an incentive, and also in a minor way the wages of the staff involved in administering the incentive. Finally, the provision of insurance and savings facilities operate in a different way again, not by discouraging loan default as such but by transferring the costs which it imposes on the lending agency to borrowers and others willing to bear risk. The key point is that there is no free lunch: to implement each of them is beneficial, according to Table 3.4, but each of them has a cost.

Given that the different resources required to implement each of the 'technologies' (unskilled labour, skilled labour, equipment, and risk capital) have different costs and different leverage in the countries under examination, it follows that the mixture of incentives used in each environment should be different. Specifically,

1 the lower the relative cost of labour, the more intensive the use that should be made of the 'labour-intensive' technology of loan collection on the borrower's premises;
2 the more work that is done to reduce default by a combination of intensive loan collection and incentives to repay, and the more that is done to combat the moral hazard problem through deductibles and no-claim bonuses, the smaller the risk premium that needs to be loaded on to the interest rate;
3 the higher the level of insurable risks[8] to which the activity financed by the lender is subject, the higher will be both the pay-off to, but also the costs of, insurance.

The three technologies should be seen as mutually supportive safety-nets which, between them, substitute for the absence of collateral: the cheaper the resources required for the construction of each 'net', the stronger it can be made, and the stronger each is, the less work the others have to do. A logical decision tree for determining the specification of each of them is set out in Figure 3.4. We now examine the design of the individual safety-nets.

Loan collection methods

Since the pioneering initiative of the Grameen Bank of Bangladesh in the late 1970s, the principle of weekly collection of loan instalments at a public meeting place in the immediate neighbourhood of the borrower's house has been widely accepted as canonical, and has been adopted by, amongst our 'successful' institutions, Bangladesh BRAC and TRDEP, Kenya KREP Juhudi, and Indonesia BKKs and KURKs (which sometimes come literally to the borrower's door); it has also been consciously copied from Grameen by the much-less-successful Malawi Mudzi Fund. The logic of this procedure is often presented as being to minimise the borrower's 'transactions

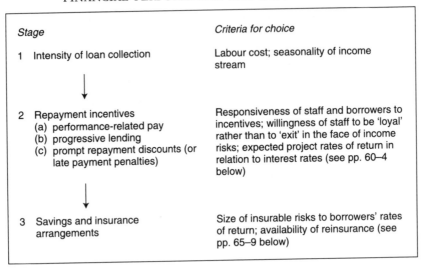

Stage	Criteria for choice
1 Intensity of loan collection	Labour cost; seasonality of income stream
2 Repayment incentives (a) performance-related pay (b) progressive lending (c) prompt repayment discounts (or late payment penalties)	Responsiveness of staff and borrowers to incentives; willingness of staff to be 'loyal' rather than to 'exit' in the face of income risks; expected project rates of return in relation to interest rates (see pp. 60–4 below)
3 Savings and insurance arrangements	Size of insurable risks to borrowers' rates of return; availability of reinsurance (see pp. 65–9 below)

Figure 3.4 Decision tree for DFI 'safety-nets'

costs' – the cost of doing business with a lender. As will be demonstrated empirically in the next section, however, the cost increase in terms of *time* of appearing at fifty-two compulsory weekly meetings, by comparison with one block repayment to a moneylender, generally outweighs by a large margin the cost decrease from having the lender come to one's village, rather than the other way about. What intensive repayment on the Grameen model does, rather, is to make repayment into a regular, ritualised and public process. The regular ritual minimises the perceived financial cost of repaying the loan, and ingrains habits of 'good practice', much as training and visit (T&V) methods of agricultural extension ingrain 'good' agricultural practices; the fact that the ritual takes place in public maximises the reputational cost of not repaying and makes public knowledge of repayment problems at an early stage so as to increase the likelihood that such problems can be tackled.[9] Both characteristics tend to give loans of this type seniority over borrowers' other debts.

That measures of this type work well across the broad range of schemes surveyed here is amply illustrated by Figure 3.5; the partial regression coefficient of intensity of loan collection on arrears rates $(\partial p / \partial a_1)$, is, it will be recalled from Table 3.4, 0.61, which is well above the critical level required, from equation [2.5], to make investment in this form of expenditure pay for itself.[10] But there are of course diminishing returns, and, in any given country, the higher the cost of the labour required to collect the loans, the sooner they will bite and wipe out any advantage from making loan collection more frequent. It is not surprising, therefore, that in Bolivia,

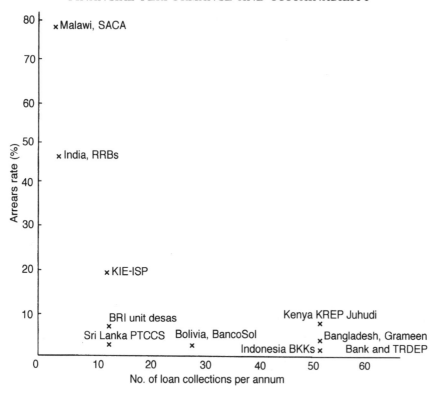

Figure 3.5 Intensity of loan collection in relation to arrears rates

where wage levels are higher than in the other countries sampled, loan collections by BancoSol are fortnightly or monthly according to the group's choice, rather than weekly.

All the schemes so far discussed lend mainly to micro-entrepreneurs in the service, trade and manufacturing sectors, although all except KREP Juhudi do have an agricultural element in their loan portfolio. By contrast, India Regional Rural Banks and Malawi SACA lend mainly or exclusively to farmers, and coincidentally or otherwise they have poor repayment rates. It has often been suggested that the seasonal nature of arable farmers' income patterns requires that crop loans be repaid in one balloon payment after the harvest.[11] But this does not have to be so, given that most borrowers are in multi-enterprise households, particularly if the lending bank also offers a savings facility, witness the ability of the 'success' institutions (Indonesia BRI unit desas, Sri Lanka PTCCS and, more recently, BancoSol) to lend for agriculture and to collect loans on a weekly or monthly basis. We speculate

59

that if the 'mainly agricultural' lending institutions shifted to monthly loan collections their repayment rates would improve.[12]

Repayment incentives

Incentives to repay, in their simplest form, extend the reach of intensive loan-collection systems. Just as weekly public repayment combats moral hazard by raising the reputational cost of default, so incentives to the borrower do the same by raising the financial cost of default, either by offering a discount for consistent on-time repayment (as in all Indonesian systems) or by charging a higher interest rate on overdue amounts (for example, Thailand's Bank of Agriculture and Agricultural Co-operatives). One way of extending this approach, practised by seven of the nine 'financially successful' institutions, is to increase the credit limit of borrowers by a proportion dependent on their previous repayment record, a practice we describe as 'progressive lending'. In all the Indonesian systems, Thailand BAAC and Kenya KREP, some or all of employees' pay is profit-related, and in Indonesia BKKs and KURKs the local officials who countersign and monitor loan applications are co-opted into the system through being awarded a share of any profits made.

How effective are these incentives? Although the regression coefficient of the 'incentive dummy' variable (Table 3.4), at 0.16, is once again positive and sufficiently high to suggest that such incentives, once again, pay for themselves, a dummy variable is a blunt instrument and tells us little about how they should be designed; the more so since most of the observations are clustered around one point ('progressive lending' only). In the appendix to Vol. 2, Chapter 11, we show how the process of fine-tuning these incentives can be taken further by picturing a utility-maximising lender using them as bargaining chips in a game of strategy with a borrower who is trying to maximise his or her own family's utility. To reduce the argument to its simplest terms, imagine that the lender's problem is to choose which, if any, of the following instruments to deploy:

- an element of bank staff's pay which is profit-related (denoted henceforward as γ);
- a rebate to those borrowers who repay on time (denoted as β);
- a 'coefficient of progressive lending', or increase in the credit limit for those who repay on time (denoted as α).

Let us visualise the relationship between borrower and lender as a game in three stages which may or may not repeat themselves: initial agreement, implementation, decision on whether and on what terms to grant repeat finance. Henceforward, we refer to these stages as Acts 1, 2 and 3 respectively. In Act 1, let us suppose the lender makes a loan of standard

60

size X at a standard interest rate r. In Act 2 the borrower received a return s on the project which the loan is being used to finance and repays a proportion of this loan; in the event that repayment is not made in full, the lender either punishes this behaviour by refusing to provide repeat finance, or not. The extensive form of the game is as set out in Table 3.5, ignoring all italicised figures for the time being (see also Figure 3.6). It will be noted that in the bottom left-hand corner of the table the pay-offs for the case where the borrower does not repay the loan in Act 2, but the lender still provides a loan in Act 3 (which we call the 'exploitative solution') are given in two different forms. This is because the lender's strategy of 'lending into the recipient's arrears'[13] is a gamble which may or may not come off in the sense of persuading the borrower to use the increased liquidity made available by the loan to pay back the arrears on the previous loan. The result of this gamble turns out to be crucial to the outcome of the game. If it is successful the game has a 'dominant strategy equilibrium' – that is, an outcome where the optimal strategies of each player are mutually compatible, and neither player has an incentive to deviate from these strategies – in the bottom left-hand corner, since the lender has no incentive to deviate from the strategy *Refinance* and the borrower has no incentive to deviate from the strategy *Not repay* as long

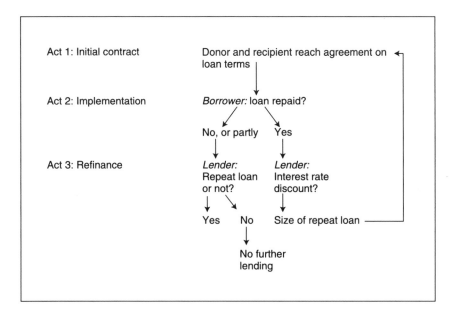

Figure 3.6 Incentives to repay and 'progressive lending': the game in extensive form

Table 3.5 Incentives to repay and progressive lending: pay-offs to different points on the 'game tree'

Lender strategies (Act III)/ Borrower strategies (Act II)	Refinance [1]	Partial refinance (repeat loan, but no increase in size) [2]	No refinance [3]
Repay 100 per cent of Act I loan ($\lambda = 1$)	Act II Lender: rx Borrower: $(s-r)x + \mathbf{\beta}$ Act III Lender: $r(1+\gamma)x - \mathbf{\beta}$ Borrower: $(s-r)\mathbf{(1+\gamma)}x + \mathbf{\beta}$ [4]	Act II Lender: rx Borrower: $(s-r)x + \mathbf{\beta}$ Act III Lender: rx Borrower: $(s-r)x + \mathbf{\beta}$ [5]	Act II Lender: rx Borrower: $(s-r)x + \mathbf{\beta}$ Act III Lender: 0 Borrower: 0 [6]
Partial repayment: repayment percentage $0 < \lambda < 1$	Act II Lender: λrx Borrower: $(s - \lambda r)\mathbf{(1+\gamma)}x$ Act III Lender: $\lambda r\mathbf{(1+\gamma)}\,x$ Borrower: $(s - \lambda \mathbf{r})\mathbf{(1+\gamma)}\,x$ [7]	Act II Lender: λrx Borrower: $(s - \lambda r)x$ Act III Lender: λrx Borrower: $(s - \lambda \mathbf{r})\,x$ [8]	Act II Lender: λrx Borrower: $(s - \lambda r)x$ Act III Lender: 0 Borrower: 0 [9]
No repayment ($\lambda = 0$)	Act II Lender: 0 Borrower: sx Act III Lender: 0 *or* $r(1+\gamma)x$ Borrower: sx *or* $(s-r)\mathbf{(1+\gamma)}x + \mathbf{\beta}$	Act II Lender: 0 Borrower: sx Act III Lender: 0 *or* rx Borrower: sx *or* 0	Act III Lender: 0 Borrower: sx Lender: 0 Borrower: $-\mathbf{\mu}$

Notes

The amounts in **bold** are included in the pay-off when incentives to repay (β, γ) exist, and excluded when they do not exist.

x = loan size; r = interest rate; s = rate of return on borrowers' projects; λ = proportion of loan repaid; μ = loss of reputation from non-repayment; β = borrower's bonus for on-time repayment; γ = increase in loan size for on-time repayment.

as $rx > \mu$, that is, the short-term financial gain from default exceeds any financial loss to the borrower from loss of reputation.[14] If, however, the gamble is foreseen as being unsuccessful the game has no equilibrium at all since the *Refinance* strategy is no longer dominant for the donor. In other words, under the assumptions of Table 3.5 the equilibrium of the game is either perverse, in the sense that it involves exploitation of the lender by the borrower,[15] or non-existent. It is to prevent this kind of breakdown of trust and to channel the game into a stable 'refinance, repay' equilibrium at the top left-hand corner of the table that incentives to repay were introduced in Indonesia and Thailand; we now consider the circumstances in which they may be expected to work.

The figures in bold in Table 3.5 spell out the consequences of introducing a premium β which, like the Indonesian HAT or IPTW[16] is refunded to the borrower in the event that a loan is paid back in full and an increment which is the percentage by which the borrower's credit limit in Act 3 is expanded in the event of successfully paying back the Act 1 loan. These devices may secure the desired result of a dominant strategy equilibrium in the top left-hand corner of the table, but not automatically. The recipient will prefer to *Repay* as long as the net financial advantage conferred by the bonus and by the loss of reputation on the decision to repay – that is, $\pi(\beta + \gamma - rX) + (1 - \Pi)(\beta - \mu - rX)$, where Π is the likelihood of refinance – is more than zero. The lender will unconditionally prefer to *Refinance* if, in the event of the borrower implementing *Not repay*, his gamble of lending into her arrears is successful in eliciting repayment. But we can already see the key determinants of the effectiveness of the bonuses β and γ, apart from their magnitude; namely the interest rate r, the loan size X and the loss of reputation μ. The last of these can be influenced, as earlier described, by intensive loan-collection practices which make the act of repayment more frequent and more public. In this way the optimum incentive to repay interlocks with the technology for loan collection which the bank has previously chosen: the more work that is done by intensive loan collection methods (or other devices such as peer monitoring by members of borrower groups) by giving teeth to social sanctions against non-repayment, the smaller the resources which need to be sacrificed in offering incentives to repay. In Vol. 2, Chapter 11, we calculate a formula for the 'optimum incentive to repay' which suggests that the BRI system in Indonesia has its incentives about right, but that even the BKK system of that country and the BAAC system of Thailand have both their β and γ incentives too low to optimise repayment performance. The same applies *a fortiori* to those institutions which at present have no performance incentives at all.

We now consider the incentive of linking the wages of bank staff to its profits (or its recovery rates, or some other element of bank performance). If the relationship between the 'flexible' element in pay and the repayment

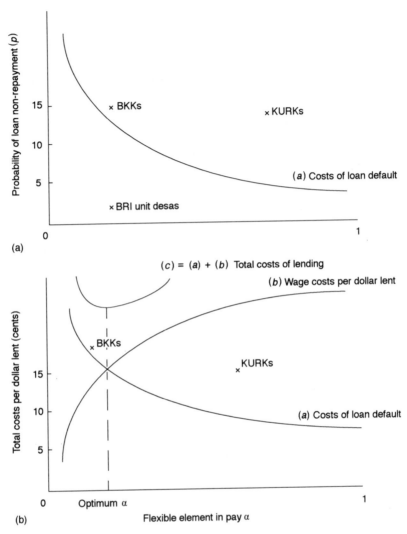

Figure 3.7 Possible relationship between pay flexibility and loan repayment
(a) Wage effects excluded (b) Wage effects included
Source: For empirical data: Table 3.3

rate is continuously downward-sloping, as in Figure 3.7a, then the optimal design is for all pay to be performance-related ($\alpha = 1$): the smaller the guaranteed element in the bank worker's pay, the stronger his incentive to collect repayments. This was the solution originally adopted by the KURKs of East Java for all staff in 1983, but it has been subsequently modified by allowing head office and regional office staff to receive fixed salaries subject to a performance-related bonus. In fact the relationship between α and the bank's efficiency is likely to consist of two components. On the one hand, it acts as a deterrent to the moral hazard that bank staff will get away with slack monitoring of loans, which is likely to be a wholly negative influence on banks' costs (that is, a positive influence on their profits), as in curve (*a*) in Figure 3.7b. On the other hand, it raises the instability of bank staff's earnings by relation to their salaried counterparts; if they are even moderately risk-averse, they will demand a risk premium, and this effect will bring about an upward influence of α on the bank's costs, as in curve (*b*) in Figure 3.7b. Once account is taken of this second effect, the optimal performance-related element in pay is no longer 1 unless staff are risk-neutral or risk-loving; it is that level of α which, as in Figure 3.7b, minimises the total level of costs associated with pay flexibility, that is, minimises the vertical sum of the 'loan default' and 'wage cost' curves.

Savings and insurance arrangements

Savings and insurance schemes offer additional protection to the lender by offering the possibility of repayment of a loan if a borrower becomes financially distressed. In the simplest case, the bank takes *voluntary savings* in the form of deposits, which provide borrowers who are also savers with a financial buffer; if some of these savings are automatically taken by the bank from all borrowers in the form of a surcharge on the interest rate and invested in an insurance fund, we have the second model, that of *compulsory saving*; if insurance against named risks is provided by an institution extraneous to the bank, we have a formal *insurance contract*. As frequently lamented by the Ohio School,[17] development finance institutions worldwide have been slow to perceive the advantages of taking voluntary savings, as discussed in Chapter 2, and of the institutions studied in this book, only the BRI unit desas, the Sri Lanka thrift and credit co-ops and Bolivia BancoSol – three out of thirteen – have what may be described as fully fledged voluntary savings schemes. All the Bangladesh institutions, Kenya Rural Enterprise Programme, Malawi Mudzi Fund and the BKKs and KURKs of Indonesia (which also have embryonic voluntary savings institutions) take a compulsory savings deposit into an 'emergency fund' as a part of the charge for credit, whereas borrowers from the India Regional Rural Banks can claim on a private-sector insurance scheme in respect of yield shortfalls on specific crops only – cereals, pulses and oilseeds. It is clear from Tables 3.3 and 3.4 that institutions practising some sort of savings or insurance have a significantly better financial performance than those which do not; and across all the schemes on which we have data, the regression coefficient of 4.19 on the insurance dummy variable in Table 3.4 satisfies the condition of equation [2.5′] (p. 26) for the resource cost of insurance to pay for itself in terms of its impact on the lender's balance sheet. What remains unresolved is what form the savings/insurance package should take.

There are many arguments for developing a voluntary savings capacity within a development finance institution which go beyond the protection of the institution's loan portfolio, the most important of which is the development of a sustainable source of finance which does not depend on the whims of a particular sponsor. Other relevant arguments were presented on p. 26, and will not be rehearsed here. The key question is whether such voluntary schemes need to be supplemented with a compulsory insurance scheme. It has now become a conventional wisdom that such schemes, unless confined to a very narrow range of risks, are doomed to failure in a developing country context. A typical statement of this position is provided by von Pischke (1991: 138–40):

> Development assistance agencies promoted agricultural insurance programs in a number of developing countries in spite of theory and practice that indicated that the conditions required for these programs' success are extremely rigorous. Problems included a lack of basic data, heterogeneous agricultural practices contributing to wide dispersions in yield levels, small and geographically scattered risks that would make administration difficult, the limited ability of some farmers, lack of staff trained in insurance, poor infrastructure inhibiting field administration, and limited financial resources to support introduction of agricultural insurance. These data indicate that the economic argument for agricultural insurance is not realized in practice.

Von Pischke in fact presents very few data, but there is now abundant evidence (for example, Hazell 1993) that agricultural insurance in developing countries is often unable to cover its costs. The point at issue is threefold:

1 whether such insurance provides benefits, over and above those provided by voluntary saving, which counterbalance these resource costs – the issue of desirability in principle;
2 whether the provision of such benefits is feasible in practice;
3 how, if feasible, such provision should be made.

On the first issue, the only scheme within our thirteen which offers both voluntary saving and a separate crop insurance scheme is the India Regional Rural Banks, discussed in detail in Vol. 2, Chapter 14. Our finding there is that the insurance scheme, although loss-making and often ill-administered, managed to deliver resource allocation benefits which exceeded the costs of the scheme to the extent of about 0.3 per cent of the total portfolio, or about $8 million, in 1992 (Vol. 2, Chapter 14; see also Mishra 1994), over and above the benefits provided through voluntary saving. In general there are likely to be many cases where disasters are unforeseen and where as a result borrowers are unable to meet their financial obligations to banks from voluntary savings. One source of such unforeseen disasters, namely drought, is particularly important, and we believe that in those cases where banks lend to unsecured farmers in semi-arid, rainfed areas the case for schemes to insure their portfolios against the consequences of natural disaster is particularly urgent. It will be remembered from Table 3.3 that the financial performance of schemes lending to small farmers is generally worse than the performance of schemes lending to small businesses.

This brings us to the questions of what is feasible and what is best. Problems of 'heterogeneous agricultural practices contributing to wide dispersions in yield levels, small and geographically scattered risks, poor infrastructure' and so on undoubtedly prevail in India as elsewhere in the developing world, but they have not precluded the creation of an institution which, as earlier noted, manages to deliver a positive balance of benefits over costs; nor need they preclude the creation of such institutions elsewhere. However, lessons can be learned from the Indian experience. In the first place, loan collection effort is slack and incentives to repay non-existent, which imposes heavier burdens on the insurance scheme than it is reasonable to expect it to carry. Second, the scheme is subsidised to a ludicrous degree (claims paid out over the last eight years have been eight times premium income). Third, insurance is voluntary on a state basis, with the consequence that the low-risk states where agriculture is mainly irrigated (such as Punjab, Haryana) are free to opt out of sharing of risks with higher-risk states, and have indeed done so, with the consequence that the scheme covers only the highest risks (the so-called 'adverse selection' problem). Finally, the Indian scheme is based on an area yield guarantee, under which payouts take place in specified areas if average yields for that area fall more than a defined percentage below the moving average yield. This was conceived as an ingenious defence against moral hazard, since no individual farmer can by his own actions influence the average yield for the area, but it has led to vast waste, because under the present scheme farmers (or rather their creditors) receive payouts if the area yield falls below the threshold whether or not their own yields fall below it, and whether or not they are suffering from payment difficulties due to natural causes. On the basis of this experience we recommend, for agricultural lending schemes, a compulsory, unsubsidised scheme against the specific peril of drought – the most serious non-culpable cause of loan default – which like the average yield cannot be influenced by any beneficiary, so that the moral hazard problem is circumvented.

Because this scheme does not exactly correspond to any currently existing,[18] it is worth spelling out in a little detail exactly how it might work and how it would interlock with the financial system. What we visualise is that drought insurance would be sold to individual farmer-borrowers, who would pay an identical premium per dollar of insurance within the catchment of any given weather station, and receive an identical payout per dollar of insurance if the season's cumulative rainfall for some specified period of the year (say an agricultural season) fell below an agreed 'drought' level (say 80 per cent of the average). In order to pursue the practical implications, let us consider a particular case where a financial institution collapsed because of failure to insure against the risk of drought. The institution in question is the Smallholder Agricultural Credit Administration of Malawi (discussed in detail in Vol. 2, Chapter 16), which had maintained repayment rates of over 90 per cent for almost twenty years, from the early 1970s to the late 1980s, but which suddenly lost its grip during the 1992 drought, when repayment rates fell to 21 per cent. From the data in Table 3.6 it appears that on the basis of data for the last twenty years the break-even insurance premium required in Malawi to restore an average farmer's crop yield to its level in a year of normal rainfall would be $7 (27 Malawi kwacha at 1992 prices, or 9 per cent of average loan value). This would have raised the average annual interest rate paid by farmers over the period 1980–93 from 18 per cent to 27 per cent; however, we calculate that during the drought year of 1992 it would have raised the repayment rate from just over 20 per cent to 82 per cent, and possibly have protected the institution against collapse.

It is significant that when north and north-west India were struck in 1987 by a drought of broadly similar severity to that which hit southern Africa in 1992,[19] the default rates of the regional rural banks increased by only 0.9 per cent (from 50.3 to 51.2 per cent); this was partly due to the fact that these banks were able to claim on the Comprehensive Crop Insurance Scheme in respect of shortfalls in yield on designated crops. The uninsured Malawi Smallholder Agricultural Credit Administration, in other words, was destroyed by the 1992 drought; the insured Indian Regional Rural Banks suffered almost no incremental damage as a result of a shock of equivalent magnitude. No insurance scheme, however well designed, can rescue an otherwise inadequate lending programme, and it is significant that the SACA was beginning to experience arrears problems at the end of the 1980s even in years of adequate rainfall. But in the case of those lending programmes where involuntary default can easily occur for reasons quite unconnected with moral hazard, in particular the weather, appropriately designed insurance should be seen as a valuable adjunct to the related financial services of lending and savings. Such insurance should contain its own defences against moral hazard, including deductibles and no-claim bonuses. As an extension of the same principle, the risks which it covers should be confined to events which the insured borrower cannot influence, in other words, not loan default as such but non-culpable causes of default. Our proposal for rainfall insurance as a supplement to small-farmer lending

Table 3.6 Operation of crop insurance: hypothetical Malawi case
(data for Blantyre ADD only)

Crop year ending	Rainfall (mm)	% of average	Premium collected		Value of payout ($)	Default rate (%) Actual	Probable, with crop insurance[b]
			$	%[a]			
1980	1073	108	5	12		3	3
1981	1017	102	5	12		3	3
1982	894	90	5	11		2	2
1983	785	79	6	11	19	14	5
1984	974	98	6	11		2	2
1985	1187	119	6	10		4	4
1986	1180	119	6	10		12	12
1987	944	95	6	10		8	8
1988	1123	113	7	10		9	9
1989	1245	126	7	9		20	20
1990	1030	104	7	9		16	16
1991	989	100	7	9		14	14
1992	450	45	8	9	53	79	18
1993	991	100	8				

Sources: Malawi Meteorological Department for rainfall data; Smallholder Agricultural Credit Administration for loan default data. Full data arrays are in Vol. 2, Chapter 16, Table 16.8.

Notes

[a] Insurance premium as a percentage of loan value.

[b] The 'probable default rate' is derived by substituting the level of family income (as it would be if insurance payouts had been made) into the regression of default rate against family income and other determinants estimated in Table 3.5:

repayment rate = 4.38 −0.00027 (family income) + 1.65 (group organisation dummy variable)
                          (0.37)
+ 0.61** (loan collection method dummy variable) + 4.19 (savings/insurance dummy variable)
  (3.36)   (2.73)
+0.063
 (2.14)
rainfall; r^2 = 0.64, Student's t-statistics in brackets below coefficients

where the savings/insurance dummy variable is the value of the insurance payout as a percentage of the loan portfolio.

schemes satisfies these conditions, and is administratively simple too. As we shall see in the next chapter, it also holds out the promise of beneficial impact on borrower's technology over and above its influence on the lender's financial performance.

POSITIONING IN THE CAPITAL MARKET

An absolutely crucial determinant of the effectiveness of banks lending 'on the frontier' is how they affect the operation of the local financial market as a whole. The first question is how far beyond the existing financial frontier they manage to penetrate – whether, in other words, they succeed in lending to new customers too poor to have been able to borrow before, or simply end up competing with existing banking institutions for their market. Supposing that they are able to penetrate into new pastures, however, the next question is what influence they have on the informal moneylenders who represent poor unsecured individuals' main alternative source of credit. Do they wilt in face of the lower transactions costs involved in dealing with a moneylender (as the Ohio School might predict) or compete successfully with the moneylender; and if the latter, do moneylenders respond by cutting interest rates and expanding lending, or by exiting from the market? The outcome clearly has an important bearing on the overall access to the capital market available to borrowers, and thence on output, employment and poverty overall. Finally, it is of importance to know the extent to which innovations generated in the course of penetrating beyond the frontier can be passed on to other banking institutions in the formal and NGO sectors.

As Table 3.7 demonstrates, all the institutions on which we have data did cross the frontier, and provided a majority of their loans to individuals who had not previously borrowed from any source. It might be expected that there would be an inverse correlation between the proportion of virgin borrowers and average loan size, on the grounds that very small loans might be both more attractive to new borrowers and less attractive to established lenders. But although such a correlation is observable in Table 3.7 it is not statistically significant: some institutions providing, on average, relatively large loans, such as BancoSol and the KIE Informal Sector Programme, were particularly effective at reaching new borrowers. Similarly, schemes with a high proportion of women borrowers, such as Grameen Bank and BancoSol, did not have either a particularly high or a particularly low proportion of new borrowers. Except in the case of the Kenya Industrial Estates Informal Sector Programme, which made larger than average loans to borrowers above the average income level for our sample, less than 10 per cent of borrowers had experience of borrowing from a commercial bank. Borrowing from informal moneylenders was commoner in rural areas only, with 15 per cent or more of borrowers having previously taken loans from this source in the case of the Indonesia KURKs, Sri Lanka PTCCS, Bangladesh BRAC and TRDEP and Malawi SACA, but in the case of the predominantly urban schemes (Kenya Juhudi and ISP and Bolivia Banco-Sol) moneylenders are an insignificant (less than 5 per cent) source of credit for the sample.

We now consider in more detail the relationship between the case-study institutions and alternative sources of credit. It is important to be aware that the credit market is segmented both by region and by purpose. Many borrowers sampled had no access to any traditional moneylenders: when interviewed, such lenders usually stated that they were reluctant to lend to anybody they did not know, or anybody from outside their own home village. [20] Similarly, if borrowers were able to locate a moneylender, they

Table 3.7 Case-study institutions by nature of previous borrowing

Institution	Average borrower income level ($)	Extent of previous borrowing (% borrowing from source named)					
		Average loan size for case-study institution ($)	No previous loan from any source	Informal moneylender	Family and friends	ROSCA or co-operative	Commercial bank
Malawi Mudzi Fund	78	57	56		3		—
Indonesia KURKs	119	—	77	14	3	3	3
Indonesia BKKs	125	38	66	2	2	19	8
Sri Lanka PTCCSs	143	50	70	25	11	16	2
Bangladesh Grameen Bank	115	80	82	6	8	2	3
Bangladesh BRAC	107	—	58	24	15	—	3
Bangladesh TRDEP	n.a.		65	20	12	—	3
Malawi SACA	197	70	61	16	34	9	2
Kenya KREP Juhudi	217	347	72	1	10	10	2
India RRBs		99	39	19	17	16	9
Bolivia BancoSol	360	322	68	5	13	8	6
Kenya KIE-ISP	445		72	3	2	—	13
Indonesia BRI unit desas	296	600	20	4	28	16	2

Sources: Tables 3.3 and 1.2, plus country case-studies, except data for Bangladesh Grameen Bank, which are from Hossain (1984). Borrower income levels are from Table 3.5.

Note: Row totals often add to more than 100 on account of borrowing from multiple sources.

could usually borrow short-term only (typically one to three months), and for consumption only: through the entire range of our samples, we found very few cases of borrowers who had been able to get credit from a moneylender for purchases of fertiliser, new seeds, modern machinery or any other element of new technology, although some respondents (in Malawi) claimed that 'moneylenders had recently become willing' to finance such purchases. Over the range of transactions where money-lenders and micro-enterprise lending institutions were in direct competition, the relative level of transactions costs is as set out in Table 3.8. In all cases, except Indonesia BRI unit desas (which has well-below-average interest rates because of their ability to take collateral) the 'pure transactions costs' of negotiation, travelling and so on, although significant, are substantially outweighed by the interest cost of borrowing. Together with the empirical evidence of Table 3.3, this casts doubt upon the common assumption that 'demand for credit by small borrowers is relatively interest-inelastic, because transaction costs often represent a greater proportion of borrowing costs on small loans' (Holt 1991: 5).

From Table 3.8 it will be understood how the institutions under review have been able to make such rapid inroads into the territory of traditional moneylenders. It is true that they generally suffer in relation to money-lenders by demanding, unlike them, time for training and group formation; they also, in many cases, make a statutory charge for a contribution to an insurance fund in lieu of a risk premium. Against this, however, they consume less time in negotiation and in travelling time than the money-lender (the importance of having bank branches near the borrower will be appreciated) and make, on average, much smaller financial charges than the moneylenders. For women borrowers, often precluded by family responsibilities and sometimes by social custom[21] from making long trips to cities to conclude a loan agreement, the difference in travelling time in favour of the non-traditional lending institution may be particularly important. It is notable that moneylenders in Bolivia, Kenya and Malawi (unlike any of our case-study institutions except the BRI unit desas) habitually took collateral, often like a pawnbroker in the form of a mortgage on jewellery or other loose assets, contrary to the conventional wisdom as presented by the Ohio School:[22] this was given by many of our respondents as a major reason for switching to the new institution. Finally, and not captured by Table 3.8, many borrowers described the experience of borrowing from an institution as 'more pleasant' than dealing with a moneylender. What this meant varied from case to case: in Indonesia it reflected the shift from a technically illegal to a legal source of credit; in Bolivia it expressed the desire to escape from the often thuggish recovery techniques of the moneylenders; in many countries it conveyed relief at the presence of an alternative source of credit to an individual who was often also the borrower's landlord, storekeeper or supplier of raw materials. All these sentiments, and also the ability

Table 3.8 Transactions costs (% of total loan value per annum)

	Bolivia BancoSol	Indonesia BRI	Indonesia KURKs	Bangladesh BRAC	Bangladesh TRDEP	Malawi SACA	Sample average	Informal moneylender
		Sample institutions					For comparison	
Negotiation	9.5	10.0	9.0	0.3	0.2		5.8	7.1
Group formation	5.6	—	—	0.5	0.2	3.5	2.1	—
Training	1.4	—	—	0.3	—	—	0.8	—
Travelling time and obtaining documents	4.5	10.0	5.0	0.5	0.5	2.3	4.5	7.8
Asset pledge	—	12.0	—	—	—	—	2.0	6.6
Interest forgone on compulsory saving	10.0	—	7.0	5.0	5.0	8.0	7.0	—
Total non-financial costs	31.0	41.0	21.0	6.6	5.9	13.6	22.2	21.5
Financial costs (interest etc.)	48.0	30.0	84.0	20.0	16.0	18.0	31.5	72.0
Overall total cost of borrowing	79.0	71.0	105.0	26.6	21.9	31.6	53.7	93.5

Source: Survey data as detailed in Vol. 2, Chapters 10–16.

Note: Transaction costs are initially estimated in terms of labour time, which is then valued at the relevant agricultural wage rate in the relevant country to derive an estimate of non-financial costs of borrowing.

of the new entrants to the market to undercut the established financial operators by so large a margin, illustrate the economist's classical picture of what is supposed to happen when a monopoly is subjected to competition. The range of choice is widened, and if the incomer can compete on some combination of price and quality, he wins the business, as illustrated in the case of agriculturists in Moneragala, Sri Lanka (Vol. 2, Chapter 13).

What is not determinate, and has been very little investigated, is how the moneylender will respond when thus challenged. One possible response is to exit, the other to stay and fight, and it is crucial to the impact of non-traditional banking institutions which of the two is chosen. We found evidence of both responses. Some moneylenders did indeed stop lending once faced with competition, a response which was made easier for a majority of them by the fact that moneylending was usually not their only, or even their major, source of income: only 28 per cent of the moneylenders surveyed, across all samples, derived their income solely from lending. Some lenders 'crossed the floor' and put their expertise at the disposal of the institutions whose intrusion into the market was making life so difficult for them, a response particularly common in East Java, where the KURKs took on many former moneylenders as commission agents (*komisi*) acting on behalf of the expanding new institution. A majority, however, as demonstrated by Table 3.9, stayed and fought, using mainly the classical weapon of shaving their profit margins and broadening their loan portfolios, with a consequent increase in risk; some used threats and intimidation, as in the Puttalam District in Sri Lanka where prospective SANASA members were warned that if they joined a primary society they would 'never' get loans from local traders or moneylenders again. In general, the rural moneylender as a species has proved surprisingly resilient, even in countries such as India and Indonesia where it has been a declared objective of state intervention in financial markets to suppress

Table 3.9 Changes in moneylenders' terms, 1988–92

Percentage of moneylenders interviewed	BancoSol, Bolivia	*Within market supplied by:* KURKs, East Java, Indonesia	RRBs, Andhra, India	PCEA, Chogoria, Kenya
Lowering interest rates following arrival of competitor	70	84	98	75
Increasing loan volume following arrival of competitor	60	74	69	62

Source: Moneylender interviews, in Vol. 2, Chapters 10, 11, 14 and 15.

him.[23] In Bolivia, some were even reported to have embarked on a charm offensive. 'It is only since the arrival of BancoSol that the *prestamista* [informal moneylender] says thank you when taking my loan instalment,' commented one borrower. Across the entire range of samples the consensus was that the volume of lending *from traditional sources* had expanded since the advent of competition even though its price had gone down. Although inference from any before-and-after comparison is dangerous[24] the likelihood must be that this improvement in access to informal credit by the poor is largely due to the arrival of non-traditional lending institutions.

Ideological battle has raged around the head of the hapless rural moneylender for nearly a century. Once reviled, and in some cases outlawed, by post-colonial governments as an agent of exploitation, he has more recently been idealised by the Ohio School in terms such as this:

> The emerging view is that moneylenders generally perform a legitimate economic function. They supply services desired by their clients without the costly apparatus of buildings, papers and staff, and they do this at low cost to borrowers because of proximity, their quick response to requests, and the flexibility they permit in repayment. Their operations are frequently more cost-effective and useful to the poor than those of the specialised farm credit institutions, cooperatives, and commercial banks that governments use to supplant moneylenders. [Because of the] substantial transactions or access costs imposed on loan applicants, poor farmers often prefer to borrow from the informal lender rather than the formal institution.
>
> (von Pischke *et al.* 1983: 8)

The data reviewed in Tables 3.8 and 3.9 suggest that the right approach to the rural moneylender, where he exists, is neither to seek to wipe him out nor to romanticise him, but rather to seek out alternative methods of risk management to his as a means of competing with him. Lacking, in most cases, all of the tools of risk management described in the previous section of this chapter, he has often been forced to adopt the alternative approach of treating the risk of lending to an unsecured borrower as a fixed cost, and of loading that very high fixed cost on to the interest rate as a loan-loss provision; and because of the conditions of local monopoly which often prevail in rural financial markets, would-be borrowers have had no option but to pay this price. Below this price (depicted as r^*_m in the right-hand segment of Figure 3.8, which is simply the left-hand half of Figure 2.7 rotated clockwise through 90°) any alternative lender faces a very elastic demand for loanable funds, limited only by the demand for the goods and services which the local economy produces. This is depicted as D_A in the right-hand half of Figure 3.8. If such a lender can supply this demand at a total cost level lower than the moneylender's (such as r^*_a in the diagram) by the use of the techniques described earlier, then the moneylender will lose

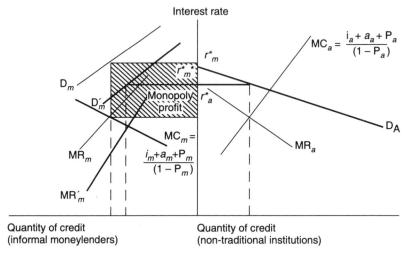

Figure 3.8 Relationships between formal and informal credit markets

some of his monopoly profit, and his demand curve will fall, forcing him to cut price and expand volume, for example to r_m^{**} if profit levels are to be maintained, as appears to have happened in the countries covered by Table 3.10. If both the moneylender's and the new institution's interest rates stay down at r_m^{**} (or can be pushed down further by cost-cutting on the part of the new lender) then investment will be increased, and poverty reduced, *pro tanto*, as depicted in Figure 2.7 above. In Chapter 4 we shall see whether this happens, if the knife-edge is successfully negotiated. But some institutions (such as the Malawi Mudzi Fund) never get to first base, because their burden of fixed costs is too high in relation to the moneylender for them to compete with him.[25] And institutions which do get to first base may conclude, like many duopolists, that the right approach is to collude with the moneylender to maximise joint profits and to continue to charge r_m^*: good for sustainability, bad for investment and poverty reduction.

The potential influence of 'innovative' finance institutions does not end with their influence on the behaviour of moneylenders. Their experimentation, and in some cases their overt research and training activities, create knowledge which other lenders can use. This knowledge takes the form both of general techniques which may be deployed to reduce risks, and of specific knowledge about the creditworthiness of particular borrowers. As an example of the former, the Grameen Bank's experimentation with the idea of borrower groups meeting weekly with other groups in a repayment centre has been successfully copied by very many other institutions in Bangladesh and around the world. As an example of the latter, successful clients of BancoSol can show their repayment record to other banks from which they wish to borrow, thereby assisting the second bank with its

Table 3.10 Kenya Rural Enterprise Programme: components of the 'optimal subsidy', 1988–93

Symbol	Externalities	Meaning	Value ($m) 1988–93	Source
$Q\ \partial a/\partial Q$		Change in administrative costs of 'client' per unit increase in lending of 'parent' multiplied by value of 'parent's' lending	−0.4	Aleke-Dondo *et al.* (1992)
$Q\ \partial p/\partial Q$		Change in default rate of 'client' per unit increase in lending of 'parent' multiplied by value of 'parent's' lending	0.9	Aleke-Dondo *et al.* (1992)
$\partial\sigma_{(TT)}/\partial Q$		Change in variance of clients' profits per unit increase in lending of 'parent'	0.3	Interviews, KREP, October 1992
$\dfrac{Q(\partial a/\partial Q + \partial p/\partial Q)}{Q\ \partial p/\partial Q} - \dfrac{\partial\sigma}{\partial q}$		Optimal subsidy	0.8	Sum of first three terms above
		Actual subsidy to KREP 1988–92	8.0	Table 3.11 below

Sources: For optimal subsidy formula, see Chapter 2, note 4. For numerical data, see right-hand column of table.

screening function. In neither of these cases does the 'pioneer' receive payment for the service it has provided by lowering the risk premium which the assisted institution needs to charge; in other words, an externality has been provided to the assisted institution. It can hardly be otherwise, because the benefits associated with the creation of new knowledge are extremely difficult for their creators to conceal from, or invoice to, their competitors. Such externalities have been cited by economists working in the spirit of 'new growth theory' as a major reason why there is under-investment in human capital, especially in developing countries.[26]

In the examples given above there does not need to be any conscious process of transmission of new knowledge; information simply floats from institution to institution like pollen on the wind, and some institutions now using the 'Grameen model' are not even aware that they are doing so, much less receiving conscious training from Grameen staff.[27] But conscious training is of course possible, and to illustrate how it may work let us consider a second stage of the diffusion process, in which an institution modelled on the Grameen Bank uses a mixture of training and condition-ality to inculcate financial discipline and sustainability in other NGOs. KREP, the Kenya Rural Enterprise Programme (over and above its lending activities, discussed in detail in Vol. 2, Chapter 15) has since 1987 provided financial support to some (twelve) non-governmental organisations, initially free but since 1990 at 7 per cent interest. In return, these institutions have to offer deposit-taking facilities, must organise borrowers into Grameen-style borrower centres with weekly repayment, must meet the accounting and reporting requirements of KREP, and must raise lending interest rates to a level specified by that institution (currently 27 per cent). Response to this regime has varied, but the KREP 'client' which we studied most intensively, PCEA Chogoria, has progressed in five years from a 50 per cent to a 96 per cent repayment rate while continuing to lend to individuals whose average income is below the poverty line – most of them farmers. This tutelage, as we saw, is now paid for, and is profitable – the externality has been internalised. However, it is a high-risk operation, which would not have been initiated without subsidy from an external donor[28] – in this case USAID. The client's lending costs were pulled down and the institution made viable, not by market forces, but by external intervention.

THE SUBSIDY ISSUE

It is the presence of these externalities which constitutes the main case for providing subsidy to non-traditional lenders. As we noted, these externalities are of two kinds:

1 'experimental' lenders lower their successors' costs by providing them with free information concerning the bankability of individual borrowers and concerning the best techniques for minimising default;
2 'experimental' lenders reduce the variance surrounding their successors' returns by carrying out research in an environment where uncertainty is very high and insurance – the conventional method of reducing risks – is often not available.

We may return at this point to the discussion surrounding Figure 2.2, which demonstrated that the socially optimal rate of interest would diverge from the 'financial break-even' interest rate by an amount depending on the rate at which administrative costs, the probability of default and the variance of returns in 'client' and 'parent' institutions fell as the volume of lending increased in the 'parent' institution.[29] The size of these three terms dictates the size of the optimal subsidy, as illustrated in Figure 3.9; as the long-term cost curve flattens out (Figure 2.2) it may be expected that the terms $\partial a/\partial Q$ and $\partial p/\partial Q$ will go to zero, and as they go to zero, so subsidies can be phased out. The problem which confronts sponsors is that it is very difficult to forecast these terms; precisely the problem of imperfect information from which we began. However, if we use past data (in Table 3.10) for one institution which sees itself consciously as a 'tutor' for other NGOs – the Kenya Rural Enterprise Programme – we find *ex post* that the

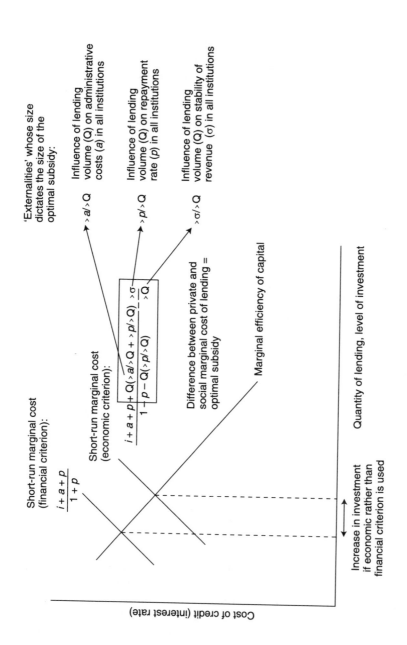

Short-run marginal cost (financial criterion):

$$\frac{i+a+p}{1+p}$$

Short-run marginal cost (economic criterion):

$$\frac{i+a+p+Q(>a/>Q+>p/>Q)}{1-p-Q(>p/>Q)}-\frac{>\sigma}{>Q}$$

Difference between private and social marginal cost of lending = optimal subsidy

Marginal efficiency of capital

'Externalities' whose size dictates the size of the optimal subsidy:

$>a/>Q$ — Influence of lending volume (Q) on administrative costs (a) in all institutions

$>p/>Q$ — Influence of lending volume (Q) on repayment rate (p) in all institutions

$>\sigma/>Q$ — Influence of lending volume (Q) on stability of revenue (σ) in all institutions

Cost of credit (interest rate)

Quantity of lending, level of investment

Increase in investment if economic rather than financial criterion is used

Figure 3.9 The case for subsidising 'informal' credit institutions

optimal level of subsidy for that institution over the years 1988–92 was of the order of $0.8 million – much less than what was actually contributed by USAID and KREP's other sponsors, but part of that could be reasonably ascribed to benefits still to materialise. In the Kenyan case one element in the 'optimal subsidy' formula, namely the impact on administrative costs $\partial a/\partial Q$, turns out *negative*: the parent imposes an external diseconomy on the client. This is the familiar case analysed earlier in this chapter, in which a lender invests in various screening devices which raise administrative cost a, in the hope that they will push down default rates p more than in proportion. In this case they do.

Indeed, if we examine the behaviour of sponsors in relation to 'experimental' lending institutions over the last ten years, we notice an interesting schizophrenia. All of them subsidise their clients; and all of them denounce subsidy, on principle, as wrong. As we see from Table 3.11, not one of the 'successful' institutions in our sample has negotiated the knife-edge without subvention from some external fairy godmother. Yet the godmothers in question often confuse the issue by making public pronouncements suggesting that such do-gooding should never happen. Consider, for example, the following remarks by one of them, Douglas Salloum, Director of Financial and Technical Services at the Calmeadow Foundation (one of the main sponsors of BancoSol):

> The history of government involvement in credit programs has been abysmal and there is no reason to suppose that any future government will perform the task of financial intermediation any better than in the past. Keeping government influence out of the business of lending to the informal sector is probably the most serious challenge that has to be addressed. Credit can be provided in a truly sustainable manner without subsidisation. Credit can be provided in a sustainable manner if the organisation is structured to be profitable and pursues that goal.[30]

Given that so good a theoretical case can be made for offering a temporary infant-industry subsidy to experimental banks, why do sponsors choose to talk in a manner so inconsistent with their actions? One explanation is that what the sponsors are attacking is the old-style open-ended subsidy on the interest rate (as still practised by the Government of India) designed to keep the cost of borrowing below some target figure; not the type of subsidy proposed, which is time-bound, tied to measurable benefits, and can be cut off by the sponsor if these benefits do not materialise.[31] Some sponsors of experimental development finance institutions (notably USAID) have sought to reconcile subsidisation and sustainability by splitting the supported institution into two parts: a 'commercial' wing which charges commercial rates, maximises profits, and is unsubsidised (BancoSol or Juhudi), and a 'research and development' wing which is responsible for research (including experimental ventures in new areas), training and out-

Table 3.11 External support for case-study institutions, 1988–93

Organisation	Sponsor(s)	Value of subsidy[a] from sponsor 1988–92 ($m)	Source
Bolivia			
BancoSol	USAID	4.6	Glosser (1994) and
	Calmeadow Foundation		sponsors
Bangladesh			
Grameen	Miscellaneous	25.0	
BRAC	Miscellaneous	29.1	Vol. 2, Chapter 12
TRDEP	ADB	1.7	
Indonesia			
BRI	USAID	20.0	Vol. 2, Chapter 11
	World Bank[b]	10.0	Boomgard and
			Angell (1994)
BKKs/KURKs	USAID		
	Indonesia Government[c]	50.0	
India			
RRBs	Government of India[d]	225.0	Vol. 2, Chapter 14
	IDA, ODA and others		
	through NABARD		
Kenya			
KREP	USAID	7.5	
	Ford Foundation	0.5	Vol. 2, Chapter 15
	ODA	1.4	
KIE-ISP	GTZ	1.5	Vol. 2, Chapter 15
	Others, inc. Government of		
	Kenya	0.4	
Malawi			
SACA	World Bank	4.5	Vol. 2, Chapter 16
Mudzi Fund	IFAD	1.5	

Sources: Vol. 2, Chapters 10–16

Notes
[a] Subsidy is defined as financial inflow less value of repayments by lender to sponsor organisation
[b] Non-concessional loan; figure quoted is the element of concessionality in IBRD loans
[c] Concessional credits provided through central bank
[d] Concessional credits provided both through central bank and through government-owned sponsor banks

reach work, and continues to be subsidised (PRODEM or KREP). This, however, by no means pins down the externality precisely, since a lot of the assistance which 'parent' institutions give their 'clients' is precisely through the knowledge which is thrown up by their commercial operations, rather than by their research or training work.

The as yet unsolved problem is how to design subsidies so that they maximise external spin-offs in 'client' institutions, and for that matter amongst informal moneylenders, in the same way as the cluster of performance incentives described on pp. 60–5 aim to maximise repayments in 'parent' institutions. What originally got subsidies a bad name is that, as designed in the 1970s and 1980s, they appeared in many cases to motivate not improvements but deterioration in financial-sector performance, undermining loan repayment and the productive use of loan funds. They also discouraged innovation, rather than encouraging social creativity. We believe that the tying of subsidies to defined external benefits through a fixed-term performance contract is only a necessary, and not a sufficient, condition to make subsidies effective. The additional condition which must be satisfied is that potential poor borrowers need to be identified and linked with the credit supplier through a process which combines the functions of social organisation and financial linkage – social intermediation, as Lynn Bennett calls it.[32] This process may be carried out through an NGO or local government organisation, through self-help groups or through individuals, as locally appropriate. It will be considered in detail in Chapter 7. For the moment, having examined the financial foundation stones on which experimental institutions seek to build, it will be useful to see the effects of the structures they have so far managed to erect.

NOTES

1 In Table 3.1 and throughout this chapter we measure the arrears rate as the value of those loans that are six months and more in arrears as a percentage of the value of the total loan portfolio. Many banking institutions use a different definition of the arrears rate, and to that extent the data in Table 3.1 will differ from those published. For further discussion of the measurement of arrears rates, see Bolnick (1988).

2 With the highly untypical exception of Malawi Smallholder Agricultural Credit Administration, which is very heavily subsidised and in which an arrears rate that remained in single figures for twenty years was suddenly raised sky-high by a catastrophic drought in 1992. This case is examined in more detail on pp. 68–9 below.

3 In terms of the notation of Chapter 2, the subsidy dependence index is measured as

$$SDI = \frac{(i - i^*)X + (i^*E - p) + K}{rX}$$

where, as in that chapter, i = borrowing interest rate, r = lending interest rate and X = loan portfolio. The new notation is: E = value of bank's equity capital; p = profit before tax; K = non-interest subsidies; and i^* = interest rate which institution would pay for borrowed funds if access to concessional funds were eliminated.

The presentation of the SDI in this way implies that raising interest rates is the obvious instrument by which financial viability should be restored. However, raising interest rates in this way may be either politically impossible or financially risky (if the level of competition is such as to deprive a nascent DFI of its market if rates go too high). In this event, the necessary adjustment if sustainability is to be achieved has to come on the cost side. This possibility is discussed on pp. 46–56 below.

4 We know of no micro-enterprise finance institution anywhere outside Indonesia with an SDI of less than 100 per cent, with the exception of the Bank of Agriculture and Agricultural Co-operatives (BAAC) in Thailand, which is estimated by Yaron (1990) to have had an SDI of 23 per cent in 1988.

5 It is also notable that in those schemes where the lending interest rate was raised sharply as part of a restructuring programme (for example, lending to the BRI unit desas in 1985, to Grameen Bank borrowers in 1984, and to Malawi SACA borrowers in 1987), this was followed in Malawi and Bangladesh by no change, and in Indonesia by an increase, in the recovery rate.

6 Recall the data in Table 2.1 above.

7 For example, Khandkar *et al.* (1993) report that amongst Grameen Bank borrowers 'the recovery rates for loans have been found to be higher for female members compared to men. For example, the loan recovery rate for general loans for women was 97 per cent compared to 89 per cent for men in 1992.' This has been a consistent feature of the Grameen Bank's loan recovery performance, and has induced the Bank to establish only new women's groups since the mid-1980s. Other arguments in support of favouring women borrowers have been advanced, including the proposition that women, being more family-orientated and less egoistic than men, would be more likely to repay on time, being more concerned about the consequences for their entire family if the lender should foreclose on loans made to them as a result of late repayments (Fernando Romero, founder of BancoSol, in speech to conference on Micro-enterprise Credit, Santa Cruz, Bolivia, 25 April 1993).

8 An insurable risk is a risk which (a) can be predicted reasonably reliably from past data and (b) cannot be deliberately increased by the insured in order to claim indemnities. Drought is an insurable risk; failure to repay loans is a non-insurable risk. See Hazell (1993).

9 This is as true in the individual-lending schemes of Indonesia as in group-lending schemes, because village administrators in Indonesia take responsibility for recommending, and monitoring the performance of, borrowers within their village. See Vol. 2, Chapter 11.

10 From equation [2.5] (p. 25), the criterion for a particular category of administrative expenditure to be effective is

$$\frac{\partial p}{\partial a} > \frac{1}{r}$$

To convert the regression coefficient (0.61) in Table 3.5 into a value for $\partial p/\partial a_1$ we need to divide by cost of loan collection per visit, since the independent variable in Table 3.5 is number of visits. This is $0.2 (from Table 3.8). Hence across the sample as a whole,

$$\frac{\partial p}{\partial a_1} = \frac{0.61}{0.2} = 3.02; \quad r = 40\%. \text{ Hence } \frac{1}{r} = 2.5. \quad \text{Hence} \frac{\partial p}{\partial a_1} > \frac{1}{r},$$

and expenditure on a_1 (loan monitoring is effective).

11 Livestock farmers, of course, have a much less extreme seasonal fluctuation to their incomes, and can repay much more easily on a weekly or monthly basis.

12 However, loan instalments in the Bank for Agriculture and Agricultural Co-operatives of Thailand, one of the most successful banks lending to small

farmers and the only one to our knowledge to have a Subsidy Dependence Index of less than 100 per cent. See Nattaradol (1995).

13 We borrow this phrase from staff of the World Bank and IMF who encounter a similar dilemma when deciding whether or not to extend a further loan to a client (usually a national government) already in arrears.

14 If (as may often be the case for a poor unsecured borrower) the borrower cannot borrow from any source other than the banks under examination, then his or her reputation with other lenders will be of no account, and $\mu = 0$ by definition.

15 In the course of 'exploitation of the lender by the borrower', of course, the lender will lose much of his capital through non-repayment of loans, and a third player, namely a sponsor, will need to enter the game if the lender is to continue to lend.

16 HAT = Hadiah Angsuran Tepat Waktu = rebate for timely BKK loan repayment. IPTW = Insentif Pembayaran Tepat Waktu = incentive for timely repayment of BRI (KUPEDES) loans.

17 See, for example, von Pischke et al. (1983: 11); von Pischke (1991: 96–7).

18 It draws freely on (but is not identical to) the scheme proposed by the World Bank (1991). It has historical roots which go back a long way, for example to the scheme proposed by Mysore State, India, in 1918: see Mishra (1994: ch. 2).

19 In the northern provinces in Rajasthan, Gujerat, Uttar Pradesh, Bihar and Madhya Pradesh 1987, rainfall was 62 per cent of the 1948–92 average: compare the Malawi data in Table 3.8.

20 Vol. 2, Chapters 10, 11 and 16; see also Udry (1990: 259–60) for the comparable Northern Nigerian case.

21 'In many areas it is considered inappropriate for a woman to travel alone the long distance between her rural home and a bank in the town, or to offer the occasionally necessary bribe to a male official in charge of credit applications' (Holt and Ribe 1991: 11).

22 'In general, the provision of security will not be an important feature of lending in the informal money market' (Bottomley, in von Pischke et al. 1983: 247).

23 For persuasive data demonstrating the resilience of the rural moneylender in the Indian case, see the essay by Bell (1990).

24 Because the difference between moneylenders' behaviour before and after the advent of competition could be due to factors other than the competition: for example, new infrastructure, autonomous changes in moneylenders' costs.

25 In terms of the diagram: the D_A curve is below the MC_a curve in the right-hand part of Figure 3.8.

26 The usual approach employed in new growth theory is to depict the creation of new knowledge as being subject to diminishing returns, but to depict returns to that knowledge as increasing. See Romer (1986) and, for empirical evidence, Levine and Renelt (1992).

27 Compare Molière's Bourgeois Gentleman, to whom it came as a surprise to learn that he was speaking prose.

28 Interview, Managing Director KREP, Nairobi, 30 September 1992.

29 In Chapter 2 we calculated the optimal subsidy as:

$$\frac{Q(\partial a/\partial Q + \partial p/\partial Q)}{Q\ \partial p/\partial Q} - \frac{\partial \sigma}{\partial q}$$

where a = administrative costs per dollar lent, p = costs of loan default per dollar lent, σ = variance of profits, Q = volume of lending. For full derivation see Chapter 2, note 4.

30 Often as a device to simplify this calculation, donors use a rule of thumb, such as the provision of finance to cover the expected costs of new bank branches for five years – the period it usually takes for a new branch of the Grameen Bank or BRAC to achieve sustainability. This is a crude approximation, as it takes no account of effects on institutions outside of that subsidised.

31 Salloum (1993: 7 and 10). For more on social intermediation, see Bennett (1993).

32 An analogy may be drawn with the type of infant-industry protection offered by the governments of South Korea and Taiwan, which is conditional on the protected firm fulfilling its part of a performance contract requiring it to improve productivity, or some other performance indicator, by a specified percentage, on pain of such protection being withdrawn. For more detail, see Chang (1993) or Wade (1990).

4

THE IMPACT ON PRODUCTION AND TECHNOLOGY

INTRODUCTION

From the previous chapter we know that sustainable banking with poor customers is possible. But the ultimate test of any institution is not whether it exists or sustains itself, but whether it manages to do something useful. Do the institutions considered here pass this test? In this chapter we consider what influence experimental banking institutions have had on technology (using that phrase to include employment and all other factors of production) and on incomes; in Chapter 5 the focus is sharpened to examine how the impact on incomes and employment divided between rich and poor, and thence the impact of the schemes on poverty.

We presented an initial picture of the linkage between financial market intervention and the output and technology of borrowers in Figure 2.6 above; this diagram is reproduced, unaltered, as Figure 4.1. From the diagram it will be seen that the number of income-earning opportunities that borrowers are able to create in any time period should in principle depend:

1 on the rate at which the barriers to access which they face (represented by the budget constraints AA′, BB′) are removed, reflecting the various forces on the supply-side of financial markets discussed in the previous chapter and also the growth of demand;
2 on the state of technologies available to borrowers, represented by the isoquants R_1, R_2;
3 on the relative prices of capital, labour and other inputs (represented by lines p_1, p_2), which determine where borrowers end up on these production functions.

Previous research on the impact of agricultural credit on technology and output (for example, David and Meyer 1980: tables 3 and 4; Desai and Mellor 1993) has confirmed that because of imperfections in the capital market, credit had an influence on production going beyond the influence of conventional factors of production, as hypothesised in 1 above. What

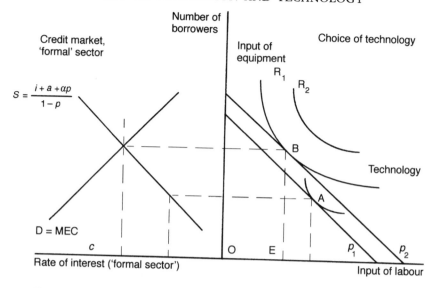

Figure 4.1 Interlinkage between credit market and choice of technology

such research has not yet done is to explain why that impact varies so widely between schemes and countries. In what follows we suggest that over and above the effects described as 2 and 3 above, the riskiness of expected output in relation to the size of borrowers' capital stocks and complementary government policies (particularly in the area of infrastructure and extension) play a crucial part in influencing allocation decisions. This will require us to modify the simple picture presented in Figure 4.1.

IMPACT ON PRODUCTION AND INCOMES

First the good news: as shown in Table 4.1, both the absolute incomes (in all cases except BRAC and Malawi Mudzi Fund) and, more importantly, the increase in the incomes of borrowers are substantially greater for borrowers in all the schemes we examined than for a control group of non-borrowers. As shown in Table 4.2, this was due more to an increase in the profitability of the assisted enterprise, rather than to income deriving from outside that enterprise. In other words, there is every likelihood that the receipt of credit did directly increase the income of assisted enterprises, both for borrowers above the poverty line and to a markedly lesser extent, for borrowers below. The tendency of poor borrowers to benefit less will preoccupy us in Chapters 5 and 8. Amongst both rich and poor borrowers, there is enormous variance in impact from 0.5 per cent in the case of the Kenya Industrial Estates Informal Sector Programme to nearly 40 per cent in

Table 4.1 Loan impact on family incomes: summary

	(1) 1992 family income ($)	(2) 1992 family income ($)	(3) (2)/(1)%	(4) Annual average change in family income[a] 1988–92	(5) Annual average change in family income[a] 1988–92	(6) (5)/(4)%
	Borrowers	Control sample		Borrowers	Control sample	
Bolivia						
BancoSol	3028	1121	270	28.1	14.5	193
Indonesia						
BRI unit desas	1722	1074	160	20.7	3.8	544
BKK/KURKs	702	570	123	5.2	2.4	216
Bangladesh						
Grameen Bank	418	341	123	—	—	—
BRAC	517	552	94	19.8	13.8	143
TRDEP	1138	816	139	38.7	30.6	126
Sri Lanka						
9 sampled PTCCSs	1301	981	132	15.6	9.9	157
India						
2 sampled RRBs	505	496	102	46.0	24.0	191
Kenya						
KREP Juhudi	1756	1307	134	1.5	1.1	133
KIE-ISP	2807	1759	159	0.5	0.4	125
Malawi[b]						
SACA	830	276	301	2.8	1.6	175
Mudzi Fund[c]	655	669	98	1.4	1.2	117

Sources: Bolivia: Table 10.12; Indonesia: Tables 11.7 and 11.11; Bangladesh: Tables 12.15 and 12.19, also Khandker *et al.* (1993: Table 7.7); Sri Lanka: Table 13.21; India: Tables 14.7 and 14.8; Kenya: Tables 15.20 and 15.21; Malawi: Tables 16.16 and 16.27, with some supplementary data from Conroy (1993)

Notes
[a] Real changes in family income; deflator is the difference in inflation rates between the national currency and the US dollar
[b] For Malawi, data in cols 1 and 2 are for 1993 and income changes reported in cols 5 and 6 are for the period 1989–93
[c] Data for 1990–3 only (Mudzi Fund created in 1990).

case of Bangladesh TRDEP, and we now wish to investigate the causes of these differences in impact. Table 4.3 begins this task.

It is immediately apparent that the short-term productive impact of particular schemes had a direct connection with their financial performance or long-term sustainability as analysed in the previous chapter. Financially sound schemes which were able to pull down the real cost of lending were thereby able to attract more borrowers (in terms of Figure 4.1,

Table 4.2 Loan impact on borrower family incomes: decomposition

	(1) Average annual income increase, 1988–92		(2) Decomposition by income percentile Percentage annual income increase for:		(3) Decomposition by source of income	
	Absolute ($ p.a.)	%	families above poverty line	families below poverty line	% of income increase from assisted enterprise	% of income increase from other sources
Bolivia						
BancoSol	665	28.1	58.0	100.8	86	14
Indonesia						
BRI UDs	303	20.7	24.7	12.2	69	31
BKKs	36	5.2			61	39
Bangladesh						
BRAC	102	19.8			92	8
TRDEP	440	38.7	24.5	33.9	89	11
Sri Lanka						
9 sampled PTCCSs	320	15.6	19.0	12.3	—	—
India						
2 sampled RRBs	46	9.1	19.6	−1.1	—	—
Kenya						
KREP Juhudi	19	8.7	3.2	0.2	74	26
KIE-ISP	14	—	—	—	77	23
Malawi						
SACA	23	2.8	4.1	0.1	84	16
Mudzi Fund	9	1.4	9.1	−0.1	71	29

Sources: As for Table 4.1

an eastward shift in the supply curve of credit, and thence an increase in the number of borrowers); in general, the high-turnover schemes were also those with the highest margin of benefit per borrower, as may be seen from the first two columns of Table 4.3. All the high-margin schemes in Table 4.3 (growth of beneficiary family income more than 150 per cent of income growth within the control group) have more than 100,000 borrowers except Bolivia BancoSol; all the low-margin schemes have less than 100,000 borrowers except Bangladesh BRAC. Also apparently related to scheme impact, according to Table 4.3, is:

1 the rate of growth in the local economy (in terms of Figure 4.1, the speed at which the demand curve in the left-hand part of the diagram is moving outwards). Unsurprisingly, the benefit which borrowers are able

Table 4.3 Average increase in borrower family income, 1988–92, in relation to possible causes

	Average increase in income of borrowers (as % of income of control group)	*No. of borrowers (thousands)*	*Rate of growth of personal incomes 1988–92 (% p.a.)[a]*	*Possible causes*	
				% borrowers investing in new technology	*% increase in intra-family employment*
Bolivia					
BancoSol	193	45	5.2	26	4.5
Indonesia					
BRI unit desas	544	1800	3.1	36	—
BKKs[b]	216	700	3.1	24	8.2
Bangladesh					
BRAC RDP	143	598	2.7	8	1.3
TRDEP	126	10	2.7	11	2.4
Sri Lanka					
9 sampled PTCCs	157	700	2.1	11	5.1
India					
2 sampled RRBs	200	25	—	12	7.5
Kenya					
KREP Juhudi	133	1.1	2.2	4	—
KIE-ISP	125	1.7	2.2	7	—
Malawi					
SACA	175	400	1.4	71	4.5
Mudzi Fund	117	<1	2.8	—	—
Average, 'high impact' schemes[c]	257		3.0	33.6	5.6
Average, 'lower impact' schemes[d]	128		2.5	7.5	1.9
t-statistics for difference between sample means[e]			0.87	1.93*	4.33*

Sources: Increase in borrower incomes (col. 1): Table 4.1 above; rate of growth of personal incomes (col. 2): World Bank, *World Development Report 1994*, tables 2 and 8 (see also note [a]); other columns: Bolivia, Tables 10.12 and 10.13; Indonesia, Tables 11.7, 11.8, 11.11; Bangladesh, Tables 12.15, 12.17, 12.19, 12.21; Sri Lanka, Tables 13.21, 13.24, 13.25; Kenya, Tables 15.20 and 15.21; Malawi, Tables 16.16 and 16.27, with supplementary data from Conroy (1993)

Notes
[a] For urban schemes (BancoSol, Juhudi and Kenya Industrial Estates ISP) relevant rate of growth of personal incomes is taken as annual average increase in private consumption for 1988–92. For all other schemes, relevant rate of growth is taken as average rate of growth of agricultural GDP 1988–92 in country stated.
[b] Data for 1990.
[c] Schemes for which growth in borrower income 1988–92 was more than 50 per cent higher than in the 'control group': Malawi SACA, Bolivia BancoSol, Indonesia unit desas and BKKs, Sri Lanka PTCCs.
[d] Schemes for which growth in borrower income 1988–92 was less than 50 per cent higher than in the 'control group': Kenya KREP Juhudi and KIE-ISP, Bangladesh BRAC and TRDEP, Malawi Mudzi Fund.

to derive from microcredit is greater in rapidly growing Indonesia and Bolivia than in relatively stagnant Bangladesh and Kenya;

2 the rate at which credit is being invested in new technology (in terms of Figure 4.1, the speed at which the isoquants in the right-hand half of the diagram are being moved outwards by the uptake of credit);

3 the extent to which credit creates employment *within the assisted family*.[1] From the point of view of overall poverty reduction, employment outside the family is obviously more important, but we come to that in the next section.

In general, as we see, 'high-impact' schemes, defined as those with the biggest difference between the growth in incomes of borrowers and the control sample of non-borrowers, had a higher growth of demand, a higher rate of hiring of family members, and a higher rate of investment in new technology; but the first of these is not statistically significant. This definition of impact is inadequate, since it considers only the margin of net benefit per borrower as listed in the first columns of Table 4.3; but as earlier noted, this correlated with number of borrowers. It begins to look as though, in most cases, schemes need to negotiate the financial knife-edge, as discussed in the previous chapter, and achieve a state where the number of borrowers is high and growing rapidly before they can get into a position where they can offer a substantial margin of benefit to borrowers. At all levels of turnover, schemes which enable many borrowers to invest in new technology have higher margins of benefit per borrower; but the opportunities for such investment vary between sectors, and even where feasible, technology-enhancing investment will generally raise the risks to which borrowers are subject, which is precisely what poorer borrowers, in particular, are seeking to avoid. We now examine in more detail the uses to which loans were put, and in particular the relationship between income, technology and risk.

TECHNOLOGY, RISK AND LOAN IMPACT

The justification generally given for credit schemes of the type examined here is that they will raise the borrowers' incomes in a way which would not otherwise be available to them. In terms of Figure 4.1, they move the

---

[e] Student's *t*-statistic is measured

$$\frac{\bar{X}_1 - \bar{X}_2}{\sqrt{\frac{s_1^2}{n_1} + \frac{s_2^2}{n_2}}}$$

where x_1, x_2 are the two sample means, s_1, s_2 the two sample standard deviations and n_1, n_2 the two sample sizes.

* denotes significance at the 5 per cent level.

budget constraint outwards by enabling them, in spite of their lack of collateral, to purchase capital assets from which an income is expected. This income, however, may materialise in either of two ways: as a result of additional purchases of equipment within the existing technology, so that returns per unit of capital remain constant (known by economists as 'capital widening') or as a result of purchases of new technology so that not only is the capital stock expanded, but its productivity increases ('capital deepening'). Those schemes which made possible a substantial amount of capital deepening, on the evidence of Table 4.3, reaped a benefit in terms of higher margins of benefit per borrower family. However, there is no free lunch: higher returns can, as a rule, only be bought in return for the acceptance of higher risks. Since the poor cannot afford to bear high risks, it follows that schemes of the type examined here will have two types of beneficiaries: richer beneficiaries who use credit for capital deepening, which increases their expectations of income and risk at the same time, and poorer beneficiaries who use credit either for capital widening which involves unchanged risks and income, or even to reduce their capitalisation and their risks – that is, their vulnerability – at the same time. The first of these behaviours corresponds to what has been described as the 'promotional' role of development programmes and the second to what has been called their 'protectional' role (Dreze and Sen 1991).

Figure 4.2, which is a free adaptation of a diagram in Weeks (1971), illustrates this. The borrower – who may be either farmer, micro-entrepreneur or (like many of our interviewees) both at once – faces a trade-off between the expected value and the variance of his or her income. A 'disaster point' D, below which the borrower's family faces food shortage or loss of assets, is defined on the expected-value-of-income axis; the borrower chooses technology so as to keep the risk of an income below D down to an 'acceptable level'. (This risk can never be reduced to zero – in other words, 'fail-safe' business plans enabling the borrower to climb the vertical axis above D are generally not available.) If the maximum acceptable risk of disaster is 33 per cent, and income is normally distributed, expected income must be at least one standard deviation above D, and a 45° line from D will define the boundary between the acceptable region to the north-west of DR and the unacceptable (because the risk of disaster is excessive) region to the south-east. If the maximum acceptable risk of disaster is reduced to 5 per cent, expected income must be at least two standard deviations above, and the boundary DR' between the acceptable and the unacceptable region will be defined by a line at an angle of 22.5° to the vertical axis; and so on: the greater the degree of risk aversion, the smaller the risk of disaster that can be afforded and the steeper the slope of the boundary. In what follows, we shall arbitrarily assume that there are two groups of would-be borrowers, one with a 5 per cent tolerance of 'disaster' and one with a 33 per cent tolerance. Since

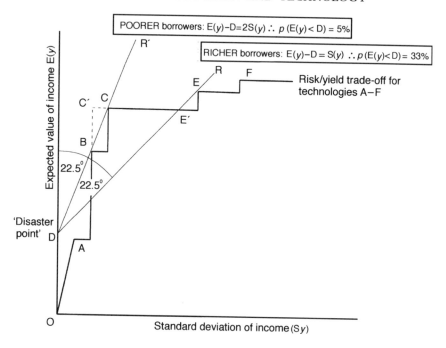

Figure 4.2 Risk/yield relationship for potential borrowers

the poor have more to lose in the event of a disaster, we shall call the first group 'poorer' and the second group 'richer'. (Data are presented in Table 4.4 which suggest that, both within and between schemes, richer borrowers are more likely to borrow for new technology.[2]) Indeed, we now have a precise definition of vulnerability: the further to the south-east an individual moves, the more vulnerable he or she becomes to the risk of income below the disaster level, and vice versa.

Let us now consider what is feasible. We shall assume that a range of technologies exists within each sector (true in agriculture and informal-sector manufacturing, less true in trade), and that to move to a technology which offers a higher income implies an increase in the standard deviation of income, so that the trade-off between expected yield and its riskiness is upward sloping. This trade-off has been drawn jagged rather than smooth in Figure 4.2: only the five technologies A, B, C, E and F are available. For any individual, the optimum technology is defined by the highest level of income which satisfies both the feasibility and the risk-aversion constraint: as these constraints have been drawn, this is point B or C for the poorer group of would-be borrowers and point E for the richer group. Even these optima, of course, cannot be attained if the producer is constrained by inability to borrow, or for that matter by lack of other assets such as land.

Table 4.4 Growth of productive assets and uptake of new technology: between-scheme comparisons

	Average beneficiary income 1992 ($/family)	*Growth in productive assets 1988–92 (%)*		*Proportion adopting 'new technologies' during loan period (%)*
		Borrowers	*Non-borrower control group*	
Primarily non-agricultural schemes				
Bolivia: BancoSol	3,028	22	12	26
BRI unit desas	1,722	24	7	36
Bangladesh: TRDEP	1,138	—	—	11
Bangladesh: BRAC	517	61	36	8
Kenya: KREP Juhudi	1,756	2	−11	4
Kenya: KIE-ISP	2,807	4	−1	7
Malawi: Mudzi Fund	655	50	29	—
Primarily agricultural schemes				
Malawi: SACA	830			71
India: RRBs	505	12	8	12

Sources: Beneficiary incomes: Table 4.1; proportion adopting new technologies, Table 4.3

In such an environment, credit for poor producers has multiple responsibilities thrust upon it. By simply loosening a liquidity constraint it can enable producers to simply enlarge the scope of operations; for example, from B to C for a poor producer or from E′ to E for a richer producer, so that vulnerability is not increased; we refer to this as the *protectional* role of credit. Examples of this might be a farmer increasing the area under a food crop, or an informal-sector manufacturer increasing stocks of raw materials. However, if their income is successfully increased through a series of loan operations, *this may itself influence their attitude to risk*, so that the risk-aversion constraint rotates clockwise. In this event borrowers, emboldened by the success of previous loans, may choose to borrow again for the purpose of capital-deepening (for example, the purchase of modern varieties of a crop, or a switch from manual to electrical equipment). Such a move (for example, from C to E) will increase their expected income, but at the same time also increase their vulnerability;[3] we describe credit operations which have this effect as *promotional*. (If things go wrong, these processes are reversed: assets have to be sold to keep the risk of disaster at an acceptable level, and the borrower may have to retreat from the technical frontier.) There exists, in fact, a third option, because there are some investments which have the ability to reduce the variability of income without reducing its expected level – in other words to move the risk/yield trade-off westwards over the parts of its length, for example from point C to C' on the diagram. This can be done by both non-financial means (such as investment in boreholes and other minor irrigation equipment[4] and by financial means (such as the purchase of insurance). Lending of this type which has the function of *reducing* the borrower's vulnerability is of course super-protectional.

We can now use Figure 4.2 to explore the technological impact of different credit schemes, and the strategic choices which face their managers and sponsors. First, we may recall, the use of micro-enterprise loans to upgrade technology is actually the exception rather than the rule: as shown by Table 4.3, only within Malawi SACA did the majority of borrowers use their loans to upgrade their technology, and in all the other schemes the proportion of borrowers who did so was one-third or less: most lending, in this sense, was 'protectional'. Table 4.4 additionally suggests that in general the rate of innovation was higher among those schemes catering for a less poor clientele, for example, the BRI unit desas in Indonesia and BancoSol, as predicted by Figure 4.2. *Growth of productive assets* was higher amongst borrowers than amongst non-borrowers in all schemes; but not noticeably higher among schemes lending to richer borrowers.

Within schemes, once again (Table 4.5) we see a correlation between borrowers' initial income and the adoption of new technology, but it is possible to take the analysis further by comparing cohorts of borrowers according to the number of loans they have taken. Within all the schemes that have been operating for a number of years (that is, all except KREP Juhudi and the Malawi Mudzi Fund) it is possible to identify a group who have taken a series of loans. Technical innovation is generally confined to this group; but only to a minority within it: the others continue to use their loans mainly for protectional purposes, and some do not even increase their loan size with successive loans.

Table 4.5 BancoSol, Bolivia: adoption of new technology and asset acquisition in relation to income: within-sample comparisons

Number of loans received	Average income per month, 1992 ($)	Average asset holdings 1993 ($)	Proportion who had adopted new technology during loan period
6 or more:	392	4,148	40
1–6	205	3,165	24
0 (that is, control group)	282	163	10

Source: Vol. 2, Chapters 10 and 11

External sponsors of micro-enterprise lending schemes have generally espoused the promotional model of credit, and much of their illustrative case-history material focuses on exemplary individuals who use successive loans, progressively increasing in size, to approach the technical frontier.[5] As Table 4.5 illustrates, these are exceptional cases, even for lenders operating at the upper end of the micro-enterprise income spectrum. It is therefore the more important to emphasise that the demand for small-farm and micro-enterprise loans consists mainly of borrowing for protective purposes, sometimes indeed to finance consumption or to pay off existing borrowing from moneylenders. This not only should not be discouraged but often lays the basis for a subsequent attack on the technical frontier. Figure 4.2 once again illustrates. Consider an individual at point A: because of resource constraints (let us assume that the potential borrower is landless) his or her income is actually below the 'disaster' level D. Any borrowing undertaken is likely to have, as its primary purpose, to raise the family's consumption level above D, for example by buying raw materials which can be resold at a profit, or by financing a search for work by a member of the family, or simply by paying off existing loans from moneylenders so that the pattern of repayments is stretched out over a longer and more manageable period. If this strategy is successful, it may get the borrower to point B, where income has risen to the point at which the balance between income and its uncertainty is where the borrower wants it. But if it can be maintained there for a time, the borrower's risk-aversion frontier may move; in other words, he or she may contemplate investments which allow an increase in vulnerability, including technical innovations such as the purchase of new seeds or equipment. The key point is that borrowing for consumption is what started this entire process off, and may have been a necessary precondition for it; institutions lending to the poor are therefore ill-advised to treat small loans for consumption as being 'unproductive'.

One of the major technical changes which micro-enterprise lending institutions have attempted to bring about is the acquisition of green revolution technology in the growing of food crops: it requires particular attention on account of both its potential implications for poverty reduction (discussed in the next chapter) and its unusual risk/yield mixture. Both BIMAS (the predecessor of the BRI unit desas in Indonesia) and the IRDP (the main conduit for loans from the Indian Regional Rural Banks) were set up in the 1970s deliberately as vehicles for bringing the green revolution to hitherto unbankable small farmers, as were the farmers' clubs in Malawi from which the Smallholder Agricultural Credit Administration eventually grew. In a smaller way, the Sri Lankan thrift and credit co-operatives, the Bangladeshi TRDEP and the Indonesian BKK and KURK schemes also serve as vehicles for bringing modern cereal varieties to very small farmers.[6] But the green revolution has followed very different patterns in Asia

Table 4.6 Characteristics of the green revolution in selected African and Asian countries

	ASIA	Indonesia	India	AFRICA	Kenya	Malawi
Growth of grain output per ha 1988–90 in relation to 1961–3		4.8	3.6		1.1	0.8
Grain output per ha. 1990–2 average	2,580	3,843	1,861[a]	1,160	1,722[a]	1,110[a]
Large farm yields as % of small farm yields (all cereals 1987)	104	—	90	245	290	186
Area irrigated (% of area under arable and permanent crops, 1990)		25.9	25.4		2.1	0.9
Percentage of rural people borrowing from rural financial institutions	32.8		25.0	10.3	17.0	8.0

Sources: Mosley (1994: Table 11), except percentage of people borrowing from rural financial institutions: from Desai and Mellor (1993: 28, Table 3).

Note: [a] Data for 1988–90.

and Africa, being both more widespread and less biased towards large farmers in Asia. It is also the case that institutional credit is much less widespread in Africa, as illustrated by Table 4.6. We should like to suggest that these facts are related.

Green revolution technology consists of high-yielding, mostly hybridised, seeds of particular foodcrops, of which the most important are rice, wheat (in Asia) and maize (in Africa), which for maximum yields need to be accompanied by appropriate fertiliser applications and predictable levels of water supply. Potentially the most exciting feature of such technology, as explained by Lipton and Longhurst (1989: ch. 3), is that it is scale-neutral: in other words, unit costs per ton of grain are in principle the same for small as for large farmers, and the variance of yields to which crops are subject is in principle the same for modern as for traditional varieties, possibly even less if the modern varieties are more disease- and drought-resistant than the traditional varieties they replace. If this is right, investment in modern crop varieties, unlike investment in most new technologies, *can be seen as a protectional rather than a promotional strategy*: in other words, as recommendable for poor farmers as for rich farmers, because it does not increase their vulnerability. In terms of Figure 4.2, the ratio of income variance to expected income is not increased by the shift to the new technology.

Whether this is in fact so depends on a number of factors, not all of them biological. The variability of the income stream derived from the decision to adopt a particular modern variety over the years depends on weather and soil type, but it also depends on whether new seeds, fertilisers and indeed credit reach the farmer on time, and on the relationship between their price and the price of the final output. If any of the latter are more favourable, in particular years, for traditional varieties of grain than for modern varieties, the expected value/variance ratio for *net income* may be such as to increase the farmer's vulnerability if he or she adopts green revolution technology, even if *crop yields* will both increase and stabilise if the modern variety is adopted. For example, if hybrid seeds cannot be delivered to the farmer at the right time, any yield advantage they have over local seeds is purely notional; this can easily happen if the marketing of inputs is in the hands of a monopolistic authority such as Malawi's ADMARC. In other words, whether the adoption of green revolution technology can be presented as a protectional strategy, and who benefits from it if it is adopted, is not a datum, but depends on local administrative arrangements.

All this has relevance to the African/Asian divide, as illustrated in Table 4.6. For reasons discussed in detail by Lele and Goldsmith (1989), the 'shelf' of modern varieties recommendable to small farmers in the 1960s and 1970s expanded much faster in Asia than in Africa, even though research expenditure per unit of agricultural output was actually higher in Africa throughout (Lipton 1988b). But the response of the respective banking systems was also quite different. Whereas in both India and Indonesia in the 1970s, state-owned banking systems sponsored a determined drive to place modern farming inputs in the hands of the small farmer (IRDP and BIMAS respectively), the banking systems of Africa remained in the hands of commercial banks, cash-crop co-operatives and rural moneylenders, none of them willing to finance the purchase of seeds and fertilisers by unsecured small farmers. The results can be seen in Table 4.6: not only higher yields in Asia, but also more stable yields on account of the very high concentration of the investment financed by the banks in minor irrigation works in rainfed areas. In most Asian countries, including the four featured in this book, the resulting green revolution stimulated a surge in agriculture-based rural industries and trades which constitute the main market for micro-enterprise lending institutions. In African countries, the adoption of modern varieties of maize and (in a small way) wheat and rice has been very much more confined to large farmers with the necessary access to credit and knowledge; the growth of off-farm enterprises has been restricted *pari passu*, and micro-enterprise lending institutions find themselves lending to a smaller and a much more urban-biased market.

Within this context we can now discuss the limited success of the Malawi Farmers' Clubs (subsequently Smallholder Agricultural Credit Administration, or SACA), an institution designed to fill precisely the hole in the market described above, and also the one institution in our sample explicitly committed to use its credit to force the pace of technical change. As noted in Table 4.3, 71 per cent of sampled borrowers – a much higher proportion than in all our other lending institutions – used their loan to upgrade their technology, and specifically to purchase fertiliser and/or hybrid seed. This is not an astonishing finding, since SACA credit is explicitly linked to such purchases, and indeed given in kind: the 29 per cent who 'did not innovate' are simply those who were using hybrid seeds and fertiliser before becoming SACA members. What is interesting is that the pattern of adoption of new technology by income group appears to correspond locally to whether such adoption would or would not increase the borrower's economic vulnerability. Table 4.7 suggests that in the central districts of Kasungu

Table 4.7 Malawi: maize yield and variance trends

	Malawi yields (kg/ha)		Kasungu and Lilongwe ADDs yields (kg/ha)		Blantyre ADD yields (kg/ha)	
	Local maize	Hybrid maize	Local maize	Hybrid maize	Local maize	Hybrid maize
1982–3	1,180	2,700				
1983–4	1,037	2,757	1,200	2,800	1,080	1,700
1984–5	1,034	3,111	1,200	3,000	820	1,050
1985–6	958	2,941	1,100	2,850	800	1,300
1986–7	953	2,306	950	2,500	800	2,754
1987–8	1,094	2,667	1,350	2,800	950	3,000
1988–9	1,052	2,855	1,462	2,800	600	2,450
1989–90	813	2,555	1,450	2,400	600	2,500
1990–1	872	2,908	1,050	3,175	700	2,000
Mean	999	2,755	1,220	2,790	793	2,444
Standard deviation	106	222	175	232	154	580
Coefficient of variation (CV) (%)	10.6	8.1	14.3	8.3	19.4	23.7
(Change in CV)		(−2.5)		(−6.0)		(+4.6)
Average total family cash income, 1991 ($/annum)		52		67		39
Proportion of very small farmers (<1.5 ha) using hybrid seed, 1988		1.5		13.6		0.4

Sources: Conroy (1993, Tables 6.14, 6.15, 9.8, 9.9); Department of Agriculture, Malawi (1988).

and Lilongwe, over the years 1980–93, the switch from local maize to a SACA-financed seed–fertiliser package could be presented as a protectional measure which would not increase the average small farmer's coefficient of variation (variance/income ratio), whereas in the southern districts, particularly Blantyre, it would, for largely administrative reasons, increase the variance of income even more than expected income for adopters of modern varieties, and thus increase their exposure to disaster. Consequently, adoption of green revolution package varieties has in the south of the country been confined to the top of the pyramid of small farmers (those willing to increase their risk and accept a 'promotional' loan), whereas in the centre, smaller farmers (those farming less than 0.5 ha) have also been willing to adopt them; such green revolution as has occurred has therefore been a much more elitist affair in the south than in the north and centre. This has implications for the ability of institutions such as SACA to reduce poverty, a point which will be considered in the next chapter. It also partly explains the difficulties faced by the ill-starred Malawi Mudzi Fund, which was based in the southern districts of Chiradzulu and Mangochi. Lacking any broad-based increase in rural incomes to 'lean on', it found itself short of profitable projects to lend for, and these demand-side problems may have hampered it as seriously as its much-publicised problems on the cost side (Hulme 1993, and Vol. 2, Chapter 16).

We can summarise our general argument on the technical impact of credit by reference to Figure 4.3, which sandwiches the risk/yield relationships of Figure 4.2 between the two halves of Figure 4.1, the credit market and the technical changes to which it is expected to give rise. The increase in credit availability, KM in the left-hand part of the diagram, leads, as before, to an outward movement of the budget constraint and to consequent technical changes in the right-hand part of the diagram (from R to R') which we have represented as increased acquisition of green revolution technology. But who gets the benefit of these changes will depend on their impact on potential borrowers' vulnerability, as depicted in the middle panel of the diagram. If only a small proportion of the increase in lending is given for protectional purposes (KL in the middle part of Figure 4.3, leading to a change from B to C' in the position of risk-averse borrowers), with the remaining credit LM being allocated to promotional lending which moves risk-accepting richer borrowers from B' to E, the shift in the budget constraint, from LL to L'L' in the right-hand part of the diagram, will be confined to the larger operators who can bear the risk, while smaller producers continue to face the former relationship between the cost of capital and other productive factors, and use the traditional technique P: a not very poverty-reducing, and what we would describe as an 'African', pattern of technical change. If on the other hand most of the increased lending (KL' in the middle part of the diagram) is allocated to protectional lending, leading to a shift from B to C' for risk-averse poor producers, the

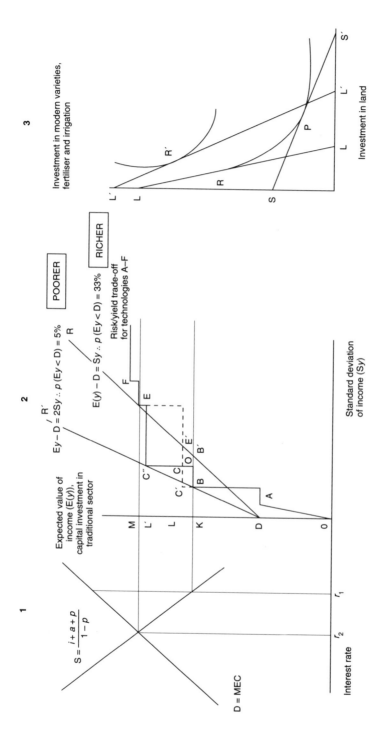

Figure 4.3 The risk/yield trade-off in relation to the 'frontier' capital market

Note: Case 1 (mainly promotional lending): 'protectional' lending = KL, 'promotional' lending = LM; constraint moves for richer farmers only to LL″
Case 2 (mainly protectional lending): 'protectional' lending KL', 'promotional' lending = L'M; constraint moves for all farmers to SS'

shift in the budget constraint will be more widely diffused, and the prospects for poverty reduction will be better, as they have been in south-east and increasingly in south Asia.

EMPLOYMENT EFFECTS

The impact of borrowing on employment is a natural consequence of the technology in which that borrowing is embodied. Across the sample as a whole, as we have seen, the technical change induced by borrowing was not dramatic, and neither as a consequence have been its influences on employment outside the family. As Table 4.8 shows, there was a difference of less than one employee per enterprise between borrowers and the control sample of non-borrowers, and a change over time of about one employee per enterprise, on average, since the first loan was taken out. Only the Indonesian BRI unit desa scheme, which caters to businesses larger than the sample average, recorded employment increases much larger than this.

Table 4.8 Loan impact on employment and possible determinants

	(a) Over-time comparisons: average increase in paid non-family employment since first loan (persons per enterprise)		(b) Differences between borrowers and control group at time of survey(persons per enterprise)	Average borrower household income, 1992 ($)
	Borrowers below national poverty line	All borrowers		
Bolivia BancoSol	−0.1	0.8	0.7	360
Indonesia BRI unit desas		5.8		296
Kenya KIE-ISP		1.1	1.1	445
Bangladesh TRDEP		0.1		
India RRBs				
Bangladesh BRAC	0.7	0.8		107
Kenya KREP Juhudi	0.1	0.3	0.5	217
Sri Lanka PTCCs		0.3		143
Malawi Mudzi Fund		0.0	−0.5	78
SACA		no data		197
Mean	0.2	1.0	0.5	196

Sources: Country studies in Vol. 2; borrower household incomes from Table 3.3.

Table 4.9 Bolivia, BancoSol customers: changes in employment and incomes by initial income of borrower

| Income change since loan | Monthly income one year ago (Bolivianos) | | | | | |
| | 250ᵃ | | 250–1,000 | | >1,000 | |
	Income	Employment	Income	Employment	Income	Employment
Decrease/no change	0	100	0	82	22	34
Increase less than 50 per cent	11	0	81	0	42	13
Increase more than 50 per cent	89	0	19	18	35	54

Source: Vol. 2, Tables 10.11 and 10.13.

Note: ᵃ Below poverty line.

This change over time was smaller still – although on average still positive – if only borrowers below the poverty line were considered.

Further examination of the hiring patterns of different types of enterprise confirms the impression that rising levels of output financed by loans were initially accommodated by increased demands for family labour only, with significant hiring of non-family labour carried out only by larger enterprises. In the BancoSol sample summarised in Table 4.9, no borrower households with incomes below the Bolivian poverty line had hired any additional labour at all, even on a casual basis (and some had shed labour) during the loan period, even though on average their incomes had gone up by more than the sample average, whereas more than half of the borrowers with incomes in excess of 1,000 bolivianos per month (four times the poverty line), had hired additional labour from outside the family. In other samples, such as Malawi SACA, seasonal peaks in output were met by the hiring of labour on a casual or on an exchange basis, but the general pattern across all schemes was that it was unusual for first-time borrowers or for firms with a turnover of less than $10,000 per annum to hire labour from outside the family on a year-round basis.

The schemes with the largest average increases in employment (Table 4.8) were Indonesia BRI unit desas and Kenya KIE-ISP: not the most 'successful', either in terms of financial performance or direct poverty reduction, but those with the most prosperous customers. In addition, as revealed also by Table 4.8, the propensity of borrowers to take on labour tended to increase as the wage fell in relation to the cost of capital. To the extent that such labour is likely to be hired from poor income groups, therefore, a low relative real wage is likely to be favourable for poverty reduction on schemes such as these.

Putting the findings of this section together with those from the previous section, we see that it was unusual for credit to trigger a continuous increase in technical sophistication, output or employment: it was much commoner for each of these variables to reach a plateau after one or two loans and then remain in a steady state. So long as household survival needs to be given priority over enterprise development, and access to training, new technologies and growing markets is restricted, the capacity for dynamic entrepreneurial behaviour is bound to be restricted also. This has important implications for the ability of micro-enterprise credit to reduce poverty, which will be explored in the next chapter.

NOTES

1 This appears also to be true at an intra-sample level: 'The most important factor correlating with increased income was labour. There is a moderate correlation (0.39) between increases in the number of employees paid by a respondent and increases in income. More significant was the level of intra-household employment – that is, the number of [household] members working in the loan-assisted activity. This labour–income correlation (.61) is not only relatively high, but is statistically significant' (Sri Lanka study, Vol. 2, Chapter 13, p. 000).

2 Data on the relative risk-aversion of different income groups for a range of developing countries are presented in Table 2 of Binswanger and Sillers (1983). These suggest that most individuals throughout the Third World are clustered within the category of 'moderately risk averse'. But high levels of risk aversion are commoner among the poor than among the well-off.

3 The question of whether the adoption of modern crop varieties increases the farmer's yield risks from disease and climatic variation is highly controversial. Until recently it was widely assumed that the adoption of modern varieties of all cereals increased both the expected yield and the variance of the crop, and hence that the green revolution was regressive. But this claim has been disputed by Lipton and Longhurst (1989: ch. 3, esp. pp. 55–74 and 119–21), Singh (1990) and, most recently, Heisey (1994). If the counter-argument is true and the adoption of modern varieties is not risk-increasing, this has a fundamental importance for our argument, since a major barrier to income generation by very poor farmers' families is removed if the barrier of access to credit can be removed at the same time.

4 Sixty-seven per cent of all rural lending refinanced by the Indian National Bank for Agriculture and Rural Development (NABARD) over the years 1987–93 was for the finance of investments in minor irrigation (NABARD, *Annual Reports* 1987–93, various).

5 Several case-histories of this kind are also provided by Patten and Rosengard (1991: for example, 31, 38, 59, 72, 75).

6 In Indonesia, however, both the conversion of BIMAS into the BRI unit desa scheme and the 1979 remodelling of the BKK system in Central Java involved a deliberate retreat from agricultural lending. See Vol. 2, Chapter 11.

5

FINANCE FOR THE POOR
Impacts on poverty, vulnerability and deprivation

INTRODUCTON

This chapter focuses on the impact that innovative financial services can have on poverty, vulnerability and deprivation. Such an analysis is central to our study as developmentally successful institutions must contribute to poverty-reduction. However, the definition of what is meant by 'poverty', how it might be measured and who constitute 'the poor' are fiercely contested issues. In this introduction we identify the meaning used in this chapter and discuss the influence of definitional issues on the analysis of poverty-reduction strategies.

At the heart of the debate about defining poverty stands the question of whether poverty is largely about material needs or whether it is about a much broader set of needs that permit well-being (or at least a reduction in ill-being).[1] The former position concentrates on the measurement of consumption, usually by using income as a surrogate. Although this approach has been heavily criticised for its 'reductionism' and 'bias to the measurable' (Chambers 1995) it has considerable strengths in terms of permitting quantitative comparisons and the analysis of changes in the access of different people to their most pressing material needs (Townsend 1993). Greeley (1994: 57) has strongly defended the use of income-poverty measures: 'an absolute and objective poverty line is a form of information that empowers the poverty reduction agenda and encourages appropriate resource allocations'. The case for adopting an income-poverty approach to the study of poverty is further strengthened by the fact that the majority of national governments and development agencies use this concept for their analyses of poverty and anti-poverty policies.

The case is far from absolute, however, and even adherents acknowledge that 'there is a broad agreement that income is an inadequate measurement of welfare' (ibid.: 51). Chambers (1983, 1995) has recorded the many forms of deprivation that very poor people identify themselves as experiencing that are not captured by income-poverty measures. These include vulnerability to a sudden dramatic decrease in consumption levels, ill-health and physical weakness, social inferiority, powerlessness, humiliation and isolation. Such dimensions of poverty are significant in their own right and are also essential analytical components for the understanding of income poverty. The failure of income measures to capture such deprivations can be illustrated at the macro level by the 'weakness in the correlations between income-poverty and some other deprivations' (Chambers 1995: 12).[2] At the household level it is illustrated by Jodha's (1988) finding that households in Rajasthan who became income-poorer over the period 1963–6 to 1982–4 regarded themselves as being better off in terms of their self-defined criteria of the quality of their lives. Such evidence is used to argue for a more holistic concept of poverty that recognises its multi-dimensionality and accepts that some important components can only be captured qualitatively.

Although the debate about reductionist or holistic approaches is commonly presented as an 'either . . . or' argument we do not believe this to be the case. In the materials that follow we adopt an integrated approach. Initially, the analysis focuses on the income-poverty impacts of the institutions studied. Following this, we examine the effects of case-study institutions on vulnerability and other forms of deprivation including physical weakness and mental disability, social inferiority (particularly in relation to gender), powerlessness and isolation. Much of the data on these issues are qualitative and were acquired by interviews with a sub-sample, from key informants and from secondary materials. While we believe that the adoption of such a broad approach is essential if the impact of financial innovations on poor people is to be better understood, the reader should recognise the analytical complexity that this introduces. Most obviously, having multiple criteria makes it less easy to judge an innovation or service simply as 'good' or 'bad'. Instead, the likelihood arises of institutions reducing poverty and deprivation in some respects while being neutral or negative in others. Thus policy implications may need to be qualified, rather than dropping as neat messages out of the analysis.

The definition of poverty and deprivation is not merely of analytical significance: it also has a strategic dimension. A concentration on poverty as 'income poverty' is usually associated with a conceptualisation of poverty-reduction as moving households from a stable 'below poverty line' situation to a stable 'above poverty line' situation (Figure 5.1). This leads to a focus on promotional strategies 'raising persistently low incomes' (Dreze and Sen 1989: 60–1) which, in terms of financial services, emphasise (often exclusively) the provision of credit for income-generation through self-employment. By contrast, a broader view of poverty that conceptualises income levels as fluctuating and the dampening of dramatic reductions in income (and other entitlements) as a major means for poverty reduction, introduces quite different strategic emphases (Figure 5.2). Protectional strategies (ibid.) become significant: in terms of financial services

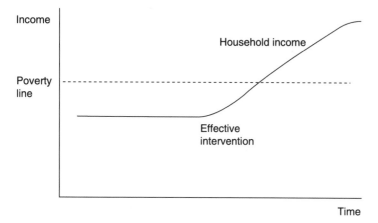

Figure 5.1 Poverty-reduction as conceptualised by an income-poverty approach

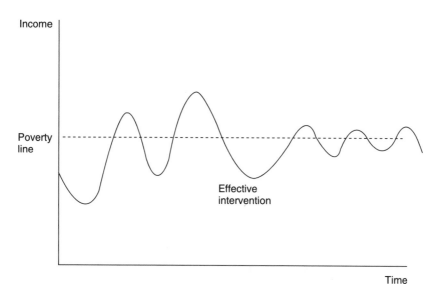

Figure 5.2 Poverty-reduction as conceptualised by an income-poverty and income-vulnerability approach

this fosters a focus on voluntary savings mechanisms, emergency consumption loans and relatively low-risk income-generation activities that are unlikely to create indebtedness.[3] Distinguishing between promotional and protectional approaches does not require that they are seen as unrelated or as competing directly against each other. Effective promotional strategies, that raise household incomes and create additional assets, can make the protection of a minimum standard of living much easier. Conversely, effective protectional strategies may permit households to undertake investments that they had previously regarded as being too risky.

The real 'crunch' between the reductionist and holistic conceptions of poverty arises not over the relationship between income promotion and income protection, however. It is over the relative prioritisation of material and non-material needs. From the reductionist perspective, then, meeting basic material needs takes preference over non-material needs. From the holistic perspective, at times non-material needs may be pursued at the expense of pressing material needs and poverty reduction could occur while material living standards are stagnant or even dropping. For us there is no scientific basis for choosing between these two positions: it is a matter for judgement on the basis of personal values. We concur with Michael Lipton (quoted by Greely 1994: 57), that 'you must be before you well-be'. Where absolute poverty exists we believe in the primacy of material needs.

Two further points must be made in this introduction. The first is to note that, contrary to much recent writing, micro-enterprise and/or small-enterprise development should not be equated with poverty-reduction. At times the two will coincide but this needs empirical validation and should not be assumed, as is commonly the case. The second point, related to the first, is that most of the poor households that we have studied cannot be viewed simply as micro-enterprises, self-employed poor or labouring poor (for example, see Remenyi 1991: 8). The vast majority of households that we have studied are 'foxes' not 'hedgehogs' (Chambers 1995: 23). They do not have a single source of livelihood support: rather, depending on season, prices, health and other contingencies, they pursue a mix of activities that may include growing their own food, labouring for others, running small production or trading businesses, hunting and gathering, and accessing loans and subsidies (from the state, friends or NGOs). In terms of economic behaviour, they are closer to the manager of a complex portfolio than the manager of a single-product firm.

FINANCE FOR THE POOR: IMPROVING INCOMES

The primary process by which financial services are envisaged as reducing poverty is by the provision of income-generating loans. According to Muhammud Yunus of the Grameen Bank a virtuous circle can be established: 'low income, credit, investment, more income, more credit, more investment, more income' (quoted in International Development Support Services 1994: 6). As is discussed below, this notion of sustained growth in income, production, credit and investment captures a part of the experience of poor households that borrow, but only a part. The differing abilities of borrowers, their initial economic and social positions and the wider economic environment (and its fluctuations) ensure that no simple model can explain the complex empirical findings of our research.

Not unexpectedly, assessing income changes proved a difficult task. In Malawi, the recall method for estimating income proved inoperable for some agriculturalists whose activities are only partially monetised. In Bangladesh there are widely differing estimates of the inflation rates experienced by poor people (Vol. 2, Chapter 12) and consequently questions about 'real' changes in income, while in Indonesia the widespread perception that the official poverty line is 'too low' made it necessary to construct an alternative.[4] Finally, there are the problems of attributing causality: although in all the cases where we associate credit with changes in income a logical cause-and-effect relationship could be identified, it was not possible for us to control for the influences of other variables. These caveats mean that often the directions of the changes we describe are of more significance than the absolute figures presented.

The obvious starting point in examining the impacts of credit on the incomes of the poor is to see the degree to which they can access loans (Table 5.1). All our case-study institutions, with the exception of the KIE-ISP in Kenya, make loans to some people with incomes below national poverty lines. As one would anticipate, institutions that target the poor have much higher rates of participation by the poor than open-access schemes. SANASA is the only non-targeted scheme that manages to incorporate a majority of poor members. Only the BRAC-RDP, Grameen Bank, BRI's unit desas, BKK and SANASA have reached coverage rates that make it possible for them to have significant impacts on poverty at the meso- and micro-level. Notably, three of these institutions are non-targeted, illustrating that mass coverage open-access schemes, with appropriate policies,[5] may play a role in poverty-alleviation despite the preference of many donors for targeted interventions. The income impacts recorded (Table 5.1) are only a snapshot of a constantly changing situation and evidently different schemes are achieving quite different results. Nevertheless, three general points can be drawn:

1 Well-designed lending programmes can improve the incomes of poor people and for a proportion of cases can move the incomes of poor households above official poverty lines in large numbers (BRAC's RDP, Grameen Bank, BRI's unit desas, BKK and SANASA).

2 There is clear evidence that the impact of a loan on a borrower's income is related to the level of income (Figure 5.3 and Table 5.2). For rural Asia the Bangladeshi cases (BRAC and TRDEP) illustrated this most clearly and the available data on Sri Lanka and Indonesia confirmed this picture. This finding should not be unexpected given that those with higher incomes have a greater range of investment opportunities, more information about market conditions and can take on more risk than the poorest households without threatening their minimum needs for survival. Such data confirm the argument made in the Bangladeshi case-study

Table 5.1 Finance for the poor: impacts on income for case-study institutions

Organisation	Target group	Proportion of borrowers below poverty line	Number of borrowers (1992)	Status of sample	Average borrower income as per cent of poverty line before last loan	Impact of last loan on borrower income (real terms)	Per cent of borrowers crossing poverty line in 1992	Estimate of numbers crossing poverty line	Other information
BRAC-RDP	Poor, especially women	Vast majority	650,000	Completed 1st loan Completed 3rd loan	68 (117)[a] 58 (99)[a]	1.1 per cent increase 6.4 per cent increase	— —	— —	Evidence that it is moving away from a focus on the core poor
TRDEP	Poor families	Vast majority	25,000	Completed 1st loan Completed 3rd loan	80 (136)[a] 103 (197)[a]	23.0 per cent increase 18.8 per cent increase	— —	— —	Lends to non-poor and poor households, but not core poor
Grameen Bank	Poor, almost exclusively women	Vast majority	1,400,000	(See Hossain 1988)	—	Members have incomes 43 per cent above target group in control villages, and 28 per cent above non-members in target groups of assisted villages	—	—	Difficulties in working with core poor – agricultural labourers are 60 per cent of target group but only 20 per cent of membership

BancoSol	No	29 per cent	—	Half about to borrow, half 6 or more loans	8.0	91 per cent of borrowers had increase in income: 89 per cent of borrowers below poverty line experienced an income increase greater than 50 per cent	—	To achieve financial viability BancoSol is promoting larger loan sizes; this is likely to further distance it from the poor
BRI unit desas	No	7 per cent	2,400,000	See Vol. 2, Chapter 11	8.4	20.7 per cent (1990)	48,670	Only 7 per cent of borrowers poor but has wide coverage
BKK	No	38 per cent	499,000	See Vol. 2, Chapter 11	6.6	Poor borrowers increased income by more than 18 per cent	36,932	—
KURK	No	29 per cent	158,000	See Vol. 2, Chapter 11	3.3	Poor borrowers increased income by more than 2 per cent	3,753	—
KREP Juhudi	Small entre-preneurs	—	2,400	Completed 1st loan / Completed 1st and 2nd loan	—	Associated with 24 per cent increase in income / Associated with 44 per cent increase in income (both loans)	—	Evidence of increased incomes and assets (see Vol. 2), Chapter 11

Table 5.1 Continued

Organisation	Target group	Proportion of borrowers below poverty line	Number of borrowers (1992)	Status of sample	Average borrower income as per cent of poverty line before last loan	Impact of last loan on borrower income (real terms)	Per cent of borrowers crossing poverty line	Estimate of numbers crossing poverty line in 1992	Other information
KIE-ISP	Not the poor	0 per cent	1,700	Completed 1st loan Completed 1st and 2nd loan	— —	Substantial increases in enterprise profitability	0	0	No direct poverty impact – 'second round' effects only
MMF	Poor, especially women	Vast majority	223	—	—	Evidence that on average MMF borrowers increase income	—	—	Scheme in experimental phase only
SACA	Small farmers	48 per cent (7 per cent)[b]	400,062	—	—	Highly variable	2	—	SACA has had little involvement with the core poor
SANASA	Rural people – no specific target group	52 per cent	702,000	Kurunegala District Moneragala District	192 154	26.0 per cent increase 18.9 per cent increase	25 per cent of those below poverty line	30,000	Has a policy of encouraging low-income members

Notes
[a] As a percentage of the 'core poor' poverty line (Rahman and Hossain 1992).
[b] Core poor.

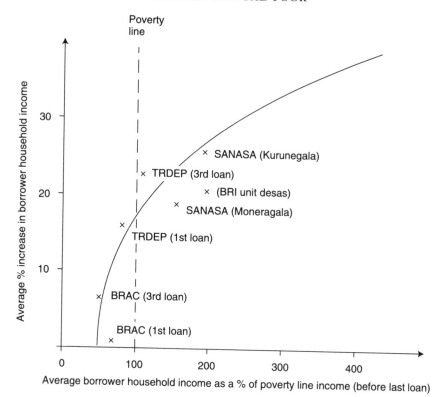

Figure 5.3 The relationship of average borrower income to average increase in household income since last loan

(Vol. 2, Chapter 12) that income-generating credits are not 'scale neutral', but have differential utilities and effects for different groups of poor people. This is an important finding as it indicates that:

(a) credit schemes are most likely to benefit the incomes of what may be termed the 'middle' and 'upper' poor;

(b) the poorest or 'core poor' (see Rahman and Hossain 1992, and see pp. 130–2 for a discussion of the 'minimum economic level' that defines them) receive few direct benefits from income-generating credit initiatives and so alternative assistance strategies (in the finance and other sectors) need to be developed;

(c) institutions seeking to provide income-generating credit to the poor, while pursuing their own financial viability will have a tendency to concentrate on the 'upper' and 'middle' poor[6] (see Chapter 8 for a discussion of these trade-offs).

3 The impacts of income-generating credits in the medium term cannot be simply understood in terms of a promotional model of credit, investment

Table 5.2 A comparison of the average incomes of borrowers and the average increase in household income since last loan for case-study institutions

Institution	Borrower group	Average borrower household income as per cent of national poverty line ('before' last loan)	Average per cent increase in borrower household income (real terms)
BRAC (RDP)	First loan	68.5	1.0
BRAC (RDP)	Third loan	58.0	6.4
TRDEP	First loan	79.6	16.0
TRDEP	Third loan	102.7	23.2
SANASA	Kurunegala	191.7	26.0
SANASA	Moneragala	153.9	18.9
BRI (BUD)	Sample[a]	195.0[b]	20.7
BKK	Sample[a]	152.9[b]	—
KURK	Sample[a]	167.8[b]	—
BancoSol	Sample[a]	480.0	39.0

Notes
[a] For details, see Vol. 2 of this study.
[b] Using the US$39 per month poverty line (see Vol. 2, Chapter 11)

and income. A significant minority of investments fail (leading to decreases in income) while many investments that increase income soon reach a plateau (for example, operating a rickshaw, manually hulling rice, adopting HYVs and inputs on a small farm). For the latter, credit schemes give borrowers an important 'one step up' in income; however, 'survival skills' rarely provide the technological or entrepreneurial basis for poor borrowers to move on to the 'escalator' of sustained growth of income. During fieldwork in Bangladesh, Kenya, Malawi and Sri Lanka respondents persistently commented on their desire for lending agencies to develop new forms of income-generation that would permit borrowers to move beyond their present levels of income. Even for urban-based BancoSol (for which the most dramatic increases in income were recorded) only 11 per cent of long-term borrowers had been able continuously to achieve income growth, while at least 41 per cent of borrowers had (at best) reached a static income situation.

In sum, while our study confirms the emerging consensus that well-designed credit schemes can raise the incomes of significant numbers of poor people, it also indicates that such schemes are not the panacea for poverty-reduction that has been claimed. There are trade-offs between the goals of poverty-alleviation and institutional performance, and credit has differential impacts on different groups within 'the poor'. This latter issue is examined in the following sections.

FINANCE FOR THE POOR: REDUCING VULNERABILITY

Poor people suffer not only from persistently low incomes but also from 'the precarious nature of their existence, since a certain proportion of them undergo severe – and often sudden – dispossession, and the threat of such a thing happening is ever present in the lives of many more' (Dreze and Sen 1991: 10). Poverty, in this sense, involves both the fear of and the operation of events that drive down existing levels of income. Such events include the illness or death of a member of the household, medical expenses, funeral costs, crop failure, the theft of a key asset, a dramatic change in prices or the payment of dowry. Often such events are linked together, as illustrated by an MMF member in Malawi: 'I failed to repay because my business failed because my spouse fell ill and I had to pay for a doctor, and there was little money because we had to buy more food than usual because our crop was spoiled by the drought.' In Chambers's terminology, another 'ratchet' clicks and a poor household slips deeper into poverty. Can financial services reduce the vulnerability of such households so that such ratchets are less likely to operate?

The evidence available from our case studies reveals their relatively limited contribution to reducing the vulnerability of poor households to a sudden dramatic decline in income and consumption levels (Table 5.3). The schemes explicitly targeted at 'small enterprise' and 'small farms' (KIE-ISP and SACA) basically bypass vulnerable households because of their loan screening and membership procedures. If they impact on vulnerability then this must be through second-round effects on the labour market. Such effects were very limited for our case-studies (see Chapter 4). The main contribution of the non-targeted programmes (BKK, BRI's unit desas, KURK and SANASA), all of which offer services to the rural population in general terms, is on the savings side of the financial market. These schemes provide relatively low transaction cost savings services that permit vulnerable households to 'store' cash, which earns interest but which can be rapidly accessed in times of crisis. SANASA's Federation-level policies to shift its services more towards the needs of poorer people have led to it extending its services into loans for very poor households, particularly for small seasonal agricultural production credits and for 'instant' short-term consumption loans (Vol. 2, Chapter 13). Both of these activities extended its contribution to the vulnerable poor well beyond those of the Indonesian institutions.

The most effective interventions might be expected to come from programmes that exclusively target the poor, but here again the evidence is mixed. BRAC, the Grameen Bank and MMF all managed to provide credit to core poor households, whereas TRDEP, while having 79 per cent of its borrowers in the 'poor' category, systematically avoided the very poor. Its membership was focused around the 'poverty line' of ownership of 50

Table 5.3 Case-study institutions and vulnerability

Institution	Do vulnerable households have access to the institution?	What are the institution's impacts on the incomes and assets held by vulnerable households?	Does the institution influence investment in risk-reducing activities or technologies?	Does the institution provide vulnerable households with accessible savings/storage facilities?	Does the institution give access to additional entitlements at crisis periods?
BRAC (RDP)	Yes – 20 per cent of sample either absolutely landless or divorced/widowed	3rd-time borrowers report 95 per cent increase in assets of loan-assisted activity. Poorest borrowers have only small increases in income but security of income is increased	Most activities based on pre-existing 'survival skills' but encouraging diversification. Problems with deeptube well loans	No – compulsory savings, but these are very difficult to access	No – but 10 per cent of respondents report using income-generating loan for essential consumption
TRDEP	No – membership is not for 'core poor'. Only 2 per cent of borrowers are female-headed household and only 2.5 per cent wage labourers	3rd-time borrowers report an 80 per cent increase in assets in loan-assisted activity, but very few of these borrowers are in vulnerable groups	No	No	No
Grameen Bank	Yes – but has difficulties in lending to agricultural day-labouring households which are its main target group	Hossain (1988) reports that borrowers with more than 3 years' membership have fixed assets 2.5 times greater than new members	Most activities based on 'survival skills'. Problems with irrigation projects	Limited – savings not easy to access	Yes – through group fund and 'intensive care' after floods (Fuglesang and Chandler 1993: 165–75)

SANASA	Partial – participation in SANASA at national average for vulnerable households	Mixed – benefits recorded by small farmers who have been able to reduce tied transactions	No	Yes – poorest members use savings services more than credit services	Yes – poorer members report value of 'instant' consumption loans
BKK, BRI and KURK	Despite innovations the poorest households cannot access credit but can make savings	Not known	No	Yes – especially BRI SIMPEDES scheme	No
MMF	Yes	Mixed – 20 per cent of borrowers' loan-assisted activities failed	No	No	No – but a minority of borrowers report using loan for essential consumption
SACA	Limited – only 7 per cent of respondents are 'core poor'	May be negative – SACA-financed larger farmers are increasing their landholdings	No	No	No
KREP	A small proportion	—	No	No	No
KIE-ISP	No – works only with secure businesses	None	No	No	No
BancoSol	Only 29 per cent of borrowers below poverty line	Mixed – 25 per cent of borrowers experience significant increase in income and assets. However, 10–15 per cent go 'bankrupt'	No	Started a voluntary savings programme in 1992, but information on use not available	No

decimals of land, so that it did not work with day labourers, the landless or widows and divorcees who headed households. BRAC, Grameen Bank and MMF all provided income-generating credits to a proportion of very poor people who on average raised their incomes and assets during the course of these loans. Worryingly, both BRAC-RDP and the Grameen Bank recently appear to be moving away from working with significant proportions of the core poor and focusing their activities on the middle and upper poor, rather than the most desperate. The institutions that target 'the poor' have generally performed less effectively on the savings side of the market: whilst both BRAC and Grameen Bank have generated large volumes of savings these funds are not easy to access when member households find themselves facing a crisis, and members are very critical of this situation.

Rahman and Hossain (1992) propose that the vulnerability of the poor can be understood in terms of a set of 'downward mobility pressures'. These are

- structural factors within the economy, particularly demand for labour, demand for the products and services of poor people and seasonality;
- crisis factors, such as household contingencies or natural disaster; and
- life-cycle factors, particularly the proportions of economically active and dependent persons in a household.

What contribution have the case-study institutions made to reducing downward mobility pressures and strengthening household security in terms of this framework?

Downward mobility pressures 1: Structural factors

In terms of structural factors then our case-study institutions have had, at best, only a marginal impact. The data available on the impact of loans on employment outside the family are very limited and, where it occurs, it is associated with a rapidly growing formal economy (such as Indonesia) and with lending to the non-poor or less-poor (Chapter 4). While the main employment gains were intra-family, these were also small, ranging from 1.9 per cent for 'lower-impact' schemes to 5.6 per cent for 'high-impact' schemes (Table 4.3). There are thus no grounds for believing that in any of our case-study countries innovative financial services have sufficient impact on demand for labour at regional or local levels to lead to raised wage rates.

The impact of credit-financed activity on the demand for the products and services of borrowers has been examined by other writers, particularly with regard to Bangladesh. Osmani (1989) has pointed out that in a rural economy in which agricultural output is growing at a very slow rate the demand for the goods and services produced by poor people's

118

enterprises – which are not traded internationally and are only marginally traded into urban centres – is likely to be a constraint on both the volume of production and returns. For some sectors loan-induced activity may expand supply to a position at which 'the rate of return [is] below the cost of borrowing' (ibid.: 16). This factor might well explain why the Grameen Bank and BRAC have significant numbers of dropouts each year (see p. 122). Even those who have queried Osmani's gloomy prognosis accept that in many lending sectors demand is a fundamental constraint on loan expansion and enterprise returns and that much of the income generated by trading activities might be simply a redistribution of income from existing traders to new traders (Quasem 1991: 131). So, as with employment, there is no evidence that structurally based constraints on demand for the products and services of the poor are likely to be removed by credit-induced activity: rather, they are dependent on changes in the wider economy.[7]

With regard to seasonality there is only limited evidence that any of our rural-focused case-study institutions have been able to stimulate new activity in the 'off-season'. SACA's lending programme focuses only on peak-season activities. TRDEP, the Indonesian institutions, MMF and SANASA rely upon borrowers using their 'survival skills' to identify investment opportunities and do not supply technical assistance. For all these cases the basic mode of project identification by borrowers could be described as 'copying' what others are doing. One of the main causes of the initial failure of MMF related to the seasonal problems (drop in demand, need to divert income-generating loans to food purchases) encountered by borrowers in the period preceding the harvesting of the maize crops. The Grameen Bank and BRAC have financed research and development (R&D) operations in an attempt to diversify investment opportunities, and some of these R&D initiatives have focused on activities that generate employment and income in the 'off-season'. Although the Grameen Bank has encountered difficulties in its R&D work (particularly for deep tubewells, fish-farming and the use of HYV rice), its loans have stimulated large increases in milch cow ownership amongst members. In 1991, 12 per cent of Grameen Bank loans (140,317) were for milch cows, creating the possibility for an income flow during the troughs of the agricultural cycle. BRAC-RDP has promoted sericulture and poultry production through large-scale training and technical assistance programmes and is increasingly lending for these activities. Such initiatives have created opportunities for new income flows during the lean months of mid-September to mid-November. It must be noted, however, that the costs of providing borrowers with training does add significantly to overall operational costs. So, for those institutions involved in research and development, there is some evidence of a capacity to enhance the income security of a minority of borrowers in the lean season. However, for most institutions, and the vast majority of borrowers, seasonal problems of low demand for labour, products and services have not been reduced by the provision of financial services.

Downward mobility pressures 2: Crisis and contingency

Turning now to downward mobility pressures caused by crisis (sickness leading to loss of earnings and medical bills, theft of assets, flooding, drought) a number of mechanisms by which financial services, and loan-financed activity, might enhance security can be identified. The first of these occurs when loan-financed activity is associated with an increase in the assets controlled by vulnerable households. This extends crisis-coping mechanisms as the possibility of selling or pawning assets, to bridge a consumption deficit, is increased. For BRAC, Grameen Bank and SANASA – for which increases in assets were reported and significant numbers of poorer households were borrowers – there is some evidence of asset growth providing an additional buffer against contingencies.

A second way in which financial services, and in particular loans, might reduce crisis-related vulnerability would be by encouraging borrowers to invest in risk-reducing technologies or income-generation activities that have a lower risk than pre-existing activities. The identification of risk-reducing technologies is difficult because of differing contexts, but the most obvious is irrigation which permits cropping when rainfall fails. In the drought-prone areas covered by our study (Malawi and the Moneragala District of Sri Lanka) the loan size and conditions of the institutions studied (SANASA, SACA and MMF) were insufficient for a 'lumpy' investment such as a tubewell and pump. In Bangladesh,[8] both the Gram-een Bank and BRAC have experimented with group loans for deep tubewells (DTW). Both agencies have encountered severe difficulties and have withdrawn from such activity: the Grameen Bank now directly manages its DTWs, while an evaluation of BRAC's seventy DTWs has revealed that only a small proportion are viable and that many borrowers, and particularly the poorer, have lost assets or have suffered income reductions because of involvement in such activities (van Koppen and Mahmud 1995). In effect, the poor have absorbed the risks of the DTW experiment.[9]

The question of whether loans are associated with encouraging bor-rowers to operate in lower-risk activities is complex. According to the conventional wisdom of finance, borrowers seeking to increase their income will take on additional risk, as returns on investment are partially a function of increased exposure to risk. If this is the case, then lending to poor people is likely to raise their average incomes but will, for a proportion of borrowers, increase the likelihood of a crisis because of 'business failure'. Although we do not have systematic data on such incidences, considerable evidence was gathered during fieldwork that a minority of borrowers become worse off because of borrowing, that is credit from a case-study institution increased their vulnerability. This situation is vividly illustrated by the case of a TRDEP borrower documented in a report to donors (Box 5.1). There is also much additional evidence:

- BancoSol staff estimate that 10–15 per cent of borrowers' enterprises go bankrupt (Vol. 2, Chapter 10);
- BRAC borrowers reported the forced seizure of defaulters' assets (such as livestock and cooking pots) and their sale in order to cover the costs of loans that members had not repaid (Vol. 2, Chapter 12). A more dramatic example is provided by Khan and Stewart (1992) who write of a conversation with BRAC women in which they described pulling down a member's house because she had not paid back a loan;
- in the last two years there have been several reports in the Bangladeshi media of 'Grameen Bank suicides' when Bank members have committed suicide, allegedly because of peer group pressure to repay failed loans;
- 20 per cent of TRDEP members drop out before their third loan – 'usually the most vulnerable who drop out as a result of failing to use the loan successfully' (IDSS 1994: 3);

Box 5.1 When a loan goes wrong: driving into debt

Kawser Ahmad was a hard-working young day-labourer, married, with two small children. Because he was the cousin of a prosperous bazaar trader who became a TRDEP *kendra* chief, he found himself a member of his cousin's *kendra*. His wife did not join him, because the group animator (GA) felt that, as a poor man, Kawser would not be able to make more than the smallest weekly repayment. His cousin advised him to buy a rickshaw-van, which he did, but because his loan was 2,500 taka, he had to borrow another 500 taka from his cousin in order to buy a rather run-down machine. Kawser had never ridden a van before, and was also very cautious about giving up his day-labouring work. He therefore tried to combine the two, which meant hiring the van out on days that he got work in the fields. This didn't work – he had trouble hiring the van out to drivers who had no certainty of access to the van every day. So he gave up that strategy and tried full-time driving himself. This worked more or less well for a few months, but then the rains came and customers fell away. This coincided with a lean time for day-labouring, so for some weeks his family got by through eating less and borrowing. There was no question of keeping up with the loan repayments, so he had to borrow again from his cousin. At the end of the loan cycle the other members removed him from the *kendra*. He was obliged to sell the van – at a considerable loss – to settle his debts.

Source: IDSS (1994: 65)

- for KREP Juhudi scheme, peer pressure is reinforced by the 'unofficial' pledging of assets within groups (though this is known by KREP staff). Some borrowers have forfeited significant assets to other members when loan-financed activities failed;
- around 25 per cent of MMF-financed activities (in its early phase) failed – scheme planners and managers misunderstood the nature of borrower risks;
- at the time of survey a growing number of KIE-ISP borrowers were being classified as Class D on the organisation's A to D scale for investment risk. Many are likely to be taken to court or lose key assets in the future.

While the present study focused on new and continuing borrowers, the findings point to the need for further research examining why borrowers leave innovative financial institutions and if such departures are associated with increased levels of debt or reduced asset levels. Given the scale of 'dropping out' (15 per cent per annum for the Grameen Bank, which is 300,000 members a year; 10–15 per cent per annum for BRAC, or 181,700 members, in 1992 and 1993) there may well have been significant under-reporting of credit-induced crisis in most studies of finance for the poor. The virtuous circle of 'low income, credit, investment, more income, more credit, more investment, more income' is seductive: unfortunately, it does not mirror the reality that the majority of very poor households face in sustaining a livelihood.

A third way in which financial services may reduce vulnerability is by providing facilities for very poor households to 'store' windfall and seasonal cash and earn a return. The institutions we studied had very different approaches to savings (Table 5.3). At one extreme stand SACA and the KIE-ISP, which only provided loans. At the other stand the BRI unit desas and SANASA in which savings activities are as important as lending activities. The unit desas have proved that the main demand for financial services from poorer Indonesians is for safe savings facilities. Similarly, in Sri Lanka, SANASA's experience illustrates that the highest priority of poorer households for financial services is for easy-withdrawal saving programmes. In between these two positions come BRAC,[10] the Grameen Bank, TRDEP, KREP and BancoSol: all of these have compulsory savings programmes but limit member access to these savings. In the cases of BRAC-RDP and Grameen Bank, members regard such 'savings' as a borrowing cost because of their non-accessibility. The aversion of the Grameen Bank, and schemes modelled on it, to accessible savings accounts for members is hard to understand, given the substantial demand by poorer people for such services and the clear evidence that savings schemes can contribute to an institution's financial viability.

The final mechanism by which financial institutions can reduce the effects of crises on vulnerable households is by extending the entitlements[11] of such households when a crisis occurs. The only institutions which systematically offered such services were SANASA in Sri Lanka through its 'instant loans' service and the Grameen Bank through its Group Fund and Emergency Funds.[12] The SANASA facility provides members with access to a Rs500 loan for a three-month period, usually within twenty-four hours of application, for any purpose. Although conditions vary from village to village, the usual requirements are that an applicant has a savings account, has a good repayment record from earlier loans and pays interest at a rate of 5 per cent per month (more than three times the usual rate). Such loans are in high demand from the poorer members of SANASA groups who reported that instant loans permit them to cope with emergencies (such as medical bills, lack of food and meeting the costs of essential social obligations) at lower cost than alternative coping mechanisms (such as mortgaging crops, land or labour, a distress sale of assets or borrowing from a trader). Our focus on income-generating loans meant that we did not gather sufficient data to comment quantitatively on the effects of consumption loans. Nevertheless, there was a substantial 'voice from the village' that such loans are a significant addition to the survival strategies of vulnerable households.

The Grameen Bank's 'group fund accounts' serve a similar role for Grameen Bank members, although in this case members borrow from a portion of their own forced savings. The compulsory 1 taka per week savings and 5 per cent group tax that members pay on each loan are credited to a group fund account. Group members can borrow up to half of the funds in this account – with group approval. In 1991 some 162,000 such loans were made to a total amount of Tk189 million: 59 per cent of these loans were for social, household or medical needs (Grameen Bank 1992: 102). While these loans clearly benefit many Bangladeshi households, Bank members report that group funds are not as accessible as they would like. The Bank also operates an 'Emergency Fund' financed by a 5 per cent charge of all loans over Tk1,000. This is intended to cover death, disability, accidents and crisis-induced defaults. Although it has accumulated to Tk145 million, disbursements to date are minimal (Fuglesang and Chandler 1993: 106) and, consequently, the fund is unpopular with members, being seen as a disguised borrowing charge.[13]

The SANASA and Grameen Bank schemes both illustrate the possibility of financial services extending the entitlements of poorer households when contingencies occur. Although both schemes require further development (and detailed study of who accesses them and for what uses), other institutions could well enhance their poverty-alleviating impacts by the introduction of small-scale, rapid-access consumption loans.

Downward mobility pressures 3: Life-cycle factors

This study sheds little light on the ways in which innovative financial services may help or hinder households to cope with the stresses of demographic change in household structure. This is for two reasons. The first is a lack of data, as any detailed commentary on such matters would demand longitudinal information that was beyond the resources of our research. The second relates to the sheer complexity of such factors. This can be illustrated by the findings of a recent study of the impacts of Grameen Bank and BRAC on contraceptive usage (Schuler and Hashemi 1994). It found that participation in the Grameen Bank's credit programmes was associated with dramatic and statistically significant changes in contraceptive behaviour (59 per cent usage for bank members compared to 43 per cent usage for a matched control group in 1992). Such a situation is almost certainly likely to lead to Grameen Bank members having smaller families than non-members. In theory, in the medium term of five to ten years, this should lead to Grameen Bank members having lower household dependency ratios and thus having more resources for investment, income enhancement and asset growth. In the longer term, though – given the fact that the elderly in rural areas rely heavily on the support of their sons – the medium-term benefits may be outweighed by the long-term consequence of having fewer sons (or no sons) to provide support during old age. The possibility of greater 'child quality' in smaller families (better education, better nutrition, better health, and so on) might partially offset this if the children of smaller families ultimately derive higher incomes (and use a proportion of these higher incomes to help their parents in old age).

What is clear, however, is that none of our case-study institutions generates a sufficient income for more than a handful of its poor borrowers to amass an asset base that could generate a quasi-pension when they are too old or infirm to operate their own income-generating activities. For the 'micro-entrepreneurs' of developing countries security in old age remains a function of social relationships with family, kith and kin and 'neighbours' rather than an earnings-financed private entitlement.

FINANCE FOR THE POOR: INFLUENCES ON OTHER FORMS OF DEPRIVATION

Poverty is not purely about material conditions. It also refers to other forms of deprivation, and in this section the effects of innovative financial services on those who suffer from social inferiority, powerlessness and isolation[14] are considered. These variables are closely interlinked (with each other as well as with income and vulnerability) and so we examine them together in relation to three groups who commonly experience relatively intense levels of deprivation and discrimination: women (particularly female-headed households); the very poor (particularly the assetless, the landless and those dependent on agricultural labouring); and the disabled.

Women, women's empowerment and gender relations

In all case-study countries significant female–male gaps occur, indicating the unequal economic and social relations between women and men.[15] Giving women access to credit, it has been argued, is a means by which both their economic standing within the household and social position within society can be improved. This argument has been particularly significant in Bangladesh where women's position is so poor *vis-à-vis* men (see note 15) and where female participation in credit schemes has now reached very high levels (Table 5.4). Two forces have been particularly significant in increasing women's involvement in credit programmes. The first relates to the financial viability of institutions. As revealed in our case-studies and the work of others,[16] in many contexts female borrowers have proved more reliable than male borrowers: consequently, some lenders have found that their financial performance can be improved by focusing on female borrowers. The second force stems from aid donors who 'discovered' women in the early 1980s and have subsequently encouraged recipient agencies to provide women with more assistance. For credit this has meant pressures to increase the proportion of female borrowers, to at least 50 per cent, and sometimes to focus exclusively on women. Behind the belief that 'loans for women' will lead to their economic and social advancement are a number of assumptions: that women will use loans for their own enterprises; that these enterprises will be successful; that women will control the profits derived from such enterprises; and that greater involvement in economic activities will strengthen the social and political position of women in society. Our work reveals that in practice lending to women is much more complex than this assumption chain posits. The following discussion focuses on the situation in Bangladesh, where such an emphasis has been best developed and where a number of other studies looking in detail at the empowerment impacts of credit have been conducted.

Turning first to isolation, there is a strong case that credit programmes can reduce the relative isolation of women. Anyone who has witnessed the village-level meetings of BRAC and Grameen Bank (and other agencies) cannot but be impressed by the bringing together of large groups of women. In these regular meetings women conduct their savings and loans activities and have an opportunity to share information and discuss ideas. Such opportunities previously did not exist. Measuring the results of such association was beyond the limits of this study but the creation of a regular

Table 5.4 Indicators of women's involvement in case-study institutions

Institution	Per cent of female borrowers/members (1992)	Per cent of credit to women (1992)	Coverage of women from vulnerable groups (widowed, divorced, female-headed households)	Institution's policy on gender	Other comments
BRAC	74	67	10 per cent	Favours recruitment of women members, but also recruits men	Female membership was only 34 per cent in 1986
TRDEP	30	30	Less than 5 per cent	Works with 'families' – no policy on gender	Female borrowers are commonly 'token' family members
Grameen Bank	93	92	Significant	Virtually all new members since mid-1980s have been women	Female membership was only 39 per cent in 1980–3
BancoSol	75	—	Low	No specific gender policy	Although it does not target women, the small loans it provides are particularly valued by female micro-entrepreneurs
BRI unit desa	24	—	Low	No specific gender policy	

BKK	55	—	—	No specific gender policy	
KURK	72	—	—	No specific gender policy	
KREP	54	54	—	No specific gender policy	
KIE-ISP	18	—	0	None	Targets established businesses, which are usually male-headed
MMF	99 (of new borrowers)	99 (of new borrowers)	10–20 per cent	Initially focused on women; subsequently exclusively focused on women	Has stopped loans to male borrowers because of delinquency problem
SACA	28	—	33 per cent of female borrowers are head of household	Seeking to increase per cent of female borrowers	Donors pushing for share of loans to women to be increased
SANASA	51	—	13 per cent	Open membership, but a policy of encouraging female members since early 1980s	Female membership and borrowing has rapidly increased since early 1980s

forum at which large numbers of poor women can meet and talk represents a 'breakthrough' in the social norms of rural Bangladesh.

In terms of empowerment (that is, reducing 'powerlessness') our study reveals the naivety of the belief that every loan made to a woman contributes to the strengthening of the economic and social position of women. The evidence on this issue is mixed and contradictory. Goetz and Gupta's (1994) work indicates that some 39 per cent of the loans provided to women by four agencies (Grameen Bank, BRAC, PROSHIKA and BRDB) are either fully or significantly controlled by men, while a further 24 per cent are partially controlled by men (that is, men control the productive process while women provide substantial labour inputs). When women do fully or significantly control loans, this is most commonly associated with 'traditional' women's activities (particularly livestock and poultry) so it represents the reinforcement of existing conceptions of the economic role of women. White (1991) has reported similar observations for other credit schemes in Bangladesh, while studies of TRDEP report that 'wives, sisters or daughters' are often token members of groups and that 'in general TRDEP does not serve women's interests well' (IDSS 1994: 3). Such high levels of male appropriation of female loans led Goetz and Gupta (1994: 1) to conclude that 'gender relations and the household are in effect absorbing the high enforcement costs of lending to men in Bangladesh's rural credit system because women have taken over the task of securing loan repayments from their male relatives'. From this perspective credit schemes are doing relatively little to empower women, though one important exception must be noted. By contrast, the same study reports that 55 per cent of widowed, separated or divorced women fully control their loans (compared with 18 per cent for women in general) and that only 25 per cent of such loans are fully appropriated by men (ibid.: 13). Given that such women are usually regarded as the most vulnerable in Bangladeshi society this suggests a significant advancement in their capacity to engage in economic activity.

Schuler and Hashemi's (1994) study of Grameen Bank and BRAC female members sought to measure their degree of empowerment[17] and relate this to contraceptive usage. Their data on the effects of credit programmes on the position of women presents a very positive picture (Table 5.5). The proportions of Grameen Bank and BRAC female members who were 'empowered' were at much higher levels than the control group, and the proportion of women 'ever beaten by husband' who had been beaten in the previous year was significantly lower. However, while Grameen Bank membership is associated with statistically significant higher levels of contraceptive use, BRAC's positive impacts are not significant. This difference is explained in terms of the Grameen Bank's greater effectiveness in strengthening women's economic roles and its more disciplined and regimented approach to group activity.

128

Table 5.5 Credit programmes, women's empowerment and contraceptive use in Bangladesh

Indicator	Grameen Bank members	BRAC members	Comparison group
Mean empowerment score[a]	5.0	4.9	3.5
Per cent of sample 'empowered'[a]	64	56	23
Per cent beaten in last year by husband	9	15	27
Per cent beaten in last year by husband as a share of per cent ever beaten by husband	27	35	46
Currently uses contraception	59	47	43

Source: Schuler and Hashemi (1994)

Note: [a] The indices used to compute this index are listed in note 17. For a full definition, see Schuler and Hashemi (1994: 67–70).

Despite the contradictory nature of the evidence cited above, important conclusions can be drawn. The first is the refutation of the claim that every loan to a woman is a step forward in the empowerment of women. This means that female participation rates in financial schemes cannot be treated as an indicator of female empowerment. Although donors are keen to count female scalps (and as a result microfinance agencies are usually keen to count female scalps), programmes that genuinely seek to empower women will need to research loan usage much more carefully and will need to place a greater emphasis on developing new and more productive economic roles for women. A simple emphasis on disbursing to women is likely to encourage tokenism and the reinforcement of established gender roles (as in the case of loans to women in TRDEP and SACA).

Secondly, the exact nature of 'who' women's empowerment is to be judged against needs to be clarified. Our work on BRAC led to the finding that 'those women who do particularly well as a result of credit are much more likely to be empowered *vis-à-vis* other (less well off) women, rather than *vis-à-vis* the menfolk in their household (or in wider society)'.[18] A similar case could be made against the Grameen Bank whose members have significantly higher educational levels than the wider female population (29 per cent of GB female members have attended school as compared to only 18 per cent of a comparator group: Schuler and Hashemi 1994: 69). So agencies need to pay much greater attention to their capacity to assist target groups within the female population (particularly the assetless, widowed and divorced) rather than treating women as a homogeneous group.

Finally, our study indicates the need for further research on the question of whether credit groups are also 'women's groups' (that is, associations of women that seek to promote women's needs and interests outside the field of credit). The accounts (Lovell 1992; Fuglesang and Chandler 1993) of BRAC and Grameen Bank groups acting autonomously and asserting women members' interests *vis-à-vis* their menfolk are fascinating but are premissed on the erroneous assumption that such incidences did not occur in earlier times (see Vol. 2, Chapter 12). If anything, the scaling-up and professionalisation of BRAC and Grameen Bank has weakened the position of female (and male) *shomitis* and has strengthened the position of field staff. Members increasingly perceive *shomitis* as belonging to the credit programme and not as belonging to the members. This situation contrasted markedly with our Sri Lankan case, where SANASA's primary co-operative society members controlled society activities (Montgomery (1995)).

The poor amongst the poor

While case-study institutions have extended the reach of the formal financial sector into 'upper'- and 'middle'-income poor households, as discussed in earlier sections, they have been relatively ineffective in reaching the poorest. Several factors have frustrated such efforts. First and foremost is the emphasis on credit delivery by many institutions: for the poorest people and households the opportunities for credit-financed self-employment are very limited, and the risks are unreasonably high. As Stuart Rutherford (1993) argues from his research with the very poor in Bangladesh, the poorest commonly practice 'self-exclusion' from income-generating credit initiatives which they do not perceive as a solution to their livelihood problems.

Second, for group schemes, processes of social exclusion are important: that is, group members (most often people below the poverty line) deciding that some prospective members are 'too poor' to be given group membership. This may be on the economic grounds that such folk are 'too risky' or on social grounds as the poor differentiate amongst themselves. Direct cases of such exclusion were reported for SANASA, BRAC, TRDEP and SACA where members identified some people in their villages as being unsuitable for group membership because of the intensity of their poverty.

Third, there is evidence that as credit programmes are expanded and management is professionalised, the incentive structures for staff (bonus payments and promotion prospects) favour a concentration on groups other than the core poor.[19] This was clearest in the case of BRAC (Vol. 2, Chapter 12) where the average value of new members' assets was higher than the asset levels of successful third-time borrowers. Field staff find that headquarters-set performance targets can best be achieved by working with the poor rather than the core poor (ibid.). In Sri Lanka, SANASA is currently wrestling with this dilemma as it shifts from a predominantly voluntary staffing basis to a more professional one.

Extending financial services to the poorest will require innovations beyond those developed by the present generation of 'finance for the poor' institutions. The starting point for such experiments lies in easy-access savings and small contingency loans.

The disabled, the old and the infirm

None of our case-study institutions was observed to provide services for people with significant disabilities[20] during the course of fieldwork. This should not be a surprise, as the emphasis on self-employment in low-demand–high-competition markets for goods and services made many programmes irrelevant in terms of the opportunities available to the disabled. Removing the need for collateral makes little difference to the disabled who face many other obstacles. Interestingly, even BRAC's Income Generation for Vulnerable Group Development (IGVGD) programme – targeted on the core poor – has a physical-fitness criterion for access which ensures that the physically disabled are screened out.

The point of the above observations is not to argue that innovative financial institutions should service the needs of the disabled or infirm (it would be unreasonable to expect them to meet all social welfare needs), rather, it is to point out that explicit and implicit claims that such programmes reach the 'poorest of the poor' need to be tempered. If we update Doyal's (1983) estimate of around 350 million physically and mentally disabled people in developing countries, then, given population growth, the emergence of AIDS and the explosion of cripplings associated with the increasing incidence of warfare (and the cheapness of landmines), there is clearly a vast army of disabled poor people who are presently beyond the reach of even the most innovative institutions.

Similar arguments apply to many elderly people. However, the demands of the elderly for accessible savings schemes was evident from Sri Lanka where almost 10 per cent of SANASA members had reached 'retirement age'. Such people used SANASA to store 'lumpy' income, from the sale of assets or gifts from friends and relatives, and to accumulate savings so that major purchases could be made (such as roofing iron and new clothes). The needs for financial services for the elderly may well be similar to those of the able but very poor.

RECONCEPTUALISING 'FINANCE FOR THE POOR' AND ITS POLICY IMPLICATIONS

Our main finding in this chapter is the need for the designers of financial services for poor people to recognise that 'the poor' are not a homogeneous group with broadly similar needs. The emphasis of the last fifteen years has been on a promotional model of poverty-alleviation through loan-financed enterprise expansion. Such a model is valid for 'middle' and 'upper' poor households, with members who have entrepreneurial flair, but is inappropriate for the poorest households, those with a high degree of income insecurity and the disabled. Commonly credit for micro-enterprise promotion and credit for poverty-alleviation will overlap, but this does not mean that they are the same activities, as is often assumed by microfinance institutions and their sponsors.

Recognising the heterogeneity of the poor clearly complicates matters for scheme designers because potentially numerous groups and sub-groups could be distinguished. For analytical purposes it is appropriate, at least as a starting point, to conceptualise two main groups within the poor: the core poor who have not crossed a 'minimum economic threshold' and whose needs are essentially for financial services that are protectional, and those above this threshold who may have a demand for promotional credit. This minimum economic threshold is defined by characteristics such as the existence of a reliable income, freedom from pressing debt, sufficient health to avoid incapacitating illness, freedom from imminent contingencies and sufficient resources (such as savings, non-essential convertible assets and social entitlements) to cope with problems when they arise. The distinction between the poor and core poor must be applied to both women and men. Although females and those within female-headed households comprise a disproportionate number of the poor and core poor in most situations, simply targeting activities on women is too crude a device to help the poorest. The female population has a range of living standards and so poverty-reduction needs. to target specific groups carefully. While these vary from place to place they will commonly include the widowed, the divorced, the disabled and the elderly. Recording the participation rates of such people with financial institutions, something which none of our case-studies regularly did, would be a useful step in the direction of more effective targeting.

If the poor/core-poor categorisation is accepted, then it indicates the need for either more comprehensive approaches to financial services than were offered by most of our case-study institutions (that is, providing investment, consumption and contingency loans and offering high accessibility savings schemes) or for specialist institutions to operate to meet the differing needs of poor households and core poor households. While the financial viability of institutions genuinely targeted on the 'core poor' remains to be tested, the profits generated by our Indonesian cases from savings schemes, by SANASA's primary societies from 'high interest' contingency loans, and by official pawnbrokers (in Sri Lanka and other countries) indicate that there are substantial possibilities for operational cost recovery.

Those concerned with the poverty-reducing impacts of financial intermediation must note two further points:

1 even if future innovations lead to the design of financial services that meet the needs of the poorest, the requirement for other social security mechanisms – employment guarantee schemes, food-for-work programmes, drought relief, indigenous welfare practices – will continue. Financial services targeted on the poor are only one element of a national poverty-alleviation strategy, not a replacement for other approaches;

2 for the 'above-threshold' poor the evidence from Bangladesh indicates that many close to the poverty line may be able to invest in activities that can offer increasing returns over time (that is, the TRDEP borrowers). For less well-resourced, less well-educated and less well-connected poor people (the middle poor) then investment opportunities are very limited and are likely to remain so, unless the formal economy experiences substantial growth. As a consequence, if a promotional strategy is being pursued, this category of small entrepreneur is likely to need assistance in the areas of product development, technical change and marketing if income-generating credit is to be anything more than 'one step up' the income pyramid. The risks of technical innovation must, at the very least, be shared between institutions and borrowers, and not simply absorbed by borrowers as in the case of BRAC's deep tubewell programme (van Koppen and Mahmud 1995).

The recognition of the heterogeneity of the poor makes the identification of 'best practice' design features for poverty-alleviation difficult. If we pose the question 'Which scheme has most rapidly pushed household incomes above the poverty line and is associated with continuing income growth from successive loans?', then TRDEP and BancoSol are highly successful. However, if we pose the question 'Which schemes have helped to raise and protect the incomes of the poorest households?', then we would judge TRDEP and BancoSol failures. The challenge of providing financial services to poor people needs to be seen not as developing a 'super institution' that meets all of the needs of all of the poor: rather, the challenge is to develop a set of institutions (in any one area or country) able to serve the differing needs of the poor. Institutional pluralism and competition (for market share and for subsidies) are required if financial services are to evolve that serve the needs of the poorest: the Grameen example, which currently dominates the field of institutional design (namely, TRDEP, BRAC's RDP, KREP Juhudi, MMF), must not be seen as the only approach, given this model's clear problems with working with the 'core poor'. Further experimentation with protectionally focused schemes for the poorest, offering savings and contingency loans services, perhaps on an individual basis or on the basis of indigenous savings societies, is needed to explore whether a 'second wave' of innovation can provide services to the poorest.

A final issue to note in this section is our finding that there has been a gross exaggeration in that part of the literature[21] on credit schemes, claiming that they are vehicles for the mobilisation of poor people that are, or will soon be, stimulating dramatic social and political change. Innovative financial services, as was illustrated in the discussion of gender relations and of relations amongst the poor, have complex socio-political impacts. Commonly, they simultaneously change some dimensions of social relations (such as reducing the isolation of women) whilst reinforcing and strengthening other relations (such as a gendered division of labour). The financial interventions studied in this volume are only one of many forces for change operating in the countries concerned and none of them have created forms of class or interest group solidarity of structural significance to date. The largest institution, the Grameen Bank, has moved away from its earlier focus on 'mobilising the poor' to being a specialist bank, while BRAC has effectively abandoned its village-level institution-building activities and is no longer attempting to federate village organisations. SANASA makes a local-level contribution to notions of democracy in Sri Lanka but it explicitly avoids a political identity. The Indonesian institutions work with individuals and make no attempt to establish new social organisations. SACA was an extension of the Malawian state and, if its members had a group position, this was conservative and orientated to the status quo. Financial institutions – even those that mobilise large memberships – can help the poor in terms of their economic impacts and influences on micro-level social change. They are not, however, vehicles for social mobilisation that will confront existing socio-political structures (see Chapter 6).

CONCLUSION

This chapter has shown that recent innovations in financial intermediation have permitted a majority of our case-study institutions to make a contribution to poverty-reduction in terms of raising the incomes of some poor people and (in a smaller number of cases) helping to reduce income vulnerability. Given this evidence, there is a strong case for their extension into new areas, allied to a recognition that such schemes are not a panacea for poverty-alleviation.

Most contemporary schemes are less effective than they might be because (a) they treat 'the poor' as an undifferentiated group, and (b) they focus largely on a promotional strategy for poverty-reduction involving a rigid loan disbursement regime rather than more diverse credit and savings services. As a consequence, the poorest people have little access to these schemes, are likely to take on unreasonable risks if they do participate, and the benefits are most likely to accrue to 'middle'- and 'upper'-income poor who have crossed an economic threshold that means a major part of their income is secure. A reconceptualisation of financial services for the poor – that recognises both promotional and protectional strategies and (at a minimum) differentiates between the poor and the core poor – is now necessary. As a result a further phase of institutional experimentation and innovation – a second wave – is required to extend financial services deeper down the socio-economic pyramid. Ironically, it is the success of the 'first wave' finance-for-the-poor schemes, and particularly the Grameen Bank, that is the greatest obstacle to future experimentation. Most designers and sponsors of new initiatives have abandoned innovation, and 'replication' is leading to a growing uniformity in financial interventions.

NOTES

1 For detailed discussions of the definition of poverty, see Chambers (1983 and 1995), Doyal and Gough (1991), Greeley (1994), Ravallion (1992) and Townsend (1993).

2 'Strikingly, the latest *Human Development Report* (UNDP 1994: 15) shows Sri Lanka, Nicaragua, Pakistan and Guinea all with per capita incomes in the $400–$500 range, but life expectancies of, respectively, 71, 65, 58 and 44, and infant mortality rates of, respectively, 24, 53, 99 and 135' (Chambers 1995: 12).

3 Although concerns about 'protection' are associated with writers of the left, the concern has also been raised by those on the right. For example, von Pischke's (1991) contention that 'credit' should be called 'debt', and that being indebted may be very risky for poor people, is based on similar premisses.

4 The whole notion of a poverty line does of course encounter logical problems because of the fact that large proportions of the populations of African, Asian and Latin American countries live below these 'minimum' levels for survival for much (or all) of their lives.

5 Important amongst these are the 'economic' policy of tapered interest rates (BRI's unit desas and BKK) and the 'social' policy of encouraging low-income borrowers (SANASA).

6 Our study of Bangladesh revealed this to be the case for TRDEP and to be the direction that BRAC's RDP has taken in the 1990s. Evidence of the Grameen Bank's problems in working with agricultural labouring households and other studies (IDSS 1994) indicate that it is also operating in this niche.

7 For example, in Moneragala, many SANASA members were benefiting from loan-financed diversification into sugar cane production. The creation of this opportunity lay in national agricultural policy, however, rather than financial service provision.

8 It is probably more appropriate to regard irrigation in Bangladesh as productivity-enhancing rather than productivity-securing.

9 For a discussion of an apparently more successful approach with shallow wells and other forms of irrigation, see Wood and Palmer-Jones (1991).

10 BRAC has experimented with a pilot voluntary savings scheme that permitted savers rapid and easy access. An evaluation found that members valued this service highly and that the scheme could contribute to branch financial

viability. For unknown reasons BRAC senior management has decided not to extend this initiative.

11 Entitlement refers to the 'set of alternative bundles of commodities' over which a person (or group of persons) can establish command through ownership or rights of use. For a detailed discussion, see Sen (1981).

12 Several of the other institutions studied unwittingly provided loans for consumption when borrowers used income-generation credit for non-approved purposes (Table 5.3).

13 Interestingly, Grameen Bank did use emergency loans for food purchase in the Rangpur area following severe floods in 1991; 18,000 members were loaned Tk300 each, from Grameen Bank funds, to alleviate their hunger.

14 Chambers (1995) also includes 'humiliation' in his conceptualisation of deprivation. While we concur with this inclusion, the nature of our field research did not allow us to capture much data on such a sensitive and methodologically difficult item. However, it was clear that in some circumstances credit groups do humiliate members who cannot meet their loan obligations and that field staff are insensitive. For example, one BRAC female borrower described how a programme assistant confronted her father-in-law when she was unable to meet instalments for a failed project and subsequently how she was stigmatised within her household.

15

	Females as a per cent of males			
	Literacy (1992)	Years of schooling (1992)	Proportion in labour force (1990–2)	Average age at first marriage
Bangladesh	47	29	69	16.7
Bolivia	84	60	69	22.8
Indonesia	85	58	67	21.1
Kenya	—	41	67	20.3
Malawi	—	46	104	17.8
Sri Lanka	90	79	49	24.4

Source: UNDP (1994)

16 For the Grameen Bank in 1985, 81 per cent of female borrowers had no overdue repayment instalments as against 74 per cent for men (Hossain 1988: 52). For the Malawi Mudzi Fund in late 1990, the on-time repayment rate for women was 92 per cent as against 83 per cent for men (Hulme 1991b). In Malaysia, Projek Ikhtiar reported 95 per cent repayment rates for women as against 72 per cent for men (Gibbons and Kasim 1991).

17 In terms of mobility, economic security, ability to make small purchases, ability to make larger purchases, involvement in major household decisions, subjection to violence, political and legal awareness and involvement in protests/campaigns (ibid.: 68).

18 It is no coincidence that BRAC field staff (the vast majority of whom are young males) report that female members are much 'easier to work with' and more 'disciplined' than male members. Female members are observing their cultural norm in relation to a male.

19 Tapered interest rates (charging smaller borrowers high interest rates) may partially offset such tendencies.

20 The definition and assessment of 'disability' are complex tasks. For the purposes of our field research 'significant disability' simply refers to observable physical attributes or behaviour that means that the mobility and capacities

of an individual are clearly well below those considered the norm in that specific setting.

21 IDSS (1994) refers to sections of the literature on the Grameen Bank as ranging from the adulatory to sycophantic. Lovell's (1992) work on BRAC falls somewhere between these two positions.

6

THE POLITICS OF FINANCIAL INTERMEDIATION FOR THE POOR

INTRODUCTION

The contemporary orthodoxy argues that 'politics' is bad for financial intermediation for the poor. Political 'interference' in such activities leads to weak targeting, low repayment rates and institutional collapse that becomes a serious drain on the public purse. Implicitly, effective financial intermediation requires a 'no politics' situation in which the state steps back and a small cadre of value-neutral technocrats select neo-liberal economic policies, and efficient institutions (that have no political life) evolve from the market forces that are released. Such situations can be explored in ideal models but, as our empirical work reveals, the 'no politics' assumption is facile as even radical neo-liberal economic policies are the result of complex political processes. Indonesia's dramatic liberalisation of financial markets (Vol. 2, Chapter 11) was grounded in domestic politics. It did not slip from a technocrat's VDU into a sector in which politicians had agreed not to trespass and other political forces had evaporated. The influences of political factors cannot simply be wished away.

In this chapter we outline the political models that have underpinned theories of financial intermediation, identify their weaknesses and argue for a contingent analysis that can accommodate the complex influences, both negative and positive in terms of the evaluative criteria utilised in Chapters 3, 4 and 5, of political activity on finance for the poor. The empirical experiences of Volume 2 are compared and the policy options available to financial institutions – for managing their political environments – are examined. Following this we reverse the causal chain and explore the influence that poverty-focused financial intermediaries, and their growing numbers of clients, have on political and social structures. Can innovative financial institutions 'empower' the poor, as has been claimed, and play a leading role in the redefinition of domestic political relationships?

The conclusion points to the complexity of the relationships between political factors and poverty-focused financial intermediation. There are no glib generalisations that can cope with the diversity of empirical evidence generated by our case-studies. Political factors are not necessarily 'bad' for financial activity; political structures do not automatically predetermine the outcomes of financial interventions; institutions, governments and donors all have some 'room for manoeuvre' in their actions; and state action can have both negative and positive effects on the evolution of the 'bottom end' of the financial market.

POLITICS AND POVERTY-FOCUSED FINANCIAL INTERMEDIATION IN THEORY

The theory that dominated the analysis of developing-country financial markets, particularly rural financial markets, in the post-war period through to the early 1970s was grounded in the concepts of market failure and the consequent need for state action and economic planning to overcome this failure. The political contexts and dynamics of such an analysis were rarely specified. In essence, they were that a public interest state (Mackintosh 1992) with benevolent politicians and impartial and competent bureaucrats could overcome this failure – the inability of the 'traditional' sector of a dual economy to mobilise resources through economic forces or political action – by the allocation of public resources and the establishment of implementing agencies. Allied to this was a wishy-washy reformism which saw informal financial intermediaries (especially money-lenders and traders) as monopolistic and evil: using their economic power to exploit poor people and small farmers. The moneylender would be displaced by government initiative or, in some countries, such as India and Indonesia, disestablished by decree. However, the assumptions under-pinning this analysis – political leaderships devoted to the social good, a clear distinction between the political and administrative realms, impartial and competent bureaucrats, a civil society that recognised state legitimacy by acquiescing to government intervention and an informal financial sector which set its charges purely on the basis of monopoly rents – have usually proved invalid.

In the 1970s the weaknesses of this model led to a search for alternatives and by the early 1980s the Ohio School had taken the high ground of theoretical debate (see Chapter 1). Its theory is largely 'economistic' (McGregor 1989) and sought to keep away from the 'messy reality' of politics (Blair 1984: 191). Its models of the operation of deregulated rural financial markets (in terms of interest rates, terms and conditions for loans and savings and market entry) and competition between formal and informal operators, indicated that allocative efficiency and increased access to finance by lower-income groups could be attained by state withdrawal and financial liberalisation. Previous policies – of loan rate capping, subsidies and sectoral targeting – discouraged private-sector activity in rural financial markets and encouraged excessive demand that led to economic rationing. This favoured larger loans to wealthier borrowers and various forms of corruption.

Subsequently, kindred spirits with interests in political science developed related frameworks of the 'political economy of the regulatory dialectic' (Kane 1984), the 'political economy of small farmer loan delinquency' (Sanderatne 1986) and the 'political economy of agricultural credit' (Blair 1984). These were not comprehensive political analyses of the Ohio School model: rather, they contributed a set of political arguments to the economic arguments that sought to criticise supply-led credit programmes and state involvement in financial services more generally.

The most sweeping model was Kane's (1984), which identified a dialectic between 'political power' (defined as 'coalition building' and exercised through legislation) and 'economic power' (secured by the accumulation of wealth and exercised by using resources efficiently so as to enhance wealth). The relative strength of political and economic forces is lagged so that a cycle of events occurs that can be characterised as regulation, avoidance and re-regulation. The initial regulation of the financial market is supported by a powerful politically based coalition that supports regulation for reasons other than those ostensibly cited (that is, its economic and political self-interest). Rational economic actors react to regulations by avoidance (for example, the use of loans for non-permitted purposes, or the diversion of credit to ineligible people) and 'in some agricultural credit programs circumvention becomes a cooperative game played by lenders and borrowers at the expense of external sponsors and the intended beneficiaries' (ibid.: 175). The staff of implementing agencies succumb to rent-seeking activities and the powerful economic actors who gain resources, through bribery and influence (Sanderatne 1986: 347), apply them to the most advantageous investment opportunities available, such as urban real estate, regardless of programme objectives. After some time growing public evidence of avoidance triggers political pressure, by domestic supporters of subsidised credit and donors. A phase of re-regulation ensues which, in turn, is followed by a further phase of avoidance. Implicitly there is only one way off this financially debilitating treadmill: total deregulation!

While Kane's model can incorporate a number of widely reported empirical experiences hampering rural credit programmes in developing countries – 'consideration money' in India (Copestake 1994), 'farmers with long pants' in Sri Lanka (Sanderatne 1986), high levels of wilful default, political rhetoric about objectives and achievements – it has fundamental flaws in its construction and implicit prescription:

- In Kane's model, political power and economic power are distinct. This is only tenable because of the omission of public expenditure (which is 'political' and 'economic') from his analysis and the assumption that the memberships of each power block are discrete. Neither the omission nor the assumption can be justified in the light of empirical evidence.

- The actions of those in his 'political' realm (politicians and bureaucrats) are purely regulatory. The possibility of non-regulatory government action – what Hoff *et al.* (1993: 22) call 'the role of social innovation' and illustrate with group lending schemes – to stimulate institutional experimentation is not recognised.

- Although reference is made to the political interests of donor agencies the model focuses almost exclusively on domestic political economy. The international political economy within which recipients and donors operate – the Cold War, the rise of Islamic fundamentalism, the promotion of ideologies, the influence of multi-national corporations looking for new markets, the need for aid agencies to keep their constituencies satisfied by moving from panacea to panacea – is not incorporated. Malign 'political forces' in this model are located almost exclusively in recipient institutions and countries.

- The model is deterministic and offers no opportunity, or explanation, for the weakening of the powerful vested interests that support subsidised credit. In practice, the late 1980s witnessed interest rate deregulation in most developing countries.

- Attempts to test Kane's model empirically (Khalily and Meyer 1993) have revealed that simple deregulation is not sufficient to modify the influence of political factors on financial activity. For example, increases in the nominal rate of interest on rural loans in Bangladesh (10.5 per cent in 1979–80 to 16 per cent in 1987–8) and real interest rates (-2.5 per cent in 1979–80 to 8.6 per cent in 1987–8) have been associated with a steady decline in recovery rates, in the following year (from 52 per cent in 1980–1 to 19 per cent in 1988–9).

Blair's model (1984) has greater analytical merit. It focuses on the desire of governments to stay in power. This leads to a quest for national political stability which in turn means retaining the support of those who could be disruptive. This is done by many mechanisms, and in rural areas one of the most common is government patronage of the rural elite (especially larger landowners) who control the mass of the rural populace through patron–client relationships based on sharecropping, tenancy, informal loans, assistance during periods of distress and labour hiring. Granting subsidised loans to this elite, which they may not need to repay, is an effective form of patronage. It encourages them to maintain the status quo and to support the incumbent regime, and it gives them additional resources to strengthen patron–client ties. Although Blair's model is clearly based on the case of authoritarian regimes in Bangladesh, it can be modified to explain the use of subsidised credit to win votes and reward supporters in democratic contexts. Moratoriums on loan repayments in Sri Lanka, India (*melas*) and contemporary Bangladesh can be seen as a device used by governments to make their retention of power more likely. Subsidised credit has rhetorical appeal and may be used to 'buy' blocks of rural votes or reward party stalwarts. However, in other political contexts – for example, African states without such a clear '*kulak*' class and where ethnicity is of significance – alternative models of the patronage process would have to be formulated. We return to this issue of patronage in the next section.

One final point on Blair's model must be noted. While his analysis illustrates the pitfalls of subsidised credit, it does not reach the economistic conclusions typical of the Ohio School, that is, that the state withdraw from the financial arena and that 'politics' will then evaporate. Rather, Blair sees some form of state involvement as inevitable and argues that those wishing to reshape financial markets will need a detailed understanding of specific political economies and of the types of political support that reform initiatives would need if they were to be implemented.

To sum up so far, we argue that while some of the political discussion that has evolved around the Ohio School work provides useful insights about processes, it can in no way be viewed as an authoritative analysis of the politics of finance for the rural poor, or the poor more generally. A less deterministic framework that can accommodate specific contexts and appreciate the possibility of experimentation and innovation by individuals, institutions, governments and donors is required. The empirical work undertaken for this study (Volume 2) shows the need for a contingency analysis that can cope with the complexity of political processes occurring in different countries. This is illustrated in the next section by a comparative discussion of our case-studies.

POLITICS AND FINANCIAL INTERMEDIATION FOR THE POOR IN PRACTICE

While no single theory can accommodate the differing political processes and experiences described in Volume 2, a methodology can be identified that aids in the analysis of the politics of financial intermediation. This requires an examination of the nature of the state, the identification of the domestic political forces that seek to influence financial policy and institutions and an exploration of both the general and country-specific influences of external actors. This approach permits the recognition of diversity and contingency and an escape from the determinism of the current orthodoxy: anything with state involvement will fail.

The nature of the state

At the heart of this approach is an appreciation of the fact that those who control the state at any particular time are not omniscient nor all-powerful. Lindblom's (1979) notion of 'muddling through' is more informative, recognising the uncertainty of much government action and the opportunity for incremental innovation by individuals and groups who can find 'room for manoeuvre' (Clay and Schaffer 1984). One could postulate that such room for manoeuvre would be greatest in democratic[1] states where, at least in theory, alternative views and a pluralist approach to institutions would be tolerated. However, the most dramatic financial innovations encountered during our research[2] occurred under authoritarian military regimes in Bangladesh and Indonesia. The most successful small-farmer credit scheme in Africa operated under Banda's one-party state. It faltered partly as a result of donor-induced moves towards democratisation (and market liberalisation) coinciding with a drought which encouraged the Banda regime to be more lenient with write-offs and rescheduling than at earlier times.[3] Tentatively, one could float a modified version of O'Donnell's (1975) thesis of 'bureaucratic authoritarianism' and argue that the difficulties of introducing new policies (such as liberalised interest rates, genuine access to credit for small entrepreneurs and farmers and a focus on savings mobilisation) are so great that they can only occur under strong authoritarian regimes that can control or withstand the domestic opposition generated by reforms. We do not have sufficient cases to substantiate such an argument, but it must be noted that the most effective state-run schemes we studied (BRI, BKK, KURK and SACA) were in Indonesia and Malawi. By contrast, in the developing world's longest-running democracy, Sri Lanka, state-operated schemes have performed poorly for forty years whilst our case-study institution reported the threat of political co-option as its greatest problem. Could it be that in democratic contexts the interplay of the processes of responsiveness (responding to popular demands) and accountability (accounting for the use of resources and the results achieved) favour short-term responsiveness (keeping interest rates low, writing-off loans, trying to buy-off the rural elite) over long-term accountability (contributing to growth and capital accumulation, ensuring the financial sustainability of institutions)?[4] If this is the case, then the recent wave of democratisation sweeping the globe might not run hand-in-hand with sustainable financial intermediation for the poor.

Our case studies revealed that under both democratic and authoritarian conditions innovative financial institutions have to consider not only the influence of (and their relationship with) those who hold state power, but also of those who, by fair or foul means, seek to hold power in the future (the opposition). In Bangladesh, BRAC kept itself formally distanced from Ershad (and his Jatiyo Party) and from opposition groups while maintaining personal and informal contacts with all of these parties. These contacts kept BRAC close enough to Ershad's regime to permit it to prosper during the 1980s, but also made it possible to jettison its links in the dying days of his dictatorship by signing an NGO petition against Ershad. This facilitated a relatively smooth transition to operating under the auspices of the incoming democratic government. It is in Sri Lanka, however, that our fieldwork revealed the most complex oppositional contexts. At election time both the UNP and the SLFP parties seek to identify with SANASA, and its large membership, at the national and the local level. The movement's leaders seek to avoid all contact with parties and politicians at such times to ensure that, whoever wins, they will not be subsequently victimised. During the 1980s and 1990s the picture has been further complicated, as 'invisible' relationships have been necessary with armed opposition forces (the Tamil Tigers and JVP) which could have closed the movement down in large parts of the country. Understandably, little is known of such contacts as the threat of assassination (by rebel groups or by state-sponsored killer squads) was a day-to-day reality for those involved. State institutions were not so fortunate, having either to cease operations or, alternatively, to respond to pressures from the armed police and soldiers involved in peacekeeping to provide loans (Zander 1992).

The nature of domestic political economy

The second key element for an understanding of the politics of financial intermediation is an analysis of the domestic political economy of resource allocation within a specific context. In case-study countries, with the possible exception of Bolivia,[5] the concept of patron–client relationships proves most useful as interest groups are usually weak and not well organised. This approach postulates that the political elite of a country will use their influence over the financial system to permit their retention of power and the maintenance of the status quo. The best-articulated example is that of Bangladesh (Vol. 2, Chapter 12). Under authoritarian rule the Ershad regime used rural loans to promote stability and win the support of the land-owning class (McGregor 1989). Under democratic regimes it has used loans to influence voter behaviour (Khalily and Meyer 1993). The multi-stranded control and influence mechanisms that large landowners have over rural livelihoods – employment, sharecropping, distress loans, tenancies – permits them to patronise large numbers of poor clients and gain control of the local government system and co-operative organisations. This landed elite is not united and factions compete to dominate local contexts. The national political elite – and nowadays competing parties – seek to win the support of the more powerful patrons by giving them privileged access to public resources. A hierarchy of interlinked patron–client relationships is thus created, and subsidised rural loans (that may be written-off informally or by moratoriums) are used by those at the top of the chain to win the support of the rural elite.

Such relationships have not only a structural but also a personal dimension, in which individuals seek to enhance their own or their families' position. Loan allocation is part of this, but for those at higher levels of the hierarchy the allocation of jobs in financial organisations (and the continuous flow of resources that ensues) may be of even greater significance. This was revealed by our study of TRDEP. This scheme managed largely to avoid the use of its loans as a patronage device, but when it was rapidly expanded (through an infusion of donor funds) it could not evade the patronage of employment allocation. The creation of 350 public service jobs at one time could not fail to attract the attention of members of the national elite, up to ministerial level. The subsequent brokering of jobs by politicians and senior bureaucrats stalled the expansion problem, demoralised the existing staff and drew TRDEP and its lending into established patronage networks.

Modified versions of this model of a hierarchy of patron–client relationships can explain aspects of rural loan provision in other South Asian contexts, such as Sri Lanka (Moore 1985: 93–4). However, alternative models are required for different socio-political structures, and in Africa ethnic factors would have to be incorporated. For example, in Kenya, whilst the use of agricultural credit was partially influenced by patronage networks targeting individuals (Leonard 1991: 195–6), there was also a distinct set of ethnic influences by which Kikuyu technical officers with political support were able to divert a greater share of the small-farmer credit budget to Kikuyu areas than would have been the case on the basis of ecological and economic considerations (ibid.: 319–20). In Malawi, SACA credits were concentrated in Central Province which, not surprisingly, was President Banda's home region and the main power base of the Malawi Congress Party.

While such an analysis illustrates the significance of the environments within which financial intermediaries must operate, it is erroneous to assume that socio-political structures will determine the performance of all financial institutions that are not purely market based, as do adherents of the Ohio School. Innovative institutions and schemes can be designed and managed so that they have a significant degree of autonomy from both national and local elites. This is not to suggest that they can escape from their political environments, but that their actions and outcomes can be more than the simple interplay of existing social forces might indicate. The examples in Volume 2, and especially that of the Grameen Bank – in what surely must be one of the world's more limiting political economies – are clear evidence of this. Such breakthroughs cannot be assumed to be permanent, however. As institutions and programmes expand they inevitably attract more attention from national political elites (as was reported in

Kenya) and need to react to the threats of capture or co-option by powerful vested interests. Also with expansion come questions about whether innovative institutions can avoid the organisational culture that dominates a national scene. A small cadre of committed staff with dynamic and charismatic leadership may be able to operate with relatively high levels of honesty, accessibility and openness in a context in which the broader organisational culture is inaccessible, closed and malfeasance is common: but as such an organisation expands from 10 to 100 to 1,000 to 10,000 staff, can it insulate itself from the context?[6]

The international environment and international agencies

While the orthodoxy is deterministic about the influence of the state and the political economies of developing countries on financial intermediation, it is very quiet about the politics of international agencies and actors. This is surprising given the effects that imported ideas and organisational forms have had on financial markets, not least in the encouragement of specialised farm credit institutions (SFCI) in the 1960s and 1970s.

At the global ideological level one can identify a shift of policy towards more monetarist, market-orientated and right-wing strategies. The implications of this can be illustrated in terms of the role that small farmers and entrepreneurs are seen as playing in national development (Figure 6.1). The far left position has withered[7] while the left of centre position is mainly vaunted by some academics (Dreze and Sen 1989) and 'leftish' NGOs (such as OXFAM and Christian Aid) but has had only limited influence on policy. At the centre of the ideological spectrum the policy of strongly assisting small entrepreneurs and farmers through subsidised intervention has been largely discredited by the experiences of the 1970s and 1980s. Thus, the contemporary ideological debate focuses on propositions to the right of centre. It can be crudely characterised as a contest between a 'soft' right position (intervene to create financial intermediaries and other services that emphasise cost recovery and can rapidly become fully self-financing) and a far right position (deregulate interest rates and market entry requirements and let intermediaries evolve in response to market forces). On this side of the spectrum the counter-revolution (Toye 1987) of the 1980s now seems to be losing steam and the policy influences on financial intermediation appear to be gently slipping from a far right towards a 'softer' right position. While the ascendancy of market-orientated policies in the late twentieth century can be presented as a technical debate, the international political context has clearly been of fundamental significance.

The swing to more right-wing governments in the USA (under Reagan), the UK (under Thatcher) and in other European countries, followed by the end of the Cold War and the collapse of communism, has had a profound

Far Left	Soft Left	Centre	Soft Right	Far Right
Production is a state function and small enterprise has only a residual role in the economy	Poor producers need access to credit at reasonable rates. They also require access to credit for consumption to reduce their vulnerability to seasonal factors and crises	Small enterprise has a significant role in the economy and should receive credit at reasonable rates (i.e. subsidised) and services to help it evolve and to reduce economic inequality	Small enterprise has a major role in the economy and interventions to promote it should keep subsidies low and should aim to remove rapidly any element of subsidy	Small enterprise has a major role in the economy and is best left to evolve in a deregulated environment

Figure 6.1 The role of small farmers and entrepreneurs: an ideological spectrum

effect on the shape of bilateral and multilateral development agency policies including financial markets. Our case-studies illustrate the major threads in this political shift.

The most obvious impact on policies is the widespread acceptance of official interest rate structures that are more closely aligned to market forces. Although only the Indonesian examples approach what appears to be full market rates, all our other cases have increased the real rate of interest they charge on their loans and the spreads between the cost of fund acquisition and on-lending.[8] This interest rate liberalisation has been a key factor in contributing to the sustainability of case-study institutions (Chapter 3).

A second major result of this ideological shift has been the accreditation of a large new sub-set of players in this area – non-governmental organisations (NGOs) or the non-profit private sector. Despite the arguments of the far right, private business has proved reluctant to experiment in intermediation for poor savers and borrowers, but this 'vacuum' has in part been filled by the non-profit sector. The rise and rise of the non-profit sector is a global phenomenon associated with the anti-statist politics of the right (Salamon 1993; Edwards and Hulme 1992 and 1995) and these organisations now play a significant role in financial innovation. In Bangladesh, the Grameen Bank's experimental and establishment phase was as an NGO, while BRAC is the country's biggest NGO. In Sri Lanka, SANASA, despite its present moves towards professionalisation, is a co-operative movement relying heavily on voluntary management and contributions from the village to the national level. KREP, and a number of similar programmes in Kenya, are all registered as NGOs, while in Malawi the initial plan of the MMF was for it to be non-governmental. The case of

BancoSol is particularly interesting. This originated as PRODEM, an NGO, but was subsequently incorporated as a commercial company. This may well be a model that will become common over the coming years, with the risk of innovation taken by non-profits which, once successful, exchange their 'mission' for a 'market' niche.[9]

But not all political debate has narrowed down to a discussion about how far right to go. History has not ended! A new political dimension has become evident in the ideological clash between Islam and Western notions of capitalism and democracy and this may become the political issue of the next century (Ahmed and Donnan 1994). It has profound implications for financial intermediation, and its influence on schemes for the poor in Malaysia has already been reported (Hulme 1993) where Amanah Ikhtiar Malaysia has opted to charge a flat 'management fee' rather than interest. It is becoming increasingly significant in Bangladesh. During 1993 and 1994 both BRAC and the Grameen Bank have found themselves competing for 'hearts and minds' at the local level with Islamic fundamentalists supported by village imams and linked to the *Jamaat Islami* and other political parties. The fundamentalist challenge focuses on the Koranic prohibitions on interest rates and the role of women in the economy. Both BRAC and the Grameen Bank are seen as abrogating the fundamentalist interpretation of these matters so that all Muslims (more than 90 per cent of BRAC and Grameen Bank memberships) should not participate in their programmes. Both institutions are encountering resistance, sometimes violent, to the creation of new branches in some areas, and the continuing rise of fundamentalism in Bangladesh poses a threat to their expansion plans. In Muslim Indonesia such problems have not arisen as yet, at least in part because of the efficiency and ruthlessness of the Suharto regime in destroying nascent fundamentalist groups.

Moving on from these general influences of the international environment, two points specific to our case-studies emerge. The first relates to the relative success of USAID in promoting and assisting commercially orientated loans programmes through non-profit organisations. Through direct involvement in founding KREP, by supporting ACCION to work with PRODEM and financing a team from Harvard University to work with BRI, the ideological preferences of the US government – small-enterprise promotion, market-based pricing, economic growth as the answer to poverty-alleviation – were effectively promoted.

The case-studies also illustrate the internal politics of international aid agencies and in particular the pressures on multilateral agencies to commit and disburse funds. The most obvious case is the Asian Development Bank's (ADB) loan for the expansion of TRDEP. At the time of agreeing this loan with the Government of Bangladesh (GoB) most informed observers warned that the scale and speed of the expansion was so great that it would destroy the programme. However, internal pressures within the ADB to meet commitment targets led to an insistence on a large loan and the GoB was in no position to refuse such funds. A senior consultant[10] to the ADB subsequently queried ADB country managers about the loan and was advised that they were aware of the likely problems but not concerned as 'rural development projects in Bangladesh never perform'. The funds were programmed, the aid administrators expected them to be squandered so there was little point in getting too involved with the detail!

The World Bank's *Janasaviya* Trust Fund (JTF) activities in Sri Lanka were clearly driven by a need to commit and disburse funds in order to demonstrate the Bank's new-found commitment to poverty-alleviation.[11] The adoption of this new mantle has been necessitated by its major sponsors questioning what it does and what it achieves now that the Cold War is over and its political role in promoting OECD interests has gone. The approach may well be less cynical than the ADB's and there is a serious attempt by committed personnel to use the funds effectively. However, the question of whether these funds would achieve more if programmed over a longer period was not permitted on this agenda: the Bank's loan was to be disbursed as close to the original schedule as possible. This served the interests of the UNP government, as the expansion of rural credit in 1993 and 1994 (before the elections due in 1995, but held in August 1994) was part of its armoury of patronage mechanisms to help increase the likelihood of electoral success. Despite the JTF's objective of 'institutional development' it was identified by the SANASA board as a major threat to the Federation's future (Vol. 2, Chapter 13). It was also a source of concern for several bilateral agencies[12] who believed that their work with other 'financial' NGOs would be damaged by the Bank pumping funds into the sector.

The final point to note about the influences of international agencies relates to the protection and support that they can offer domestic financial institutions. It is difficult to be precise about this role as, for reasons of both confidentiality and pride, institutions are circumspect about disclosures on the topic. In the Sri Lankan example just referred to, there was direct evidence of SANASA exploring with bilateral donors whether they could form a group to confront the World Bank and persuade it to get JTF to work only at Federation level. In one of our African examples the managers reported that having donors was useful because their support for the organisations reduced the likelihood of direct domestic political interference: upsetting a major donor for the 'small beer' that this organisation represented was not worthwhile. The same agency also reported working with donor agencies to achieve policy changes: 'if we go to the government we are not listened to, if a donor goes with our argument it may be listened to'.

MANAGING THE POLITICAL ENVIRONMENT: INDIVIDUALS AND NASCENT INSTITUTIONS

All the relatively successful institutions discussed in Volume 2, with the exception of SACA and MMF, demonstrated a capacity to manage their political environments so that they could design financial services that permitted them to meet their goals and remain viable. The ways in which this was achieved are complex, subtle and often hidden. However, a common element of these cases was the maintenance of a significant degree of institutional autonomy from politicians, political parties and (for the NGOs) state agencies. Key individuals figure prominently in negotiating the organisational contexts that facilitated effective financial intermediation. The analysis of the activities of such individuals remains difficult in social science, as identifying the importance of human agency often leads to 'great man' theories (Leonard 1991) arguing that institutional performance is determined by the chance involvement of an exceptional individual – in our examples, figures such as Abed, Yunus, Romero, Kiriwandeniya, Patten and Mutua. However, we must seek to go beyond personal 'exceptionality' as the explanation for institutional innovation and must note that, given the weak nature of interest groups in many developing countries, a more prominent role for individuals is only to be expected. It must also be recalled (see earlier sections of this chapter) that neither the state nor the dominant groups in the domestic political economy are all-powerful as is commonly assumed. In all countries studied, with the possible exception of Malawi, institutional managers had room for manoeuvre and could negotiate their organisational environments to some degree.

The characteristics associated with success in such negotiations vary with organisational scale. When small, leaders commonly found that they had little need to consider the political positioning of their organisations. As they expanded and attracted more interest from politicians, parties and other actors, 'getting the politics right' became more important. In at least five of our cases (Grameen Bank, BRAC, KREP, PRODEM and SANASA), the negotiating space of their leaders was enhanced by the early establishment of a reputation for success. Each of these individuals took on a 'product champion' role and spearheaded not only the expansion of the programme but also a conscious strategy to manage 'the politics' surrounding their organisation. All were aided by the existence of personal reputations for integrity and professionalism and, in at least two cases, Yunus and Kiriwandeniya, a charismatic personality proved valuable. Interestingly, all these 'product champions' were significantly motivated by non-financial factors: although all have prospered in personal financial terms through their organisations there can be little doubt that all could have earned much more had their motivations been purely economic self-interest. The problems of the Malawi Mudzi Fund relate, in part, to the lack of a product champion attempting to manage the political environment. Research on the MMF in 1990 revealed a situation in which the scheme's manager had to do what donors and the domestic elite wanted (wisely in terms of personal security) and had no capacity to influence or avoid them.

The techniques used to manage the political environment in our case-studies vary from country to country and their selection has been a matter of judgement rather than calculation. Listing those reported by managers (see below) provides some insight into the 'room for manoeuvre' that imaginative individuals can create:

1 Devote great time and effort to the construction of boards so that they are publicly seen to be 'balanced' in terms of political sympathies and members' ethnicity and religion. If possible, actively recruit board members who have a reputation for independence and integrity, but can offer protection from political interference because of their position and personal authority (for example, senior religious figures, senior academics, NGO leaders, and so on).

2 Develop relationships with a group of donors who are sufficiently flexible to support innovation and experimentation, who understand they are working with an organisation and not a 'project', who are not driven purely by disbursement targets and who may be able to offer covert protection if politicians or parties seek to manipulate the organisation. Carefully assess the advantages and disadvantages of managing donors bilaterally or as a consortium.

3 Programme operational expansion partly in terms of political factors and not simply of social and economic objectives. For example, ensure that political factions cannot argue that there is a regional or ethnic bias in operations by running services in each major region or for each major ethnic group.

4 Develop a conscious strategy for relationships with politicians and parties. This may vary from using pre-existing political contacts extensively (BancoSol) to maintaining informal and personal links with members of all main political parties so that an agency is not too closely associated with a single party (BRAC), to a strict avoidance of both formal and informal contacts (SANASA).

5 Wherever activities or policies are likely to prove controversial, then package and present them to minimise any adverse reaction. For example, in Indonesia the switch to market-orientated interest rates was disguised by moving the quoting of rates from annually to monthly (see note 8).

6 When encountering legislative obstacles, search for loopholes that will permit internal policies that are not inconsistent with the law. (This was reported as a key device in the court politics of financial innovation in

151

Indonesia where banks encountering legislative obstacles simply redefined some programmes as non-bank financial services.)

7 Identify 'like-minded' civil servants and design programmes so that the organisation works with these individuals rather than with the bureaucracy more generally.

8 Form NGO and academic support networks to increase representation and security of one's own and other sympathetic organisations. This is illustrated by the Association of Development Agencies in Bangladesh (ADAB) and the academic links that most South Asian NGOs pursue.

It is not possible to design a tool-kit from this list but it does demonstrate the existence of substantial opportunities for the leaders of innovative institutions to manoeuvre around potential political obstacles. This is a context-specific activity that is constantly changing and in which there is no guarantee that earlier success in 'walking the political tightrope' (as one case-study director termed it) will continue. The examples of our case-study institutions reveal the possibilities, however.

CAN THE TAIL WAG THE DOG?

At least four of the institutions studied (Grameen Bank, BRAC, SANASA and KREP) not only sought to provide financial services to the poor but also to 'empower' them. These organisations do not explicitly identify the mechanisms underpinning empowerment but, adapting Friedmann (1992), four strands can be identified in the theory of empowerment:

1 material advancement;
2 psychological empowerment in terms of a heightened awareness of personal self-worth and capacity;
3 social empowerment in terms of an enhanced social status within the immediate community;
4 political empowerment, in terms of a greater capacity to influence the decisions of external bodies.

The first of these has been dealt with in Chapters 4 and 5 where it was confirmed that case-study institutions improved the economic position of significant numbers of poor people, but that this was generally 'one step up' and not the establishment of a cumulative process of increasing household income. The influences of microfinance schemes in restructuring political processes by its economic impacts remains insignificant *vis-à-vis* other forces such as increasing technical change in agriculture and industrialisation. The second dimension presents considerable methodological problems in terms of assessment and the claims in the literature on the Grameen Bank (Fuglesang and Chandler 1986 and 1993) and BRAC

152

(Lovell 1992) that such changes have occurred are not backed up by any systematic evidence.

On the third, it is possible to be more specific and our empirical research on BRAC, the Grameen Bank and SANASA (Volume 2) and the work of others sheds some light on the effects of innovative financial intermediation on gender[13] and class relations. Schuler and Hashemi's (1994) finding that Grameen Bank and BRAC borrowers are more likely to be using contraceptive measures than comparable non-members – and the argument that this represents an enhanced capacity to negotiate fertility behaviour with husbands – provides evidence of credit programmes influencing gender relations within the household. However, the effects of such schemes on the position of women are far from uniform and in some situations women's access to credit may simply disguise the continuation of existing patterns of power within the household (Goetz and Gupta 1994).

In terms of political empowerment, however, we remain sceptical of the claims that financial institutions for the poor can spearhead structural transformation, be it in terms of the relationships between classes or the operations of formal political processes. The reports of Grameen Bank and BRAC members protesting against local injustices in which the perpetrators are clearly identified (Fuglesang and Chandler 1993; Lovell 1992) are not a new phenomenon, but goes back to colonial times (Wood 1994: 487–9) and probably much earlier. Such localised protest is quite different from the processes of structural transformation (ibid.) entailing the breaking of patron–client ties and the mobilisation of groups of the poor acting as a class to assert their interests over those of more dominant classes. Our field research found that BRAC and Grameen Bank members believe that the village organisations (VO) or centre belongs to the parent agency. There are no formal mechanisms (and our work uncovered no informal processes) by which VOs/centres can associate or federate[14] so that political action beyond the level of the VO/centre is infeasible. The possibility remains that the most successful borrowers will pursue individual and household strategies for advancement based on adopting the practices of the dominant social groups (such as purchasing land through distress sales, paying low wages, operating exploitative tied transactions), rather than practising solidarity with less-successful group members (Wood and Palmer-Jones 1991). Similarly the claims that poverty-focused financial institutions have impacted on the processes of political selection and voting patterns at local and higher levels have not been substantiated. In Sri Lanka, where SANASA's co-operative ideology and structure might theoretically lead it to form alliances with specific political parties, the movement conscientiously avoids any activity likely to identify it with specific candidates or shape electoral behaviour.

The most significant political empowerment that our work revealed was not that of borrower or member empowerment, but of the financial institutions themselves and particularly their leaders and senior managements. The Bangladeshi media now regularly treat the Grameen Bank and BRAC as significant players in the country's political economy and their leaders (along with the President of SANASA) could, should they wish, enter formal politics with substantial bases of popular support and uncontaminated by the routine processes of 'wheeling and dealing' to develop a career within the confines of a political party. The potential for 'alternative leaders'[15] who are not besmirched by years of party intrigues has been added to in both Bangladesh and Sri Lanka. During research in 1994 there were regular rumours in Dhaka that Professor Yunus might head the *Gono* Forum in the next elections.

For the present, there is little firm evidence that the 'tail' of financial intermediation for the poor can 'wag the dog' of local and national socio-economic structures and political relationships. Our case-study institutions respond to the political circumstances within which they operate and, at best, have only a limited capacity to reshape them. The empowerment of the leaders and senior managers of successful institutions has far outpaced the empowerment of members and borrowers.

CONCLUSION

The notion that 'politics' should somehow be removed from the field of financial intermediation for the poor, and its corollary, that any state involvement in finance will take the form of dysfunctional 'political interference', must be laid to rest. Like it or not, in real-world situations all financial institutions – as with all our case-studies – are located within a complex of socio-political relationships and formal political procedures. They must evolve within such environments and adapt to them. While these political environments may set limits to how things can be done and what can be achieved, these are not set in concrete. The leaders and senior managements of innovative institutions have an array of techniques (see pp. 143–5) by which they can seek to avoid the negative influences of individuals and groups who hold power at local or national levels and to gain resources or desired policy changes.

Politics, it has often been argued, is the art of the possible, and our case-study institutions demonstrate that much is possible with regard to financial innovation for the poor in political situations that would appear, on initial analysis, to be quite hopeless. BRI's unit desas evolved out of a failed programme under the auspices of Indonesia's repressive military regime which has manipulated state institutions to maintain its position. They have used an element of this authoritarian political framework – the village head – to help make the programme viable. In Sri Lanka, SANASA 'reawakened' and expanded against a background of the centralisation of political power, ethnic civil war, a youth uprising in the South, the state-sanctioned execution of perhaps 50,000 people, and frequent assassinations and indiscriminate terrorist bombings. And in Bangladesh – with the widespread 'quiet violence' of local-level socio-economic relationships, the subordination of women, inept and corrupt military government and discredited political parties – major breakthroughs in providing financial services for poor people have occurred and are reaching millions of clients.

Such innovations can contribute to the alleviation of poverty and can exert some influence upon power relationships within the household and the locality. However, this influence must be set against backgrounds in which other forces – the opening up of economies, technological change, the reinforcement of ethnic identities, religious fundamentalism – are of far greater significance. The grand claims of social transformation catalysed by innovative financial provision to groups of poor people have no basis in the empirical record and, at present, are at best an aspiration. The greatest 'empowerment' created by the institutions that we have studied is of the leaders and senior managements, rather than of their memberships.[16] This has been particularly evident in Bangladesh and, we also suspect, in India and Pakistan. In formal political terms the authority and legitimacy developed in these key individuals remains potential. Only time will tell whether these potentials are eventually activated and what, if any, are the impacts of such alternative leaderships on the position of poor people.

NOTES

1 The definition of 'democracy' goes beyond the remit of this volume. However, it must be noted that the simple labels 'democratic' and 'authoritarian' disguise a vast variety of differences.

2 Group lending in Bangladesh (Grameen Bank and BRAC) and individual schemes in Indonesia (BRI, BKK and KURK).

3 The unofficial seizure of quasi-collateral (roofing iron, sewing machines, radios, etc.) from defaulters that occurred in the 1970s and 1980s was not an attractive option for the Malawi Congress Party in the run up to multi-party elections.

4 This has been argued to be the case for public expenditure in general and food subsidy policies in particular (Hulme et al. 1994; Healey and Tordoff 1995).

5 BancoSol may be an exception as its founders and supporters are part of an emerging business community associating as an interest group.

6 See Chapter 7 for a discussion of this issue and also Wood (1994: 548–51) for a commentary on NGO expansion in Bangladesh.

7 With perhaps the exceptions of Myanmar, North Korea and Cuba.

8 Interestingly, respondents in Indonesia reported that the Minister of Finance at the time of interest rate deregulation could only be persuaded to make the policy change after advisers suggested that the new rates be quoted on a monthly rather than an annual basis – 2.5 per cent per month was more politically acceptable than 30 per cent (or more) per annum.

9 This form of metamorphosis has been common in the UK since the late 1980s with friendly and mutual societies becoming public companies (see Chapter 7).

10 This consultant is a reliable informant, but for obvious reasons cannot be identified.

11 More recently, driven along by US NGO criticisms, the Bank has convened the Consultative Group to Assist the Poorest (CGAP). This focuses exclusively on promotional microfinance, despite our evidence (and the belief of many in the Bank) that microfinance is not the best form of assistance for the very poor and the hungry.

12 Three bilateral agencies told us of their concern. They did not wish to be identified and believed that JTF was so 'political' there was little point in challenging it.

13 See also Chapter 5 for a discussion of gender issues.

14 BRAC's original plan to federate VOs has been abandoned.

15 This is not to suggest that this is the only source of 'alternatives' – careers in religion, businesses, working as an academic overseas and other bases also exist.

16 This process has not occurred in state-owned institutions, namely SACA, KIE-ISP, BRI unit desas and Indonesia's provincial development banks.

7

THE MANAGEMENT OF
FINANCIAL INSTITUTIONS FOR
THE POOR

INTRODUCTION

The preceding chapters and the materials in Volume 2 provide substantial evidence that a number of relatively effective financial institutions have evolved over the last two decades to meet the credit (and, sometimes, savings) needs of poor people. Such examples stand in marked contrast to the more general experience of credit programmes for the poor (Chapters 1 and 2) and of 'institution-building' and 'institutional development' supported by aid donors (Moore 1994). In this chapter the relative 'success' of several of our case-study institutions (BRAC, Grameen Bank, SANASA, BRI unit desas, BKK, KURK and BancoSol), *vis-à-vis* comparable institutions, is taken as given and we focus on the issue of the ways in which management factors have contributed to their performance.[1] While the main emphasis is on mature institutions, the more youthful cases (KREP's Juhudi, MMF and TRDEP) provide insights into the early phases of the evolution of financial institutions.

At the outset, the reader should be aware of the difficulties of making generalisations about the management of case-study institutions. In empirical terms this is problematic because of the vast range and great variations in management features of these cases. These difficulties are compounded by the fact that an element of enhancing performance in a number of our case-studies is the generation of an 'organisational myth' involving the systematic talking-up, both internally and externally, of what the organisation is achieving. While an organisational myth helps to motivate staff and sets a favourable environment for negotiating with other organisations (especially donors), it tends to obscure the nature of, and relationships between, practice and performance. Within our examples the Grameen Bank and BRAC have developed the most significant 'myths' about their practices and performance.[2]

In conceptual terms, such difficulties arise because of the current 'crises' within the sociology of organisations and the study of management. Post-modernist approaches to organisational behaviour necessitate the adoption of pluri-paradigm approaches (Hassard 1993) that demand resources beyond those of this study and focus on intra-organisational processes and not cross-organisational comparisons. At the other extreme are the management guru approaches, typified by Peters and Waterman (1982) and the recent craze for 're-engineering' organisations. These generate long lists of 'how' to manage organisations better, but eschew the systematic use of data. In this chapter an inductive approach is adopted that explores similarities and dissimilarities in the institutions examined and, where useful, relates these to theoretical perspectives on management and organisation.

The first section compares institutional features and focuses especially on structural matters. Subsequent sections examine management at different levels: the management of members and/or customers; the management of field staff; and the management of the organisation itself. The latter compares the evolution of case-study institutions from their experimental phases to their graduation to maturity. The concluding sections explore the possibility of generating a set of management 'lessons' for the different stakeholders involved in promoting financial institutions for the poor.

A COMPARISON OF STRUCTURAL FEATURES

A comparison of the key structural characteristics of case-study institutions has important implications for several areas of policy (Table 7.1). The most significant observation must be that non-profit institutions (including public-sector and non-governmental organisations) appear to have a comparative advantage over for-profit institutions in providing formal sector financial services to poor people. Three of the eight institutions in Table 7.1 are state-owned, a fourth (Grameen Bank) is jointly state- and member-owned, and a further two (BRAC and SANASA) are NGOs. The case that formal sector for-profit institutions could take a lead role in providing financial services to low-income households finds little support from our case-studies and indeed from the wider empirical literature. The only private company in our study that was providing such services, and that had reached a stage of relative maturity, was BancoSol.[3] This had its origins in PRODEM, a non-government organisation (Vol. 2, Chapter 10). Such an evolution indicates that while the private sector in developing countries may be able to deliver such services, the capacity for path-breaking experimentation and innovation required to broaden access to loans and savings resides within the public sector and NGOs.

Why should this be the case, when the maxim of the late twentieth century has been that the for-profit sector is inherently more efficient and more responsive to people's needs than the public sector? Two main reasons can be identified. The first is that private companies are simply not prepared to provide the venture capital for experimental services to low-income borrowers (and savers). While they may have a 'customer orientation' this is an orientation that prioritises meeting the needs of middle- and upper-income customers over the needs of poor (and often 'invisible') customers. The second reason relates to the erroneous assumption that features of private-sector management that are central to the effective provision of financial services (costing and pricing services, recovering costs, promoting a performance-orientation in staff, market research and new product development) are found only in for-profit concerns. All the organisations in Table 7.1 have adopted management methods and techniques derived from the private sector during their evolution: they include the use of techniques to monitor the performance of loans based upon portfolio management; systematic measures to increase trading margins; performance incentives for staff and borrowers; the treatment of branches as individual units so that their profit/loss can be monitored; and surveys of customer satisfaction (Table 7.2). The 'new' public management of the 1980s (see Lane 1993: 122–49 for a discussion) and the adoption of a more business-like approach by many NGOs have reorientated at least some state and non-profit organisations so that they have been able to link their focus on service delivery to target groups with pressures for cost recovery and financial viability. By contrast, the formal private sector has proved unable, to date, to link its push for profits with the recognition that low-income households represent a vast 'market' for financial services, as public-choice theory would suggest. For economic historians, this finding will come as no surprise, given the fact that many of Northern Europe's and North America's largest 'retail' financial institutions (building societies, friendly societies, co-operative banks) are non-profits or have their origins in the non-profit sector.

The second conclusion to be drawn from a comparison of the 'successful' organisations is that all have adopted administratively intensive operational structures. As is demonstrated in Chapter 3, the additional costs of high levels of field staff are more than offset by the reduced levels of default associated with intense loan supervision. While there are a variety of different ways in which field staff can be effectively deployed (for a review, see Chapter 3) the general point emerges that effective financial services for poor people, similarly to those for rural populations, must be based on a 'mobile banking' approach (Yaron 1991). This is not a single system as is commonly assumed (that is, adopting a Grameen Bank approach) but a broad approach which recognises that the bank worker must go to the customer and not vice versa. The provision of financial services from offices which the customer has to visit – a model introduced from the West which has dominated banking in developing countries – is clearly inappropriate in relation to most of the needs of poor people. Indeed, the surprising thing is that such a model was

Table 7.1 Management features of successful case-study institutions

	BRAC	GB	SANASA	BRI unit desas	BKK	KURK	BancoSol
Institutional status	Credit programme within an NGO	Parastatal financial institution	Three-tier member co-operative	Autonomous scheme within a bank	Non-bank financial institution	Non-bank financial institution	Private bank (originally NGO)
Ownership	Unclear	Independent 75 per cent borrowers, 25 per cent state	100 per cent members	BRI (state-owned bank)	Provincial government	Provincial government	Bolivian business (20 per cent) and interntional foundations (79 per cent)
Organisational structure	4 tier	3 tier	3 tier	—	—	—	3 tier
Lending model	Group lending	Group lending	Co-operatives	Individuals	Individuals	Individuals	Group lending
Are branches individual accounting units?	Yes	Yes	Yes	Yes	Yes	Yes	Yes
Number of clients (1992)	650,000	1,400,000	702,000	1,800,000	499,000	158,000	50,000
Number of branches	120	951	7,245				
Number of loans per staff member	—	127	—	102	272	—	—
Value of loans per staff member	$8,079	$4,863	—	$29,327	$6,933	—	—
Value of savings per staff member	$2,735	$2,833	—	$39,368	$1,387	—	—

Administration and operating costs as per cent loans (1992)		16.7 per cent	—	15.8 per cent	14.3 per cent	22.8 per cent
Staff training	Major activity	Major activity	Major activity	Major activity		
Borrower training	Major activity	Major activity	Major activity			Major activity
Active or responsive loan provision	Active	Active	Active	Active	Active	Active
'Mobile banking' features	Yes	Yes	Yes	Yes	Yes	Yes

Sources: Fieldwork; Yaron (1991); Bangladesh Institute of Development Studies (1994)

Table 7.2 Private-sector management techniques and case-study institutions

	BRAC	GB	SANASA	BRI unit desas	BKK	KURK	BancoSol
Portfolio management	√	√	√		√	?	√
Increasing trading margins	√	√	√	√	√	√	√
Incentives to staff	√	√	√	√	√	√	√
Incentives to customers	√	√	√	√	√	√	√
Branches as accounting units	√	?	√	√	√	√	√
Customer surveys	√	?	?	?	?	?	?

Source: Fieldwork

emphasised in the first place, given the importance of mobile financial services – credit unions, co-operatives and life insurance premiums collected at the door – for lower-income households in Europe and North America during the first three-quarters of this century.[4] For policy purposes such a finding has two implications. The most obvious is the recommendation that those seeking to meet the financial needs of the poor adopt a mobile approach (as is discussed in detail in Chapter 3 and later sections of this chapter). Conversely, those institutions that claim to be targeting the poor and adopt an office-based approach – probably the majority of agencies – must be forcefully challenged to explain how they will overcome the inherent problems of their approach.

The third point emerging from a review of the structural features of successful institutions is that all practice a significant degree of decentralised decision-making. Strategic decisions, such as the design of programmes and the establishment of systems, are matters for headquarters; operational decisions, such as opening a new branch or moving into a new village, are delegated to intermediary levels; and routine activities, such as monitoring loans, are left to the branch level. In both the Grameen Bank and BRAC, expansion has meant that functions have had to be steadily delegated to lower levels so that the head office can perform a limited number of core functions. By contrast, schemes that perform poorly are commonly associated with centralised decision-making structures. Perhaps the extreme of these is Sri Lanka's New Comprehensive Rural Credit Scheme (Vol. 2, Chapter 13) in which details such as loan size and use are determined by the Central Bank at its Colombo headquarters.

The main features of organisational cost structures have already been examined in Chapter 3, but one finding in particular must be reiterated. Successful case-study institutions have a clear propensity towards high levels of administrative cost (Table 7.3) reflecting their adoption of labour-intensive approaches to credit (and savings) services provision. Commonly, administrative costs are three times greater than the average cost of a sample of thirty-eight rural credit schemes computed by the World Bank (1984, Annex 13). Such investments in staff salaries and training (particularly field staff) permit the attainment of high levels of outreach and relatively high levels of loan recovery, through intensive supervision. The relatively high levels of resources committed to administration in SANASA are disguised by the absorption of the training and institutional development costs of primary societies at the district and federation level and the exclusion of many costs from society accounts because they are met on a voluntary basis. Given the significance of personnel-intensive strategies to case-study institutions, the issue of the management of field staff is of particular importance.

Table 7.3 Administrative costs and ratios for selected schemes, 1991

	Administrative costs as a % of outstanding loans portfolio	Number of borrowers per staff member	Number of loans per staff member
BRAC	—	209[b]	—
Grameen Bank	16.7	131	127
SANASA	2.8[a]	—	—
BRI unit desas	15.8	—	102
BKK	14.3	—	272
KURK	—	—	—
BancoSol	22.8	—	—

Sources: Vol. 2; Yaron (1992); Bangladesh Institute of Development Studies (1994); and fieldwork

Notes

[a] Excludes district union and federation expenses as well as voluntary administrative contributions.

[b] In 1990 the figure was 148. The 1991 figure reflects a spurt in borrower recruitment.

MANAGING FIELD STAFF

The performance of case-study institutions is heavily dependent on their capacity to recruit good field staff, train them effectively and motivate them through emoluments and promotional prospects. Early success in this area has to be followed by the development of a human resource management (HRM) system that can provide increasingly large numbers of field staff without any significantly adverse influence on their quality.

The recruitment process is the foundation for HRM activities. In the Bangladesh and Indonesian examples the focus for recruitment has been on recent university graduates for field-level managers and higher secondary school certificate holders for village-level workers. These are given field-based training, much of it on-the-job, which is associated with relatively high rates of trainee drop-out. For example, in the mid-1980s around 26 per cent of Grameen Bank recruits dropped out before their training was completed (Hossain 1988: 31). In 1994 the figure for BRAC stood at around 18 per cent of recruits dropping out in the first three months. Although costly, these high rates of initial drop-out serve as a screening process that reduces staff turnover rates at later stages. In 1993 BRAC's staff turnover rate was only 4 per cent per annum (BIDS 1994: 79) and our other examples all reported rates of less than 10 per cent per annum.

The Asian case-studies all highlight the importance of staff training in terms of both technical capacities and motivation, devoting substantial financial resources and time to this function. For the Grameen Bank

Box 7.1 Training branch-level workers at the Grameen Bank

The training of newly recruited branch-level workers lasts around six months with around 20 per cent of this period spent at the headquarters Training Institute. Following a two-day introduction and overview of the Bank (objectives, procedures, forms), small groups (two to four) of trainees are attached to a branch with an experienced manager. For a seven- or eight-week period they observe the branch's operations, conduct case-studies of a small number of borrowers, prepare a map of the branch's area and develop a knowledge of the area's road and path network. During this period relatively high levels of drop-out occur as some trainees decide that the demands of branch-level work – long days, large amounts of time spent walking and cycling, being outdoors and working with the poor – are not for them.

At the end of this period trainees return to the Training Institute for a week to present their case-studies and experiences, discuss these with peers, learn the Bank's constitution and structures, and receive feedback on their performances from trainers and branch managers.

A second period in the field follows, and for seven to eight weeks trainees observe branch operations and become involved in day-to-day work. During this time trainees visit between ten and fifteen centres and monitor loan utilisation by two or three borrowers in each, look at target group identification and mobilisation and become involved in the form-filling essential to Bank operations. A week at the Training Institute ensues, to review experiences again and to undergo detailed instruction in how to master the Bank's forms.

The third branch-level attachment runs for two months and entails less open learning about borrowers and greater involvement in actual operations. Training concludes with a final week of more formal learning and assessment at Head Office. Successful trainees are then appointed to their first branch – this must not be the branch at which they were trained.

Sources: Fuglesang and Chandler (1993); interviews with Grameen Bank staff and donors

training expenses represent around 28 per cent of annual administrative costs (Yaron 1991: II. 18) and an intensive field-based training system has evolved (Box 7.1). In BRAC more than 18,000 participant days of training were provided to new and existing staff associated with the rural credit programmes in 1993 (BRAC Statistical Report 1994) and a sophisticated training system delivers courses to employees at fourteen regional training centres and a large national-level complex. In a similar fashion, SANASA's Federation operates a large-scale training service at a national training centre and throughout the district unions. This inducts new employees and provides up-grading courses on book-keeping, auditing, savings mobilisation and group mobilisation to experienced staff. Although operating on a smaller scale than the Asian institutions, KREP has identified the development of training capacity as central to its plans for expansion and has used donor funds towards this goal. While all case-study institutions still have substantial opportunities to improve the training they offer to employees, all have managed to provide courses that are significantly shaped by demand-side forces (that is, the employee's job-related learning needs). This is particularly the case in Bangladesh, where the Grameen Bank's and BRAC's training activities stand in marked contrast to the trainer-dominated, classroom-based rote-learning that characterises training in the public sector.

Once trained, motivation is maintained by practices including competitive salaries (for example, BRAC sets its field staff pay levels at between 20 and 25 per cent above equivalent public-sector levels),[5] performance-related pay (see Vol. 2, Chapter 11) and promotion systems based upon relatively objective assessments of performance. BRAC, the Grameen Bank and the Indonesian institutions all recruit the bulk of their middle- and senior-level personnel from subordinate levels[6] with around 90–95 per cent of BRAC, Grameen Bank and SANASA head office staff coming from regional or field offices.

The theoretical means by which field staff can be motivated have two very different bases. One set is based upon the altruism generated by fostering field staff solidarity with poorer households. While both BRAC and SANASA have laid claims to utilising such a process, it is the Grameen Bank that has drawn most heavily on such an idea (see Gibbons 1992). The Bank's founder argues that young Bangladeshi graduates are keen to help villagers and that, when given a training that helps them to understand the nature of poverty and a job that allows them to alleviate poverty, they readily commit themselves to work with the Grameen Bank (ibid.).

The second means is quite distinct, and views field staff motivation as based largely upon self-interest. This has been the focus particularly for the Indonesian schemes. These organisations have spearheaded incentive schemes that encourage staff to make loans and collect repayments. Such incentives range from a modest topping-up of salary (BRI unit desas) to the sole basis of income (KURK commission-based staff).[7] Perhaps not surprisingly, given the ideological context of the 1980s and 1990s, it is the 'self-interest' model of staff motivation that has become most influential, with both BRAC and the Grameen Bank adopting this approach in the last few years and SANASA experimenting with it. Such a move may be an inevitable result of programme expansion. As staff numbers grow, the capacity of leaders to promote staff performance by the transmission of specific values is reduced and work becomes increasingly routinised. The initial performance of an organisation, based on some shared vision, may only be maintained by a more commercial orientation that relies less on personality and more on pecuniary influences.

Although these latter organisations claim that both the altruistic approach, based on a commitment to certain social values, and the self-interest approach, based on personal rewards, can be combined, such a conjunction may be more a wish than a reality, as it signals a major shift not merely in organisational systems but also in organisational culture. For both BRAC and the Grameen Bank the switch to performance-related pay has been associated with growing numbers of reports of members being bullied into making repayments when they have encountered problems (see Montgomery 1995). This is good for business (in commercial terms for the staff member and the organisation) but it may not be good for poverty-reduction.

MANAGING BORROWERS AND SAVERS

Successful case-study institutions exhibit very different models for managing borrowers and savers. Three main models can be identified: solidarity groups;[8] co-operative groups; and individual customers – although there are numerous variants of each of these. Each of these models generates a different combination of management tasks and different types of relations between fieldworkers and borrowers/savers (Table 7.4). Before examining each in turn, four points must be noted:

1 The differing financial needs of specific households and of individuals within households make it infeasible to specify a single optimal model for the needs of low-income families.
2 Following on from 1, the ideal situation in any given context would be to have a pluralist system of financial service provision which, at a minimum, would involve competition between institutions based on the three models in Table 7.4. Disappointingly, our own fieldwork indicates that pluralist institutional provision remains an aspiration rather than an actuality. Nowhere did we locate households that had a choice between solidarity group, co-operative group and individual services. The competitive forces operating in our field research areas encourage institutions to copy the models of successful pathbreakers with only minor adaptations. So in Bangladesh we found that competition was basically amongst solidarity group approaches (BRAC, TRDEP, RDRS, and so on) that copied the Grameen approach. Similarly, in Indonesia institutions compete with variations of the individual model: group approaches remain only local experiments operating in small areas. The initial success of an institution with a particular model encourages national competitors to focus on 'copying' rather than continuing with innovative experiments. Convergence on a model that is working well, rather than investment in innovation, is the *modus operandi* of market forces. *A priori*, we can see no reasons why low-income households in Bangladesh should work best with group schemes while those in Indonesia should work best with individual schemes. The main factor explaining these quite different situations is simply the nature of the initial 'breakthrough' in organisational technology in each country.

Table 7.4 Comparative features of solidarity group, co-operative group and individual approaches

Feature	Solidarity group		Co-operative group	Individual
	Grameen approach	ACCION approach		
Structure	Small groups (4–8) within larger groups (20–40)	Groups of 5–10	Large groups (50–200+)	Individuals
Members	Socio-economically very homogeneous – usually below or around poverty line	Few wealthy people, but quite heterogeneous	Heterogeneous – various income levels	Various
Employee–borrower relationships	Employee works for lender	Employee works for lender	Employee works for co-operative group	Employee works for lender
Complexity of management	Complex	Complex	Complex	Simple
Borrower transaction costs	High, as meetings are weekly and groups are large	Variable, but generally lower than Grameen approach as meetings less frequent	Moderate	Low
Borrower interest charges	Low to moderate	Moderate	Moderate	High
Savings focus	Low	Low to moderate	High	Moderate to high
Responsibility for repayment	Individual, small group and centre	Individual and group	Individual and co-operative	Individual
Incentives for repayment	Peer pressure, loss of future loans	Peer pressure, loss of future loans	Peer pressure, loss of future loans, quasi-collateral	Other

3 Each of these models can, when carefully designed and skilfully managed, create incentive structures for borrowers that foster repayment. In all successful case-study institutions senior management placed a high priority on the allocation of their personal time during the development

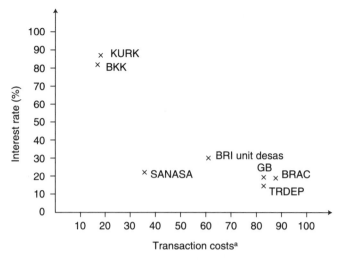

Figure 7.1 Borrower costs: interest charges v. transaction costs
Note: [a] Estimated hours per annum needed to acquire and service a loan for 12 months

phase to the identification of incentive mechanisms. (The specific combinations of incentives used are discussed in later paragraphs of this section and in Chapter 3.)

4 The fundamental similarity between the three models (when effectively implemented) is that, in various contexts, they produce combinations of financial charges and transaction costs that borrowers (and savers) find more attractive than those provided by other intermediaries. However, while the package of 'costs' to the borrower is kept attractively low, the ways in which successful institutions distribute their 'costs' varies enormously. At one extreme are BKK and KURK with high interest rates and low transaction costs; at the other are the Grameen Bank and BRAC with relatively low interest rates and heavy transaction costs (Figure 7.1). The financial market for low-income groups still awaits the breakthrough that would combine low interest rates with low transaction costs!

Solidarity group approaches

The vast majority of new schemes and institutions offering financial services to poor people in the last fifteen years have adopted the solidarity group approach (see Berenback and Guzman 1994 for a review). This approach has been popularised by the Grameen Bank and, within our sample, it was the basic model from which BRAC's RDP, TRDEP, MMF, BancoSol and KREP's Juhudi scheme had been developed.

Central to this approach is the formation of self-selected groups of borrowers (usually between four and eight, although the Grameen Bank recommends five) who take on responsibility for the loans of all group members.[9] In the Grameen variant, several groups come together to form a centre (from twenty to seventy members in our case-studies, but the Grameen Bank recommends thirty) which provides a second level of collective liability and the meetings of which are the main focus for activity. Classically, solidarity group schemes are associated with all of the regular features of mobile banking: frequent meetings, close to workplace, open procedures, and frequent small repayments. In the Grameen Bank approach such features are usually mandatory whereas in the ACCION approach local variations and member preferences are allowed to influence operations. Indeed, for BancoSol some successful groups exist only on paper and members meet bilaterally and not all at the same time.

From a lender perspective solidarity schemes have two particular advantages: (a) responsibility for supervising loans and ensuring repayment is largely delegated to borrowers, reducing risk and the administrative costs that direct supervision would entail; and (b) they aggregate clients so that the unit costs of lending and borrowing are greatly reduced. The Grameen Bank creates centres of thirty members, but KREP has expanded this to fifty and reports that this has not led to any loss of quality in group processes. Solidarity schemes are managerially demanding, however, during the stage of group formation and initial establishment. At this stage they require skilful field operatives who can provide training and guidance, but who do not overstep their role and select group members or make groups dependent on them. The Malawi Mudzi Fund (Vol. 2, Chapter 16) failed to appreciate this and, as a consequence, many of the groups formed in its first year of operations fell apart as borrowers looked to MMF staff, rather than themselves, to deal with repayment problems.

In theory, solidarity groups contribute to high levels of repayment by *supportive* actions (screening out bad proposals, assisting group members with cash-flow problems, providing free labour) and *social pressure* (persuading colleagues to make repayment of loans their top priority). In practice, very little is known about intra-group processes and the relative significance of positive (that is, supportive) and negative (punitive) actions in contributing to repayment is unclear. Our research pointed to the complexity of such processes and the need for further work that focuses exclusively on this issue. In Bolivia, the data on a sample of BancoSol borrowers refuted the *a priori* argument that the economic homogeneity of group members correlates positively with repayment performance (Vol. 2, Chapter 10). Indeed, it indicated that in some contexts non-poor members would support and assist poorer members with repayment problems rather than seeking to exploit such situations. By contrast, in Bangladesh (Montgomery 1995) there is a growing body of evidence that the positive side of solidarity group processes may have been exaggerated and that the negative side, sanctions and threats, may play a significant role in maintaining repayment rates amongst poor borrowers. In such cases the notion of financial discipline takes on a distinctly disciplinarian focus.

Higher levels of repayment by female groups compared with male groups have been documented in Bangladesh (Hossain 1988), Malawi (Vol. 2, Chapter 16) and Malaysia (Gibbons and Kasim 1990). The reasons for this are complex but include the types of activities that female borrowers finance (low return, but low risk), the lesser geographical mobility of women and the value placed upon access to credit by women who usually have fewer (if any) alternative sources. Whatever the variables explaining such results, many institutions have been keen to lend to women to improve their financial viability and because loans to women are generally classified not only as contributing to gender equality but as automatically going to 'the poor' (see, for example, Otero 1994: 98). Unfortunately, the assumption that all loans to women are used in enterprises controlled by women has proved false (Goetz and Gupta 1994), and financial intermediaries that prioritise female empowerment will need to monitor the degree to which their activities are indirectly providing loans to men while holding female household members responsible for repayment (ibid.).

Co-operative groups

The disillusionment surrounding the performance of rural co-operatives (UNRISD 1975; Lele 1981) during the 1960s and 1970s has recently begun to lift and there has been a resurgence of interest in the role that savings and loans co-operatives and credit unions might play in development (Huppi and Feder 1990; Hussi et al. 1993; Magill 1994). The case-study of the SANASA movement in Sri Lanka (Vol. 2, Chapter 13) demonstrates the capacity of co-operative groups to accumulate savings and make loans to rural people, a high proportion of whom are poor, and to achieve high repayment rates, provided that certain conditions are met. Prime amongst these conditions is that the members of primary co-operative societies must be genuinely involved in the management of their societies and must have the technical capacities to manage and oversee the management of their organisations.[10] This includes a knowledge of rules and procedures, book-keeping skills, the operation of meetings and the ability of the membership to ensure the accountability of leaders. Equally, there is considerable evidence that co-operatives are unlikely to prosper if they are used as a delivery device for subsidised loans and inputs. While government over-sight of co-operatives is desirable (in terms of externally auditing accounts to identify misappropriations or financial imprudence), attempts to control their operations, as has been common in Africa (Hussi et al. 1993) and Sri Lanka, are likely to undermine institutional development.

The autonomy commonly associated with effective co-operative management is a double-edged sword, however, and can lead co-operatives to avoid the recruitment of poor members. While Grameen Bank-type groups seek to be 'exclusive' (that is, to have only poor members) and the ACCION approach emphasises memberships in which there is a concentration on low-income households, co-operative groups are, by co-operative principle, open-membership. Commonly, in thrift and credit co-operatives and credit unions such an 'inclusive' approach leads to organisations being orientated almost entirely to middle-income groups. This is clearly the case in Malawi, Bangladesh and Indonesia where credit unions and co-operatives focus on the salaried and prosperous traders and businessmen.

Two main reasons can be identified for such a bias: co-operative procedures and social relations. A common feature of financial co-operatives and credit unions is that members must purchase a share in the organisation, must deposit a specified proportion (often 10–25 per cent) of the loan they wish to borrow in a savings account and must have two (or more) existing members of the organisation guarantee the repayment of their loan. Such quasi-collateral procedures help to ensure high repayment rates and facilitate the access of co-operatives to funds from higher tiers of their movements and from banks on a joint liability basis. However, they have an inherent 'anti-poor' bias because low-income households are commonly unable to raise the funds to purchase a share; if they do purchase a share, then they are often unable to make sufficient savings to borrow a 'normal' sized loan; and, if they manage to meet the savings requirement, they are unable to find guarantors as other members doubt the repayment capacity of poor people. Beyond these procedural barriers are the social barriers that exclude the poor and the disadvantaged. These are complex and location-specific but are based upon social class, ethnicity, religion, kinship and gender. Such obstacles are not insurmountable, however, and procedural changes allied to progressive leadership can, in some contexts, open up co-operatives to poorer people, as our Sri Lankan case-study (Vol. 2, Chapter 13) illustrates.

For decades thrift and credit co-operative societies in that country were basically clubs for middle- and upper-income male Sinhalese in the more prosperous rural areas. However, the 'reawakening' of the movement in 1978 not only expanded the membership, but also broadened it in terms of the socio-economic position of members, gender, age and ethnicity. This has been achieved by a committed leadership promoting the message that co-operative ideology (as well as religious belief and notions of social justice) means that poorer people and women should have access to primary society services and constantly emphasising that the 'best' societies serve the needs of all the major groups in a village. Allied to this are a set of relatively simple procedural changes that permit poorer households to gain membership and offer them services that they find attractive. These include permitting prospective members to purchase their share by instalments over twelve to twenty-four months, rather than with a one-off payment; introducing very small loans for which guarantors are not required; and tapering interest rates so that primary societies recoup the additional costs of micro-lending. While the bulk of co-operative management activity occurs at the primary level, it has been the district- and national-level structures that have promoted this social reorientation of the movement (along with the raising of technical capacities) through its member education programmes. The Asian Council of Credit Unions (ACCU) has recently initiated a project to encourage its members to extend their services to poorer people, using SANASA as an example, but in other socio-economic contexts this may prove difficult.

Individual approaches

Uniquely, within the countries researched in this study, financial intermediaries in Indonesia have concentrated on making loans and taking savings from individuals. This has led to programmes that charge relatively high interest rates but have relatively low transaction costs, in terms of borrower time commitments. The absence of peer pressure and joint liability arrangements by these organisations has not impaired their loan recovery performance and has permitted staff to focus their efforts on financial intermediation rather than social intermediation (namely, group mobilisation and group education). The Indonesian institutions provide individuals with positive incentives to repay, in terms of repeat loan eligibility based on repayment performance (as is common in many of our case-studies) and cash rebates and refunds for on-time completion of repayments (an innovation which has been very effective, see Vol. 2, Chapter 11). They have not focused exclusively on 'carrots' for borrower performance, however, as they also operate a set of disincentives to default. These include collateral, in the case of BRI unit desas, intense bank staff supervision (as field staff pay is partly determined by repayment performance) and, in the case of BKK and KURK, a character reference on each borrower from the *kepala desa* (village headman). The precise contribution that the *kepala desa* makes to effective screening and pressures to repay is difficult to determine, but, given his influence over many aspects of village life, borrowers who default could well anticipate that their loan is part of a 'tied transaction' in which default will negatively impact on other areas – such as access to state services, adjudication on land disputes and role in village organisations. The dependence of this mechanism on the political economy of local administration in Indonesia means that it is probably not transferable to other contexts.

While the Indonesian emphasis has been on developing sustainable rural financial services, with the assumption that these will contribute to poverty reduction, recent work on direct poverty-alleviation through microfinancial services in Bangladesh suggests that for the poorest individual approaches, emphasising savings, may be required (International Development Support Services 1994). According to this analysis self-exclusion and social exclusion keep the poorest out of group-based schemes and thus individualised approaches will be more likely to meet the needs of the very poor (see Chapter 5).

MANAGING THE ORGANISATION

The enormous variations between the organisations discussed in this volume mean that any notion of an optimal model for the management of poverty-focused financial intermediaries is impracticable. Such organisations evolve at specific times in specific contexts and have very different managerial approaches and styles. Nevertheless, it is possible to propose a number of generalisations about issues which the leaders, senior managers and advisers of such organisations will have to deal with successfully if they are to be effective and mature to a stage of mass outreach.

Most obvious is the clear evidence that quite different emphases in managerial priorities, tasks and styles are required at different periods of the organisation's development. Our findings provide support for Edgcomb and Cawley's (1994) proposals that the evolution of financial institutions can be conceptualised in terms of three main stages – development, sustainability and expansion.[11] In the first phase the key task for leaders and managers is to mount and closely monitor an experimental project that seeks to meet the financial needs of poor people and improve their living standards. As we have argued elsewhere (Hulme 1991a and 1993b) the relative success of models of financial intermediation in other localities provides a set of initial designs for experimentation. Such models cannot be directly replicated but can serve as a starting point. The experimental phase has a high likelihood of failure: even when it is successful it is likely to take several years and managers must resist any pressures or inducements to move beyond a pilot project scale until they document the effectiveness of their programme. The way in which coverage targets were set for the Malawi Mudzi Fund (Vol. 2, Chapter 16) before it was known whether or not the Grameen Bank model was appropriate in that country, provides clear evidence of the inability of multilateral donors (in that case, IFAD and the World Bank) to appreciate and utilise the simple analytical frameworks available.

The second phase, probably most accurately perceived as a focus on efficiency rather than sustainability (as this is likely to be at least ten years away in the most successful cases), involves a focus on the establishment of structures and procedures that permit a successful pilot project to be gradually expanded while unit costs of operations are brought down. This usually entails the organisation becoming two-tier (head office and branches), detailed analyses of accounts, increases in the ratios of borrowers and savers to staff, the standardisation of information and procedures and the creation of an internal training capacity. At this stage the services of professional specialists are required in financial management, management information systems, operational analysis and human resource development.

The 'final' stage expansion occurs when the organisation is both relatively effective and efficient in its operations and has a capacity to raise finance, train staff and establish new branches on a large scale. Key managerial tasks at this time include the careful management of finance, regular monitoring of costs and performance to ensure that expansion does not lead to significant loss of quality, targets for the reduction of dependence on subsidies and the establishment of some form of research and development capacity to ensure that existing services are consistent with the needs of borrowers and savers and that 'new products', to meet new or changing needs, are developed. Commonly the expansion phase involves fundamental changes in organisational culture to ensure that large numbers of staff are meeting performance standards. For our Sri Lankan case-study, SANASA, this has meant a shift from relying on a largely voluntary workforce at the local level to a professional field staff. In the case of BRAC it has been associated with the development of a 'corporate culture' (Vol. 2, Chapter 12) with field managers pursuing centrally determined targets. BancoSol, perhaps demonstrating a path that will become more common, started life as an NGO but was transformed into a company for its expansion phase.[12]

Progressing through these phases entails overcoming many challenges and, not surprisingly, reaching organisational maturity is often associated with charismatic leaders and strong personalities. While gifted leadership can guide an organisation to the mature phase it does mean that managerial succession may become a problem, as was evident in several of our case-studies. Despite serious attempts in SANASA, BRAC and the Grameen Bank to develop the 'next generation' of leaders, the strong characters heading these organisations are all very heavily involved in controlling activities and have levels of personal authority and legitimacy that place their deputies in their shadows. At the outset of our research we felt that the succession of problems facing case-study organisations were no greater than those that confront similarly sized businesses in the private sector: by the conclusion, however, we were less sanguine and viewed the planning of leadership succession as an essential but neglected activity in several organisations. This is not an easy issue for donor agencies to tackle, but one of their comparative advantages in the field of institution-building may be prodding mature financial institutions into paying greater attention to succession. Succession itself requires not merely having a choice of skilled managers who could take over the leadership, but also ensuring that they

Table 7.5 Techniques for developing and promoting an organisational myth

---

1 Computation and presentation of data
- Define profitability in a different way than is the accounting standard.
- Adopt a definition for defaults that keeps them as outstanding loans for several years.
- Present cumulative figures for lending, saving, client numbers, and so on, so that outreach is seen to be vast.
- Exclude areas of low repayment from the computation of overall repayment rates, because these are emergency or crisis areas.
- Present cameo reports of very successful clients whenever possible.

2 Accountability
- Operate under domestic accountability regimes which are undemanding, such as charitable status.

3 Public relations
- Develop a public relations capacity: videos, publications, hire English-speaking staff.
- Locate uncritical chroniclers to write histories of the organisation and use these accounts for the media.
- Identify symbols to give the organisation a strong identity: flags, roadside signs, and so on.

---

have the personal networks – with politicians, bureaucrats, businessmen and donors – that are essential for management at such a level.

A common feature of mature and well-performing organisations was the development of an 'organisational myth', usually by their leaders. Such 'myths' transmit the idea that the organisation is, and has been for many years, performing at exceptionally high levels. Management writers have observed this in business organisations, and in the non-profit sector it seems to fulfil the same objectives. Internally, it is a low-cost means of motivating staff who prefer to work for and be identified with 'the best' agency in its field. Externally, such myths make the management of relations with donors and the domestic political environment easier. Such myths are far from being fabrications: rather, they are exaggerations of what has been achieved. The myth is developed and transmitted through a series of techniques: these include the computation and presentation of data on performance in ways that are particularly favourable; national and international briefings by leaders; the chronicling of organisational histories by committed supporters who adopt an uncritical stance; accountability mechanisms that are unlikely to be demanding; and the development of symbols that raise the visibility of the organisation to clients and non-clients (Table 7.5). Promoting the myth is often beneficial for borrowers and savers, in terms of staff morale and accessing external funds and subsidies, but the danger does arise that the organisation's senior management will ultimately become 'self-deceiving', that is, they will not recognise the difference between actual performance and the myth. The Grameen Bank clearly is in danger of reaching such a position with its continuing messages of reaching 'the poorest of the poor' and the notion that most micro-entrepreneurs in Bangladesh have a set of investment options that will permit them steadily to increase profits, income and levels of investment. Myths are also an element of donor strategy, although with markedly less success than the microfinance organisations they support. The public rift between the Grameen Bank and IFAD arose from the Bank's perception that IFAD was presenting itself as the initiator of the Grameen Bank, to promote IFAD's reputation, when in reality it was a generous supplier of finance in the 'sustainability' phase.

Donors, official and non-official, can and often do play an important role in the institutional development of microfinance agencies. All our successful case-study organisations had received external finance and technical assistance – as had our less-successful cases and a large number of donor-supported development finance institutions that have collapsed. At its best, donor support can play a positive role in encouraging prospective 'product champions' in the microfinance field to commit themselves to an initial experiment, as with USAID and KREP; at the second phase of development it can help create the staff capacities and systems that facilitate efficient use of resources; and as maturity occurs it can channel subsidies into new branch creation. Donors can also play a key role in pushing microfinance organisations with weak accountability structures, particularly NGOs, to report in a systematic manner. However, constructive involvement by donors cannot be assumed. Despite their conversion to institutional development, aid agencies have 'pipelines' down which programmed amounts of aid are expected to flow. The contingent nature of institutional development often means that levels of flow planned by the donor are inappropriate for the recipient. There was clear evidence of this with the ADB for TRDEP in Bangladesh: a programme needing limited support to improve its efficiency and undertake limited expansion was swept away by a financier who needed a scheme that was in the full flush of maturity.

CONCLUSION

The contingent nature of the internal and external forces that shape high-performing microfinance schemes means that no optimal model of management can be identified. However, it is possible to identify a number of tentative lessons that the managers and advisers of such organisations should bear in mind. Most clear is the fact that quite different managerial emphases are required at different stages. Programme initiators are, in essence, operating experiments which they must closely monitor and redesign. Once programmes are effective, the senior managers must focus on creating systems that can deliver services at lower levels of unit cost and that can be easily transferred. The drive for expansion entails a decentralisation of functions to lower levels and increasing professionalisation and standardisation. Some evidence indicates that a shift to a for-profit structure may be appropriate at this stage.

The main reasons for such a shift, the need to ensure that clients have incentives to repay and save and that staff have incentives to promote on-time repayments and savings mobilisation, form a further lesson. Although at the experimental stage activities may be small enough for charismatic leaders to promote performance, once expansion occurs the incentives structures for clients and staff must be carefully designed. A variety of features discussed in this chapter and Chapter 3 can be utilised. With growth comes the need for standardisation of systems and data and the creation of a management information system. The political environment (Chapter 6) and donors will require increasing attention.

Reaching organisational maturity is likely to take fifteen to twenty-five years, when things go well. The planning of leadership succession is thus an activity that requires consideration while the original leadership feels that the organisation is only beginning to stabilise. Donors can help to encourage the analysis of succession strategies.

Finally, managers need to treat donors with caution. Despite their avowed conversion to an institutional development focus, and the benefits they can bring in finance and enhancing technical capacities, they are often insensitive to the timescales involved in establishing innovative organisations. As the managers of several of our case-study organisations explained to us: never assume that a donor has fully analysed the consequences of its proposed actions.

NOTES

1 The earlier chapters have indicated that there is no single index of performance for poverty-focused financial institutions, and indeed there are trade-offs between aspects of performance such as profitability and poverty-alleviation (Chapter 8). However, all the institutions classified as 'successful' here have achieved considerable outreach, are covering a substantial proportion of their operating costs (and have demonstrated a capacity to win subsidies, if needed), have good repayment rates and have demonstrated a capacity to improve the livelihoods of people below the national poverty line.

2 For examples of the chronicling and propagation of organisational myths, see Lovell (1992) and Fuglesang and Chandler (1986 and 1993).

3 The only other example that we have been able to identify is Bank Daman in Bali, Indonesia.

4 Interestingly, with recent breakthroughs in information technology and telecommunications, the trend in advanced economies is to return 'banking' to the residence or workplace by tele-banking. From a long-term perspective financial services based on customers visiting an office may turn out to be only a brief interval in banking history.

5 Though it must be noted that employment with BRAC has lower security than with the government, where basically entry to the service guarantees a job for life, and less generous pension provision.

6 Interestingly, when TRDEP was expanded, and the conventional processes of the Bangladesh civil service began to operate (for example, personal contacts and seniority), recruitment became much less effective and existing staff became demoralised when they realised promotion would not be performance-based (Vol. 2, Chapter 12).

7 Contexts are likely to be of great significance in determining how important financial incentives are. In Bangladesh, the lack of alternative employment opportunities serves as a strong incentive for field workers to stay with their organisation and, at the least, meet a basic set of performance requirements. In Indonesia there is a greater need to keep conditions attractive, as the rapidly growing economy is generating alternative employment options.

8 Two variants of this model exist. These are the Grameen Bank approach (common in Asia and Africa) and the ACCION approach, most common in Latin America. Table 7.5 identifies the differences between these two variants.

9 While such responsibility can entail joint liability (that is, the group members have a legal obligation to repay any group members' default) the most common form is that of group members being denied access to future loans if any group member defaults.

10 Interestingly, the Bank for Agricultural Co-operatives (BAAC) in Thailand which has been performing very well in recent years (Yaron 1991) has had severe problems with that part of its operations concerned with its vast, government-designed co-operatives. It is now shifting to a 'farmer group' model, that is in essence smaller-scale, member-controlled primary co-operatives (Nattaradol 1995: 16–17).

11 This notion is closely linked to David Korten's (1980) earlier work on institutional development. He identifies the first phase as the pursuit of effectiveness (meeting goals), the second stage as the pursuit of efficiency (meeting the goals while minimising costs) and the third phase as expansion (meeting goals at a low cost on a mass scale).

12 At the time of writing BRAC, KREP and SANASA are negotiating changes in their institutional structure to become private or cooperative banks.

8

GROWTH VERSUS EQUITY?

INTRODUCTION

The great hope held out by the 'new' development finance institutions of the 1980s was that they might kill several birds with one stone: achieve financial self-sufficiency, increase incomes and employment and reduce poverty through one and the same set of design features. Through Chapters 3 to 5 we now have some insight into how well our group of institutions achieved each of these separate objectives, and through the following two chapters we know something of the influence of political and management factors on such achievement. What now has to be established is the extent to which success in one direction prejudiced success in another. Did success in financial terms require a price to be paid in terms of poverty reduction, and if so, what was that price; did it vary as between countries and their politico-economic environments; and can the price be reduced by appropriate sleights of institutional design? These are the questions to be tackled in this chapter.

THE 'IMPACT-POSSIBILITY FRONTIER': EVIDENCE

Let us begin by bringing together three findings from different parts of the argument so far:

1 All the schemes which we consider increased average borrower income (Table 4.1) and, except in the case of Kenya KIE-ISP, moved some individuals across the poverty line (Table 5.1).
2 Both these direct income increases and indirect income increases from employment and influence on other lenders correlated positively with financial performance (Table 3.3).
3 The size of these income increases was *directly* correlated, across schemes, with the income of the beneficiary (Figure 5.3). In particular, the schemes examined had difficulty in reaching the extremely poor (Figure 5.3), raised the incomes of those below the poverty line by less than the incomes of other beneficiaries (Table 4.2), and increased the

Table 8.1 Case-study schemes: income increase, poverty impact and financial performance

	Average increase in borrowers' income (as % of control group) in year prior to survey		*Financial performance (1988–92 average) (%)*	
	All borrowers	*Borrowers below poverty line*	*SDI*	*Arrears rate*
Indonesia: BRI unit desas	544	112	−9	3
Bolivia: BancoSol	270	101	135	1
Indonesia: BKKs/KURKs	216	110	32[a]	2[a]
Bangladesh: TRDEP	138	133	199	0
Bangladesh: Grameen Bank	131	126	142	4
Malawi: SACA	175		398	27
Sri Lanka: PTCCS	157	123	226	4
Bangladesh: BRAC	143	134	199	—
Kenya: KREP Juhudi	133	103	217	9
India: RRBs	202	133	158	42
Kenya: KIE-ISP	125	—	—	21
Malawi: Mudzi Fund	117	101	1,884	43

Sources: Impact on borrowers: Tables 4.2 and 4.3; financial performance: Table 3.3.

Note: [a] BKKs only.

poverty and vulnerability of some poor borrowers (discussion surrounding pp. 115–24).

The data are brought together in Table 8.1. Proposition 1 suggests that the schemes reduced poverty, and proposition 3 that they increased inequality. Proposition 2 suggests that there exist mechanisms (as examined in Chapter 3) for making development finance institutions more sustainable and more poverty-reducing at the same time; in this sense, growth and equity march together. But proposition 3 suggests that it might be possible to focus each of the schemes more directly on the very poor, possibly at some cost in terms of profitability; in this sense, there is potential conflict between the two objectives.

The evidence of Figure 5.3 suggests that *as between* credit-based income-generation programmes, loan impact rose in direct proportion to the level of borrowers' pre-loan incomes; or put otherwise, it was relatively smaller if the borrower was close to or below the poverty line; this is proposition 3 above. The existence of this relationship imposes a limit on the extent to which it is possible to increase impact and reduce poverty simultaneously, and we therefore call it the *impact-possibility frontier.* Before seeking to interpret this relationship, let us see whether it applies within lending programmes as well as between them. Figure 8.1, reproduced for convenience alongside Figure 5.3, suggests that it does. The rectangular–hyperbola relationship of Figure 5.3 repeats itself within each scheme, and shifts north-westward as we move from schemes with bad to schemes with good financial performance: this is relationship 2 above. In other words, an increase in income impact could apparently (subject to reservations about transferability of design features) be secured *either* by lending to a higher income group, or by using some combination of the devices of Chapter 3 to improve financial performance.

What does Figure 8.1 mean? Let us ask first of all why the curves slope upwards. Our explanation goes back to Figure 4.3: the poor cannot afford to take risks, hence they avoid doing so as far as possible. For this reason they accept credit for mainly 'protectional', non-risk-increasing purposes which sustain their existing family routines, in particular the maintenance of consumption standards, rather than 'promotional' projects which will alter those routines, require experimentation and carry serious risks with them. On such projects the rate of return is small; hence the measured impact of our case-study schemes on poorer borrowers is, on average, small. Only the better-off, by contrast, can afford to take some risks, hence only the better-off borrow for promotional purposes such as the purchase of green revolution technology or other capital deepening. Hence only the better-off experience the high returns on capital which go with such 'promotional' uses of loan funds, hence the measured *average* impact of our schemes on them is larger. Needless to say, not every loan to a middle- or higher-income earner is productive: some loan-supported investments fail. But their failures, in the schemes which we have examined, are more than balanced by the successes, with the consequence that measured scheme impact is higher amongst richer than amongst poorer borrowers. This outcome will obviously feed through into borrowers' expectations, and may make it harder to persuade poor people to take the first step on to the credit ladder than to take subsequent ones.

CAN THE IMPACT-POSSIBILITY FRONTIER BE SHIFTED?

The question which we now face is whether it is possible for individual institutions to increase their poverty impact, and if so, what are the costs of doing so? For simplicity, and mindful of the discussion in Chapter 5 of the complexities of defining poverty, we shall interpret 'poverty impact' as the change in the poverty gap (numbers below the poverty line multiplied, for each individual, by the distance that she or he falls below the poverty line).[1] It will be useful, in what follows, to make use of the approximation first presented in Chapter 2 which represents this change in the poverty gap as being equal to the number of individuals whose incomes are affected by the scheme (ΔE) times the average change in their incomes ($w - w'$) times the ratio of poor to non-poor amongst these individuals (P/NP):[2]

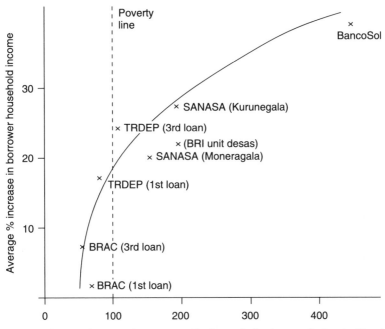

Figure 8.1a The relationship of the average borrower income to average increase in household income since last loan: comparison between schemes
Source: Copy of Figure 5.3.

$$\text{Change in the poverty gap} \; \triangleq \; (P/NP)(w - w')\Delta E \qquad [2.6]$$

Table 8.2 below sets out the estimated magnitude of each of these components for the schemes under review. We now consider their relationship to one another.

In principle, the first of these components of impact, the poor/non-poor beneficiary ratio P/NP, can easily be controlled by the lender. He can avoid what Cornia and Stewart (1993) call E-mistakes (intervention reaching the non-target population) by simply refusing to lend to all borrowers except those who declare assets or income below the poverty line; and of the institutions surveyed in this book, Bangladesh Grameen and BRAC, India Regional Rural Banks (until 1993) and Malawi Mudzi Fund do this. However, as demonstrated by Table 8.3, the institutions which targeted explicitly achieved, according to our survey results, no additional poverty focus (share of lending allocated to individuals below the poverty line) over and above those which did not. If this appearance is correct, it may arise for either of two reasons. First, lenders who are under strong pressure to meet lending targets have no incentive to be rigorous in refusing a promising borrower whether above or below the poverty line, as discussed

183

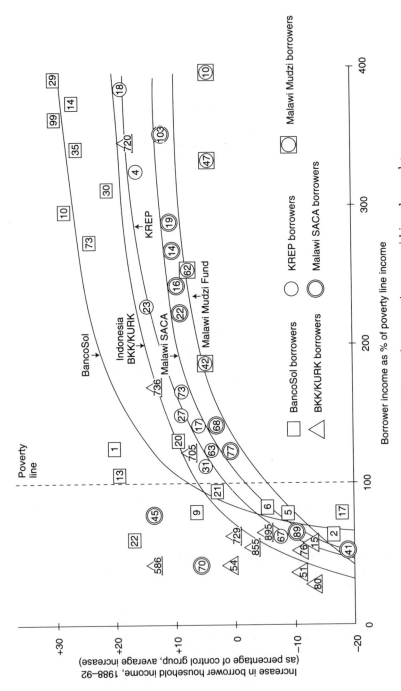

Figure 8.1b Loan impact in relation to borrower income: within-scheme data

Note: Only a few specimen data points, together with the regression line for each organisation, are indicated. Full data arrays are available from the authors on request.

Table 8.2 Twelve lending schemes: decomposition of poverty reduction

(1) Scheme	(2) Explicit targeting?	(3) Measured estimated poverty impact (P/NP) $(w - w')\Delta E$ ($'000 per month)	(4)[a] P/NP = ratio of poor to non-poor borrowers (%)	(5)[a] $w - w' =$ average income impact[b] for those below poverty line ($ per month)	(6) $\Delta E =$ number of beneficiaries (000s)
Indonesia: BRI unit desas	No	756	7	6.0	1,800
Bolivia: BancoSol	No	201	29	24.0	29
Indonesia: BKKs	No	798	38	3.0	700
Indonesia: KURKs	No	65	29	2.1	113
Malawi: SACA	No	384	48	1.9	400
Bangladesh: GB	Yes	2,160	90[a]	2.0	1,200
Bangladesh: BRAC	Yes	968	90[a]	1.8	598
Bangladesh: TRDEP	Yes	1.4	90[a]	16.0	10
Sri Lanka: PTCCSs[a]	No	3,785	52	10.4[d]	700
India: RRBs[a]	Yes[c]	3,648	38	0.8	12,000
Kenya: KREP Juhudi	No	1.6	30	5.3	1
Kenya: KIE-ISP	No	0	0	N/A	2
Malawi: Mudzi Fund	Yes	<1	98	0.4	<1

Sources: Table 4.3 for borrower numbers; Table 4.2 for income impact; Table 5.1 for poor/non-poor ratio

Notes

[a] Data in cols (4) and (5) for sampled schemes only.

[b] 'Average income impact' is defined as income change for borrowers during year following loan minus the income change experienced by a control group of non-borrowers.

[c] Since August 1993, Indian Regional Rural Banks have been authorised to make 40% of their loans to non-poor borrowers.

[d] Kurunegala: contains some non-poor members, so may be an over-estimate.

in the case of Bangladesh (Vol. 2, Chapter 12) and India (Vol. 2, Chapter 14). Second, methods of targeting other than overtly banning the non-poor are available and they may actually be more efficient. The most important of these is a small initial loan size. In all our borrower samples, loan size is positively correlated with the income of the borrower, as shown by the regressions for individual schemes portrayed in Table 8.2. The most obvious reason for this is that only poor people will want to take very small loans. If this is the case, a policy of offering very small loans only ($50 or less) to first-time borrowers may be as effective a means of raising the ratio of poor to non-poor borrowers as overt targeting, and will avoid the

Table 8.3 Seven lending schemes: relationship between loan size and borrower's income[a]

| Scheme | Constant (a) | Regression data | | r² | % of non-poor borrowing less than $100 |
		Regression coefficient (b)	t-statistic for regression coefficient		
Indonesia: KURKs (some data from Indonesia BKKs)	91.8	0.15	2.07*	0.28	7
Bolivia: BancoSol	594.7	0.29	3.83**	0.06	0
India: RRBs	273.4	0.79	2.69**	0.10	12
Malawi: SACA	120.8	0.99	6.78**	0.33	15
Malawi: Mudzi Fund	114.1	0.51	7.50**	0.44	15
Kenya: KREP Juhudi	324.1	0.001[b]	0.78[b]	0.01	0
Pooled data	216.9	0.45	3.94**	0.20	8

Source: Individual country data sets as described in Vol. 2, Chapters 10–16.

Notes

[a] The data in this table are estimates of the regression equation $Y = a + bX$, where Y = loan size and X = borrower's monthly household income, both measured in US$.

[b] Unreliable result – loans given so far in only two amounts.

* Indicates significance at the 1% level.

** Indicates significance at the 5% level.

labour associated with researching the entitlements of loan applicants. In the jargon, loan size acts as a self-targeting device, provided that appropriate incentives continue to exist for bank staff to offer and market loans of appropriately small size. The proviso is crucial – readers will remember the warnings about institutional sclerosis at the end of Chapter 5 – and we return to the issue on pp. 195–7 below.

Even supposing that a high ratio of poor to non-poor is achieved among first-round borrowers, it is only the beginning of the story, as it is possible for the intended beneficiaries to transfer the locus of benefit by giving or selling loan-financed assets to the non-poor. We have encountered cases of this both within families (poor female Grameen Bank beneficiaries acting as a front for the husband's business: Goetz and Gupta 1994) and between families (poor Malawian farmers selling SACA-financed fertiliser to tea and tobacco estates: see Vol. 2, Chapter 16). E-mistakes thus cannot be avoided even if the lending agency is 100 per cent successful in confining loans to recipients below the poverty line. Further down the chain, the strength of impact on the poverty gap depends on the number (E) and size ($w - w'$) of positive income impacts on beneficiaries; they, as discussed in Chapter 4,

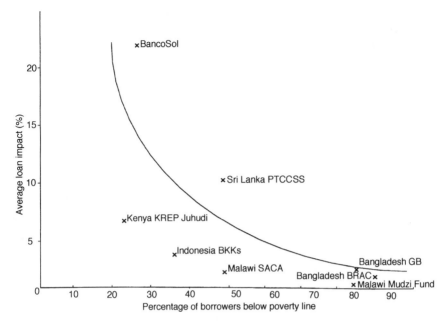

Figure 8.2 Loan impact in relation to percentage of poor borrowers

may be non-borrowers, if the schemes analysed affect the terms of finance offered by other institutions. Table 8.3 sets out the three components of poverty gap impact for each of our twelve schemes.

The components of poverty impact in columns 4, 5 and 6 of the table are graphed against one another in Figure 8.2. The poor/non-poor ratio (P/NP) is negatively correlated with scheme impact ($w - w'$): this is simply another facet of the 'unto them that hath, more shall be given' principle observed in Figure 8.1. However, the poor/non-poor ratio is uncorrelated with number of beneficiaries (E) in respect of those schemes which started off at the same time and can therefore be treated as comparable; a focus on the poor does not appear to inhibit a scheme's growth potential, as demonstrated by BRAC, the Grameen Bank and the Sri Lanka PTCCs.

At any one time, therefore, the lender faces a trade-off between the poverty of the persons reached by loan schemes and average impact per household, apparent in both Figure 8.2 and Table 8.3: in this sense, 'growth' and 'equity' are in conflict in the short run. However, the trade-off can be moved, in two senses. In the first place, schemes which possessed particular design features shown in Chapter 3 to be associated with better financial performance (savings schemes, intensive loan collection and market interest rates) had higher loan impact, *at a given level of average borrower poverty*, than schemes which lacked those attributes. For example, among those schemes shown by Figure 8.2 to target, on average, borrowers just below or just above the poverty line (Indonesia BKKs, Sri Lanka PTCCSs, Bangladesh BRAC, Kenya KREP Juhudi, India RRBs, Malawi Mudzi Fund), the first four had better financial performance, and higher average loan impact, than the last two; hence the 'impact possibility frontiers' for the first four schemes lie outside the impact possibility frontiers for the last two. This better financial performance is correlated with the fact that the first four schemes had savings schemes, intensive loan collection and market interest rates, whereas the last two lacked all of them (except savings facilities in the case of India RRBs). This is formally demonstrated in Table 8.4.

How do the design features of Table 8.4 improve impact at a given level of borrower income? Both high real interest rates and intensive loan collection procedures play a role in screening out good projects from bad: borrowers are far less likely to seek finance for unviable projects if they expect to have to pay the loans back and if the cost of such finance represents a significant proportion of their income. The role of savings mobilisation in improving loan performance is more subtle (World Bank 1990: 68).

First, savings deposits provide the borrowers with a means of protecting themselves against default in the event of misfortune and thus reduce the probability that they will have to abandon the projects in that event; second, as von Pischke (1991: 310) has argued, their existence may also assist the

Table 8.4 Schemes reaching households 'just below the poverty line': loan impact in relation to financial performance

Scheme	Average borrower income ($)	Average income impact (%)	Design features			Real interest rate (%)	Financial performance: overdues (%)
			Savings facilities	Loan collection procedure			
'Well-designed schemes'							
Indonesia: BKK	125	216	Yes	Weekly		60	2
Sri Lanka: PTCCSs	143	157	Yes	Monthly		11	4
Bangladesh: BRAC	107	143	Compulsory	Weekly		23	5
Kenya: KREP	217	133	Compulsory	Weekly		9	9
Sub-group average	148	162	Yes	Weekly		23	5
'Ill-designed schemes'							
India: RRBs	222	115	Yes	Annual		−2	32
Malawi: Mudzi Fund	78	117	No	Weekly			43
Sub-group average	139	116	—	—		Negative	38

Source: Derived from Table 4.3; all other data are from Table 3.3

Note: Average income impact per borrower is measured as income change per borrower in year previous to survey as percentage of income of control group.

188

lender in his screening function; as he puts it, 'local resource mobilisation in the form of deposits increases frontier debt capacity by generating valuable information about financial behaviour, which offers a basis for confidence creation'.

The 'impact possibility' frontier of Figures 8.1 and 8.2 can, therefore, be shifted outwards by actions which enable lenders to screen out good borrowers more effectively from bad: such actions, as we found in Chapters 2 and 3, generally pay for themselves, and if not yet implemented offer the lender the possibility of evading the growth-versus-equality dilemma. It can also be moved outwards by any measures which either lower costs for borrowers (for example, improvements in infrastructure, which reduce transport costs, or the opening of new bank branches in remote areas, which reduce transaction costs) or which raise the average benefit on a loan of given size (for example, the development of agro-industry, or any other measure which removes a demand constraint). Throughout this book we have taken the demand for loan-financed goods and services as being given and as not setting a limit on the rate at which loan-financed activities can be expanded. But such limits frequently arise, often because the attempt to expand such activities at a pre-planned rate leads to a proliferation of unviable projects. A classical case of these problems is IRDP in India (Seabright 1991).

There is a final strategic choice confronting lenders, which can only be observed over a period of time. As time passes, some borrowers in each institution graduate from being poor to being non-poor, and this presents the lender with a second dilemma: whether to traverse the knife-edge a second and third time by making new loans below the poverty line, or whether to play safe the second time round, having established a foothold in the market, by lending at less risk to clients on the safer side of the poverty line. It was suggested at the end of Chapter 5 that some institutions in our sample, having walked the tightrope once, were showing reluctance to repeat the 'institutional experimentation and innovation' which had enabled them to reach the core poor first time round. But lenders who are willing to take the risk of repeatedly soliciting applications from people below the poverty line (for example by opening offices in areas of subsistence agriculture not at present serviced by any institutional lender) can, if successful in screening, increase overall poverty impact in relation to those who do not take that risk by gradually increasing loan size for successful borrowers only. This process cannot however be accomplished by one loan only, because the very poor, by hypothesis, will not be interested in large borrowings which increase risk. It requires a continuous process of seeking out new borrowers below the poverty line and gradually building up their willingness to take risks through a sequence of five to ten loans.

Figure 8.3 gives an illustration of the dynamics at work with reference to

189

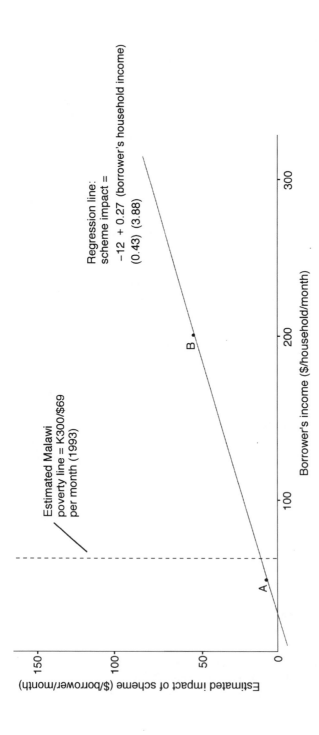

Estimated Malawi
poverty line = K300/$69
per month (1993)

Regression line:
scheme impact =
−12 + 0.27 (borrower's household income)
(0.43) (3.88)

Borrower's income ($/household/month)

Estimated impact of scheme ($/borrower/month)

Assumptions

1 All 'poor' customers have income and loan impact as denoted by A on the graph, all 'non-poor' customers have income and loan impact as represented by B on the graph. Hence overall impact is weighted average of impacts A and B, with the weights being the targeting ratio (P/NP in columns 3 and 8 of the table on p. 191) and 1 minus the targeting ratio respectively.

2 The extent of targeting on the poor under each strategy is as represented in columns 3 and 8 of the table.

3 The number of borrowers is constant as between each strategy, as represented in column 2 of the table, up to and including period 4. In period 5 it diverges as between the two strategies.

Note. Impact per borrower is inferred from borrower income by means of the regression line on the graph. This is the actual relationship estimated for Malawi SACA (see Figure 8.1).

Figure 8.3 (continued)

Outcomes

			Strategy I				Strategy II		
(1) Time period	(2) Number of borrowers (ΔE)	(3) Percentage of poor borrowers	(4) Impact per borrower (w−w')	(5) Poverty impact $P/NP(w-w')\Delta E$	(6) Overall scheme impact $((w-w')\Delta E)$	(7) Percentage of poor borrowers (P/NP)	(8) Impact per borrower (w−w')	(9) Poverty impact	(10) Overall scheme impact
1	1,000	100	4	4,000	4,000	100	4	4,000	4,000
2	2,000	50	25	12,500	25,000	50	25	12,500	25,000
3	3,000	70	15	31,500	45,000	30	31	27,900	93,000
4	4,000	50	25	50,000	100,000	10	38	15,000	152,000
5	Strategy I Strategy II 10,000 5,000	50	25	125,000	250,000	10	38	19,000	190,000

Note: Impact per borrower is inferred from borrower income by means of the regression line on the graph. This is the actual relationship estimated for Malawi SACA (see Figure 8.1).

Figure 8.3 (continued)   Diagrammatic representation

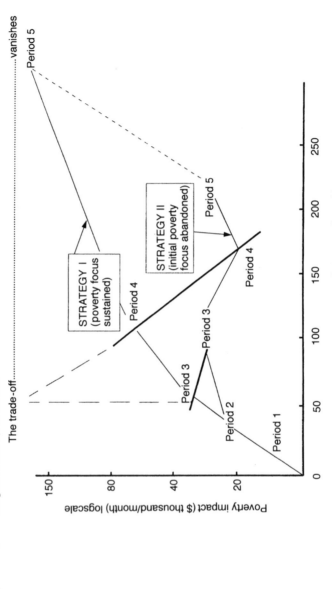

Figure 8.3 The growth–equity choice facing lenders
Source: Data in table on previous page.

Note: Impact per borrower is inferred from borrower income by means of the regression line on the graph. This is the actual relationship estimated for Malawi SACA (see Figure 8.1).

actual borrowers. Imagine two institutions, 1 and 2, which have similar design features, whose customers face similar cost-and-demand conditions, and which therefore have identical impact-possibility frontiers, drawn for simplicity as a straight line on the diagram. We have used, in this diagram, the actual impact-possibility frontier facing SACA borrowers in Malawi, which has the parameters change in income = −12 + 0.27 (borrower's income). Both begin by making all their loans to a group of borrowers below the poverty line at point A on the diagram. A substantial time passes, enough for 50 per cent of borrowers of both institutions to move, through a sequence of loans, above the poverty line, to point B. At this point, let us imagine, the policies of the two institutions diverge. Let us initially suppose that they continue to make the same total number of loans (in the notation we have been using, ΔE is the same between the two institutions). Institution 2, however, attempts to consolidate its financial position by making all new loans 'outside the frontier', that is, to new customers above the poverty line, whereas Institution 1 makes all its new loans to customers below the poverty line. More time passes, during which, once again, half of Institution 1's below-the-poverty-line customers graduate to point B; all other customers, of both institutions, remain where they are. These are not purely hypothetical examples: 'Institutions 1 and 2' correspond closely to the observed behaviour of, respectively, the Bangladesh Rural Advancement Committee (BRAC) and the Central Java Development Bank's BKK schemes between 1988 and 1992. Both have similar design features (intensive loan collection, compulsory savings deposits in lieu of insurance, 'progressive lending') but the BKKs have made very few *new* loans to persons below the poverty line over the period indicated, whereas the overwhelming majority of new BRAC loans continued to be to the poor.[3] What is particularly disturbing is that institutions currently facing the choice between the two strategies, such as Bolivia's BancoSol, continue to be advised by consultants to take the first, less poverty-reducing route.[4]

On these assumptions, Institution 1 achieves greater poverty impact (that is, reduction in the poverty gap) at the cost of lower total loan impact. However, if we assume in period 5 that Institution 1 is able to increase total loan volume more than Institution 2 by gaining access to a larger number of 'good' lending opportunities, then its strategy may, if the increase in loan volume is sufficiently higher, have *both* a greater overall economic impact *and* a greater impact on the poverty gap than Institution 2. The trade-off is now broken; the poverty-focused strategy I, by dint of faster growth of lending, has come to dominate strategy II. Note that the impact-possibility frontier relating loan impact to borrower income is assumed not to move over the entire period from time 1 to time 4; rather, the higher poor/non-poor ratio and faster rate of growth of lending in Institution 1 have acted to counterbalance the lower *average* loan impact in that institution. In this sense, Institution 1 gains a free lunch – greater overall economic impact and greater equity – *without* any shift in the impact-possibility frontier. This represents a third possible way of dodging the growth-versus-equity choice.

As a prelude to a discussion of policy options, let us bring together the threads of the argument so far. We have argued that:

1 both between schemes and within schemes, a positive relationship obtains between borrowers' incomes and the average net benefit which they derive from lending schemes. This relationship – which we call the *impact-possibility frontier* – can be rationalised in terms of the greater reluctance of poorer people to undertake 'promotional' investments which increase the risk to which they are exposed;

2 one strategy that lenders can adopt towards the choice imposed by the existence of the impact-possibility frontier is to try and select a ratio of poor to non-poor beneficiaries (P/NP), so that impact per borrower is thereby predetermined. Even this selection cannot always be done with accuracy, but fixing a small loan size appears to be a more effective way of doing so than refusing loans to the non-poor;

3 an alternative strategy consists of trying to move the impact-possibility frontier in a north-westward direction. On the evidence of our research this can be done by:

(a) measures to improve the efficiency of savings mobilisation or borrower screening as discussed in Chapter 3;

(b) measures which reduce the (transaction and transport) costs of doing business;

(c) political changes which allow greater freedom for interest-rate policy and pursuit of overdue borrowers, as discussed in Chapter 6;

(d) measures which remove demand constraints to which borrowers are subject;

(e) measures which increase the labour-intensity of loan-supported activities and thus motivate borrowers to hire more people from the pool of landless workers per unit of output (World Bank 1990; and Chapter 4).

Measures of type (b) of course lie partly, and measures of type (c) wholly, outside the control of the lending agency;

4 a second alternative strategy consists of taking the impact-possibility frontier as given, but deliberately seeking to build up business amongst poor borrowers. If this strategy is successful both in increasing customer numbers and in screening out the bad borrowers it may over time lead to *both* higher overall impact *and* greater poverty impact, than that achieved by those lenders who seek to play safe by confining their lending, after a time, to borrowers above the poverty line.

WHAT POLICY OPTIONS ARE REALISTIC?

In the light of the above, what 'win–win' options (to borrow the language of environmental economics) are available which both reduce poverty and increase overall economic impact? We shall concentrate here on instruments available to the designers and managers of development finance institutions, leaving all discussion of possible action by central government until the final chapter.

The most obvious option is to move the impact possibility frontier north-westwards by introducing those design features, amongst those identified as effective in Table 8.4, which have not yet been put into practice. These features (market interest rates, intensive loan collection, and availability of savings/insurance) help to screen out the projects that will not work, and in the case of insurance, reduce the level of risk attached to projects with a given pay-off. The contribution of insurance is potentially crucial, since risk is a major reason for the reluctance of the poor to commit themselves to projects with a high expected pay-off and hence for the upward slope of the impact-possibility frontier; but insurance schemes in practice have a chequered record. We have set out in Chapter 3 (pp. 65–9) a set of principles which we believe should inform their design.

On pp. 185–6 above, basing ourselves on the evidence of Table 8.2, we argued that the most effective way of targeting credit on the poor (raising the P/NP ratio) was not to apply an explicit means test, but rather to offer very small loans, as these would only be taken up by the poor, would inflict less risk on them and save the lender the administrative costs of targeting. But very small loans cost more to process per dollar of portfolio than large loans, so what incentives do lending institutions and their staff have to offer them, apart from pure altruism?

The answer, we believe, is a combination of interest rates differentiated by loan type and financial incentives to staff of the lending agency. What makes small loans expensive to offer is that all loans are conventionally priced by institutions at the same interest rate, so that the large loans subsidise the small; or are even *perversely* priced, as in the Indian Regional Rural Banks which are instructed to charge more for large loans than for small. If banks are to find it financially attractive to offer small loans (and hence reach the poor) the obvious step forward is for them to charge for those loans at cost, replacing standard charges for credit with a tapered tariff in which the interest rate is higher the smaller the loan. On the basis of the data in Table 8.5, taken from BancoSol, this may imply that $50 loans have to be charged at half as much again as $500 loans. Will this choke off demand for such loans? Probably not. The data of Table 3.9 suggest that when all transaction costs (financial and non-financial) are taken into account there is substantial headroom above the 'economic' charge for the smallest loans calculated in Table 8.5 before the moneylenders' terms

Table 8.5 BancoSol, Bolivia: summary of possible consequences of introducing staff incentives and 'interest rate taper'[a]

I   Calculation of 'ideal' (cost-plus) interest rate structure

Current system Flat interest rate 4 per cent per month (60 per cent a.p.r.) on all loans	*Loan size category* *(Bs)*[b]	*Proposed system* *Cost per loan*[c] *(Bs per* *100 Bs principal per* *annum)*	*Proposed* *interest rate (%)*
	0–500	65.7	70
	501–1,000	50.2	60
	1,001–5,000	39.9	50
	5,001 and up	31.3	40

II   Comparison of bank's and moneylender's transactions costs under proposed structure

	Cost of a 100 Bs loan for six months, calculated as *annual percentage charge per unit of principal*	
	BancoSol (proposed *system)*	*Moneylender*
Direct financial costs	36.4	48.0
Transaction costs[d]	16.1	3.0
Accessibility costs[e]	15.6	26.0
Total cost of credit	68.1	77.0

III   Estimated poverty and income 'impact possibilities' under existing and proposed interest rate structure

	Current structure	*Proposed structure*
Income impact[f]	1,382	1,275
Poverty impact[g]	201	332

Sources: For BancoSol direct costs, part I of this table; for all other data, Vol. 2, Table 10.15.

Notes
[a] Data for first half 1993 used in all calculations. More detailed calculations are contained in the Appendix.
[b] 4.28 Bolivianos (Bs) = $1 during the data period specified.
[c] Cost per loan is calculated from internal BancoSol data and expressed as a percentage of the total loan value. For detail, see the Appendix to this chapter.
[d] Negotiation, group formation and training.
[e] Travelling time, asset pledge if appropriate, foregone interest on compulsory savings deposit.
[f] Income impact = $(w - w')\Delta E$, where w = average without-loan (control group) income, w' = average with-loan income, ΔE = net change in income opportunities brought about by loan portfolio. For method of calculation, see the Appendix.
[g] Poverty impact = $(P/NP)(w - w')\Delta E$ where w, w' and ΔE are as defined under [f] and (P/NP) = ratio of poor to non-poor beneficiaries.

become competitive, even if no account is taken of the subjective pleasantness of dealing with each of the two institutions.[5]

Tapered interest rates will eliminate cross-subsidisation of small loans by large and get rid of the disincentive which would otherwise apply to the granting of small loans. They can usefully be supplemented by a structure of incentives to bank staff, and possibly to those local government staff involved in loan appraisal, which ties a part of the pay of these staff to the profitability of the lending institution for which they work; this would diffuse the incentive to grant small poverty-focused loans down from the management to the field staff of the lending institution. Incentives to bank staff have been offered for several years by the micro-enterprise credit institutions sponsored by the BPDs (regional development banks) of Indonesia, as an incentive to higher profitability, as described in Vol. 2, Chapter 11. What is new here is the suggestion that the incentive should be harnessed so as to motivate lending institution staff to work explicitly for higher poverty impact.

The third thing which banks can do to push the impact-possibility frontier outwards is to reduce the transactions costs of potential borrowers. By opening new branches (or simply supplying mobile banking services) in regions currently not serviced by any institutional lender, it is possible for financial institutions to cut the costs of transport, lost output, information transmission and 'social intermediation' to poor people, and thereby raise the expected rate of return on (impact of) their projects. As discussed in Chapter 3, the first, and for many the only, requirement of such customers will be savings facilities, the uptake of which helps the lender to screen those who subsequently become borrowers. 'Social intermediation' has been defined by Lynn Bennett (1993: 3) as 'the task of forming sustainable self-help groups and linking them up with formal financial institutions'.

However, as discussed in Chapter 7, the self-help group may or may not be the appropriate vehicle for lending. Depending on local conditions, lending to individuals, as in Indonesia and Thailand, may be more effective. The key point is that in remote rural areas of developing countries, often dominated for centuries by oppressive and patriarchal social structures, the lender needs not only to offer financial services, but to help organise and inform potential clients and overcome their perfectly rational suspicions of involvement with the providers of such services. This can be effectively done in a great variety of environments, as our case-studies show; but if it is not, everything that is designed on behalf of the poor by way of fine-tuning pricing and supervision structures may bear little fruit.

NOTES

1 The 'poverty gap' measure has limitations; in particular it is not sensitive to transfers *between* people below the poverty line, for example between the just-below-the-poverty-line and the destitute (Ravallion, in World Bank 1993b, pp. 14–15, box 1.1).
2 Even if we are careful to measure the specific income impact $(w-w')$ for those below the poverty line only, the formula is still an approximation, since it ignores those who slip back into poverty as a result of taking a loan.
3 Proportion of new BRAC and BKK loans made below the poverty line.

4 Boomgard *et al.* (1992: 7), USAID consultants hired to advise on how BancoSol should manage its expansion into the rural areas, suggested that 'from our projections it is difficult for the [proposed village lending] units to be profitable unless [average] loan size reaches at least $500 or unless interest rates or [village] populations are substantially higher. As loan size reaches $600 and above, units sharply increase in profitability'. This prescription would imply a retreat from the frontier of small loans to the poorest people, who mostly want loans less that $100. But, as the consultants imply, it is highly sensitive to the interest policy adopted. A policy of tapered interest rates charging more for small than for large loans, as proposed on pp. 195–7, would sharply reduce the threshold loan size at which lending became a profitable operation. Even with existing interest rates an accounting procedure which values any physical assets at their salvage value rather than zero allows the new BancoSol village units to break even at an initial average loan size of $160, rising to an average of $300 by year 3 (interview, David Lucock, Jakarta, 17 August 1993).

5 Bolivian customers preferred to deal with 'polite' BancoSol staff rather than a rude and oppressive moneylender (Vol. 2, Chapter 10, note 23). Note also the remark by borrower 35 from the SACA sample, Malawi: 'If you do not give back [the required repayments to a katapila lender] that is the end of you'. See Vol. 2, Chapter 16, for more detail.

APPENDIX: BASIS FOR CALCULATION OF DATA IN TABLE 8.5, PART III

Size categories of loans (Bs)	(1) Number of loans in each size category (ΔE)	Existing system				(6) Number of loans in each size category (ΔE)	Proposed system			
		(2) Benefit per loan per month $(w-w')$	(3) Extent to which loans are targeted on poor (P/NP) (%)	(4) Overall loan impact $(w-w')(\Delta E)$ ($'000/mnth)	(5) Poverty impact (P/NP) $(w-w')_p \Delta E$ ($)		(7) Benefit per loan per month $(w-w')$ $	(8) Extent to which loans are targeted on poor (P/NP) (%)	(9) Overall loan impact $(w-w')(\Delta E)$ ($'000/mnth)	(10) Poverty impact ($)
0–500	7,000	24	29	168	201	3,000	10	41	30	332
500–1,000						9,000	34		306	
1,000–5,000	17,500	55		962		12,500	55		687	
5,000+	4,500	56		252		4,500	56		252	
Total	29,000	—	—	1,382	201	29,000	—	—	1,275	332

Sources:

Number of loans in each size category   Col. 1: Actual figures. Col. 6: Interviews with BancoSol staff (April 1993) on the number of loans they would expect to offer if the interest rate structure given in Table 8.5, part I, were posted, together with incentives to staff to issue loans in proportion to the expected profit per loan.

Benefit per loan per month   Col. 2: Actual figures (Table 10.12). Col. 7: Average borrower's income in each loan size category is inferred from Table 8.2, and the corresponding expected benefit per loan is then read off from Figure 8.1.

Extent to which loans are targeted on poor   Col. 3: Actual figures (Table 10.12). Col. 8: Average borrower's income in each loan size category is inferred from Table 8.2; a poverty line of Bs250/family/month is assumed (Vol. 2, Chapter 10, note 20).

Overall loan impact and poverty impact   Cols. 4, 5, 9, 10: by application of the formula in Cols 4 and 5. $(w-w')_p$ is the average income increase due to the loan for borrowers borrowing less than Bs1,000 and assumed to be below the poverty line, as set out in Cols 2 and 7. The totals at the bottom of each column are reproduced in part III of Table 8.5.

9

CONCLUSIONS

SUMMARY OF ARGUMENT AND RECOMMENDATIONS

We have written this book in order to assess the achievements of micro-enterprise finance institutions from a comparative point of view. Very much of what is written about such institutions, both for good and for evil, focuses on prominent individual institutions and contains no numbers other than those demanded by accountants, so that the wider influences of such schemes on borrower income, employment and technology, on the overall financial market and, above all, on poverty are often assumed rather than measured. In the process, the success of institutions such as the Grameen Bank and BancoSol in 'walking the tightrope' between ineffective targeting and financial failure comes to be seen as something straightforward and inevitable, their many experiments and changes of direction are obscured and the failure of many institutions who have tried to emulate them have been cast into outer darkness. Walking a tightrope is what microfinance remains, and it is right to emphasise the risks run by those who undertake it and to salute the achievements of the institutions, including several described in Volume 2, who have done so successfully. They have achieved something thought by most people, until about ten years ago, to be impossible.

We have tried to analyse the correlates of that success, and at the *financial* level our observations suggest (Chapters 2 and 3) that market-determined interest rates, the availability of savings and insurance facilities, intensive loan collection and incentives for borrowers and agency staff are all positively associated with high performance. However, no one administrative model dominated the others, and both failure and success could be observed within the 'solidarity group', 'co-operative group' and individual lending models. The market is dominated by not-for-profit organisations using techniques of financial, information and personnel management often associated with the private sector. Commercial companies have been almost entirely deterred from the field by high-risk levels (Chapter 7). The degree of government intervention, again, has little correlation with project success, but most successful micro-enterprise lending institutions have needed to work out sophisticated techniques to insulate themselves against pressure by elite interest groups, and indeed against a 'loan approval culture' on the part of international aid donors (Chapter 6).

At the level of *economic and social impact,* we find that all the institutions studied had a positive impact on overall output, both directly and, in some cases, indirectly, by inducing competitive financial institutions such as moneylenders to lower the element of monopoly profit in their interest rate and widen their product-mix. They also had generally positive effects on employment and technology, but those varied according to income group: poorer borrowers, being risk-averse and having fewer opportunities, were disinclined to invest income from a successful project either in new technology or in hiring labour from outside the family, though they frequently increased inputs of labour from, and payments to, persons within the family, and this turned out to be an important channel of poverty reduction (Chapter 4). Also, the worst-off, in particular agricultural labourers, were not well represented even among borrowers from our case-study institutions, and these groups still find it difficult to borrow from any source, a predicament referred to by Osmani (1989) as the 'exclusion problem'. Material poverty, indeed, appears to have declined amongst all but one of the borrower samples we examined, and there is some evidence that those using group organisation reduced the social isolation of women borrowers. But the schemes we examined did not substantially reduce the vulnerability of borrower groups to sudden falls in income and produced few benefits for the poorest or 'core poor' (Chapter 5). We find little evidence that such schemes increase the political leverage of poorer people, and the cases we compare are best treated as financial institutions striving to alleviate material poverty: they are not social movements promoting the empowerment of subordinate classes, as some have mythologised. There is also, at any one point in time, a trade-off both between and within schemes between the rate of poverty reduction and the rate of income increase, but this trade-off can be shifted by measures which raise demand, reduce transactions costs, or increase the degree of financial control possessed by lending organisations (Chapter 8).

Our emphasis on experimentation extends across to our recommendations. Institutions of this type are like plants which need to be adapted to new soil conditions by repeated trials and sometimes by cross-breeding in order to produce optimum results. But on the evidence reported by us, the poverty impact of many microfinance institutions might be increased, without prejudicing their financial viability, if they were to adopt on an experimental basis any of the following features currently lacking from their own institutions:

- mobile banking (bank staff go to the borrower and not vice versa);
- schemes for accepting small savings and offering emergency consumption loans;
- tapered interest rates differentiated according to the administrative cost, and in particular the size, of the loan;
- a linkage between staff pay and the institution's financial performance, and between the interest rate paid by a borrower and his or her repayment performance;
- drought insurance schemes (in the case of agricultural lending programmes), which protect against the most obvious threat to poor farmers' livelihoods in rain-deficient areas, and are exempt from the moral-hazard problems which poison so many schemes of this type.

We also reiterate that in an environment characterised by market failure on a massive scale, microfinance institutions often cannot capture the value of the services they provide to clients and confer to non-clients, and that there is therefore a perfectly respectable case for temporary subsidies from government or other sponsors to compensate for such externalities. Such subsidies should, however, be provided so as to motivate higher performance through institutional development, and we discussed in Chapter 4 how this might be done. They should not be provided for direct interest rate subsidy.

IMPLICATIONS

In all of this we have deliberately skirted around the question of what microfinance contributes to the broader process of economic and social development in poor countries. Is credit, as IFAD claimed in its 1982 annual report, 'the most important single weapon against rural poverty'? Or is it, as claimed by Adams and von Pischke (1992), a mere fifth wheel on the coach, an input of only marginal relevance to the enhancement of poor people's welfare? What is its place in the structure of international capital flows from North to South, and in particular in the national economic adjustment policies implemented across the entire Third World since the beginning of the 1980s?

We incline towards the IFAD view, with some qualifications: credit is potentially a prime weapon against rural (and urban) poverty. Given the infeasibility of effective land reform in most countries (Atkins 1988), if credit is compared with the other potential weapons against rural poverty – social safety nets including supplementary feeding, employment-generation programmes, investment in primary health and education[1] – credit is the only one which places a tangible capital asset in the hands of the poor;[2] and equipment investment is still, in both rich and poor countries, the key to development.[3] Whereas it may be possible to argue that capital investment can be financed from retained profits or other current income in the case of rich people and businesses, it certainly is not possible in the case of the poor. As a specific case consider the capital investment which has probably done as much as any other to raise the standard of living of poor rural people in the Third World – the acquisition of 'green revolution varieties' of wheat, rice, maize and sorghum.

One of us has calculated that the cost of planting just *one hectare* of land to 'green revolution' varieties with the required level of associated fertiliser, weeding labour and pesticide inputs is in Zimbabwe 25 per cent, in Kenya 34 per cent and in Malawi 56 per cent of total annual rural family income (Mosley 1994: table 3). Such sums cannot be paid out of a farmer's back pocket and must therefore be bought with credit; but the credit market is often missing. Second, given the constraints on public expenditure in most poor countries, credit programmes have a potential for cost recovery and consequent extension to new households, beyond that of other poverty reduction strategies. Such are the justifications for treating credit as potentially a powerful anti-poverty instrument, provided, first, that it is properly administered and, second, that profitable projects exist – these caveats create the need for the word 'potentially'. We have devoted most of this book to the question of what 'properly administered' means. But whether the second of these conditions – the existence of profitable projects – can be satisfied is determined by conditions outside the lending institution, and in particular by government policy.

At the beginning of the 1980s the World Bank, and subsequently many other financial agencies and aid donors, reported a deterioration in project quality, which led them away from the conventional capital investment project as their main operational instrument in favour of adjustment loans linked to policy reform (Mosley *et al.* 1995: 12–13). This deterioration in project quality was particularly apparent in the case of the Bank's credit projects: the proportion graded 'unsatisfactory' by the Bank's Operations Evaluation Department rose from 29 per cent in 1978 to 55 per cent in 1990 (World Bank 1993a: 29, para. 3.22). Across all sectors the type of policy reform favoured by the Bank consisted of liberalisation: the easing or removal of controls on foreign and domestic prices, which in the case of financial markets meant the uncapping of interest rates and a clean-up of the portfolios of nationalised banks. The hope was that policy reform of this kind would stimulate a revival of output, and in particular that financial reform would create a financial sector better equipped to mobilise savings, exercise financial discipline and discriminate between good and bad projects.

As reported elsewhere (Mosley *et al.* 1995, esp. table 8.8), the realisation of these hopes has been patchy, varying according to the country and type of policy reform which is considered. So far as the financial sector is concerned, and in particular finance for the poor, it can be said straightaway that the interest rate deregulation which has occurred in many countries has been entirely helpful to the cause of enabling microcredit institutions to achieve outreach and financial sustainability, and within our sample of countries has been of specific benefit to the operation of the BRI unit desas in Indonesia, BancoSol in Bolivia, KREP Juhudi in Kenya, SANASA in Sri Lanka and, at the time of writing, even the Indian Regional Rural Banks (Mudgil and Thorat 1995). Potentially, liberalisation could also be useful in legalising financial incentives to borrowers and to operational staff in countries where these are at present forbidden by official diktat, such as India.

But liberalisation is not enough: reform needs to create and motivate, and not just rationalise and destroy. Liberalisation does not bring institutions of the kind described in this book into being, and some aspects of liberalisation may damage the very features which we have identified as causing such schemes to be viable. To give two specific examples: 'structural adjustment programmes' of price liberalisation sponsored by the World Bank have induced a cutting back of subsidies on fertilisers and other agricultural inputs in India and Malawi which has radically reduced the return on investment in green revolution technology by small farmers,[4] and they have recommended the *abolition* of the Indian crop insurance scheme rather than its reform into an institution capable of protecting the viability of the Indian Regional Rural Banks.[5] In some of its incarnations the World Bank has appeared to show little awareness of these potential conflicts of interest, recommending in its 1989 *World Development Report* that sick DFIs should be closed or merged with commercial banks rather than restructured.[6] While prescribing the closure of non-profitable institutions is relatively easy and facilitates the achievement of short-term public expenditure targets, the opportunity costs of not pursuing the 'restructure' option may be very high. More-efficient replacement institutions do not suddenly appear in the imperfect markets of developing countries: indeed, we must recognize that '[effective] institutions often take generations to evolve' (Hoff *et al.* 1993: 14). Within our sample, such a short-term focus would have terminated the BRI unit desas and the BKK fifteen years ago, and would have opposed the 'reawakening' of SANASA.

In these senses it is possible to see the prevailing policy pressures within international finance organisations as antithetical to the healthy development of the children of the 'microfinance revolution'. This view has been energetically espoused by some directors of 'new microfinance institutions', notably Muhammad Yunus, the founder-manager of the Grameen Bank of Bangladesh. In an attack on the sincerity of the World Bank's 'new poverty strategy' delivered in a speech at the 1993 World Bank Conference on Overcoming Global Hunger, Yunus said:

The World Bank was not created to end hunger in the world. It was created to help development. To the World Bank development means growth. Single-mindedly it pursues growth to the best of its ability until it is distracted by other issues like hunger, women, health, environment, etc. It adopts the rhetoric of all these issues pretty easily and quickly, but it cannot easily translate that rhetoric into action. In order for the World Bank to take poverty reduction seriously, [we must] go back to the drawing board, to design the [World] Bank from scratch. We shall also have to design a theoretical framework in which poverty reduction will have a central place. Until this restructuring of the World Bank is done, the World Bank may immediately create a window [like IDA] with an exclusive mandate [to reduce poverty]. The new window should formulate their own business practices, rather than follow the existing procedures which are not conducive to poverty reduction efforts. The hall-mark of this window will be that it will not claim to have all the answers. . . . It will have the humility to learn, experiment, and continually seek better answers. . . .

In Bangladesh we run a bank for the poor. We think of the poor differently. We think they are as capable and enterprising as anybody else in the world. Circumstances have just pushed them to the bottom of the heap. They work harder than anybody else. But that's not how conventional bankers look at the poor. To them the poor belong to the class of untouchables. At Grameen, we follow the principle that the borrower knows best, but it is quite different with the World Bank. They give you money. They give you all the ideas, expertise and everything else. Your job is to follow the yellow lines, the green lines, the red lines, read the instructions at every stop, and follow them. The World Bank is eager to assume all the responsibilities. They don't want to leave . . . any responsibility for the borrower, except the responsibility for the failure of the project.[7]

What is being claimed here, of course, is more than the conflict between 'structural adjustment' and 'finance against poverty' previously referred to. Yunus is also asserting the independence of the Grameen Bank from the pressures of international finance capital and the superiority of the 'Grameen Bank' model of poverty reduction over the 'World Bank' model.

The truth is more complex. The Grameen Bank and other microfinance institutions, although insisting on their independence from the international banks, happily recycle, and in many cases are dependent on, the capital of those banks;[8] the World Bank's 'structural adjustment' policy recommendations, as discussed earlier, both support and undermine microfinance institutions;[9] and the microfinance institutions themselves, as shown in Chapters 5 and 8, both relieve and create poverty, the latter in the sense of locking some borrowers who are both very poor and very unlucky into a deepening spiral of debt and dependency at the same time as they release others. On balance our analysis suggests that they are definitely a Good

Thing and relieve a great deal more poverty than they create, but the tendency of both micro- and macro-finance to create what Gunnar Myrdal (1967) called both 'spread' and 'backwash' effects is a matter which should be exposed rather than hidden even by the rhetoric of the most saintly.

Our argument, then, is that the relationship we have described as the 'impact-possibility curve' holds at a level beyond those previously discussed. In Chapter 5 we showed that it obtains between microfinance institutions: those which lend to established entrepreneurs (for example, BRI unit desas) achieve higher impact per loan than those which lend to the poor (such as the Grameen Bank and SANASA). In Chapter 8 we showed that it obtains also *within* microfinance institutions: all our sample institutions achieved higher average loan impact lending to their richer than to their poorer customers. What we can now add is that this trade-off also exists at a third level, namely between the World Bank (and other lenders) and their own clients, including the microfinance institutions here examined: at a given point in time they can either go for growth and put their resources into underpinning the success of established and rapidly growing institutions, or go for poverty impact, possibly through a 'new window', and put their resources into poverty-focused operations with a higher risk of failure and a lower expected return. All three trade-offs can be moved in the long term, by improvements in infrastructure and other reductions in transactions costs, but each of them represents a real choice in the short term. And at all three levels there is an issue of style as well as substance: the lender, whichever choice he makes, can either 'follow the principle that the borrower knows best' or apply conditionality and argue that any loan failure is the result of 'policy mistakes' on the part of the borrower.[10]

What has now been established beyond all doubt, however, is that the option of lending at the bottom end of the capital market exists, and is not a financial black hole, if design is correctly done and the accompanying policy environment is not actively adverse.[11] Contrary to the conventional wisdom of ten years ago, it is possible to establish lending institutions which, given the choice between poverty impact and growth, choose poverty impact and are none the less financially viable: the tightrope can be crossed. It is a privilege to pay tribute to those who through a process of 'learning, experimenting, and continually seeking better answers' have created the first wave of financial institutions that have crossed this tightrope. We express our hope that this first wave will spread successfully into areas too poor to have yet received its benefits and offer our encouragement to the next generation of innovators who are already striving for a second wave – financial institutions that can assist not only the poor but the poorest.

NOTES

1 Copestake (1995) provides a valuable comparison of the available alternative poverty-reduction strategies in relation to India.

2 Placing control over water resources in the hands of the poor is a further possibility. However, this strategy is dependent on the provision of credit (Wood and Palmer-Jones 1991).

3 De Long and Summers (1991: 445) suggest that 'over 1960–85 each extra per cent of GDP invested in equipment is associated with an increase in GDP growth of one-third of a percentage point per year. This is a much stronger association than that found between growth and any of the other components of investment.'

4 For details of the Malawi case, see the chapter by Harrigan in Mosley *et al.* (1995: II, ch. 15).

5 For further details, see Vol. 2, Chapter 14. The current crop insurance scheme is described by the World Bank (1989b) as 'neither effective nor viable'.

6 This report also treated the solidarity-group model with condescension as 'not capable of wide replication' (World Bank 1989a: 106; and Chapter 8).

7 Excerpts from speech 'Hunger, Poverty and the World Bank' to World Bank Conference on Overcoming Global Hunger, Washington, D.C., 29 November –1 December 1993.

8 In the case of the Grameen Bank, a donor consortium; in the case of the Indonesia BRI unit desas, the World Bank; in the case of BancoSol, a consortium of Bolivian and international banks including the Inter-American Investment Corporation.

9 It is not only the World Bank's policy-based operations whose effect cuts in two different directions, but its project operations. These are advised, on the one hand, by highly enlightened staff mindful of the need for building up savings capacity, for working out a proper repayment technology, and for providing proper borrower and staff incentives, but at the same time by loan officers and regional vice-presidents so keen to move money that disbursement takes priority over effective institution-building as in the case of the Janasaviya Trust Fund (see Chapter 7).

10 Some observers would regard the claim that 'at Grameen, we follow the principle that the borrower knows best' as disingenuous. Grameen borrowers are unable to negotiate the period, cost or repayment method of a loan, and the bank's style has been criticised by some as 'top-down'.

11 As illustrated in Chapter 6, 'successful' financial institutions have evolved in what would appear to be quite hopeless environments, most particularly in Bangladesh during the 1980s.

BIBLIOGRAPHY

Adams, Dale and J.D. von Pischke (1992) 'Microenterprise credit programmes: déjà vu', *World Development* **20**,1463–1470.

Adams, D.W., D.H. Graham, and J.D. von Pischke (1984) *Undermining Rural Development with Cheap Credit*, Boulder, Col.: Westview Press.

Ahmed, A.S. and H. Donnan (1994) *Islam, Globalisation and Postmodernity*, London: Routledge.

Akerlof, George (1970) 'The market for "lemons": quality uncertainty and the market mechanism', *Quarterly Journal of Economics* **84** (August), 488–500.

Anderson, Dennis and Farida Khambata (1985) 'Financing small-scale industry and agriculture in developing countries: the merits and limitations of "commercial" policies', *Economic Development and Cultural Change* **33** (January), 349–372.

Atkins, Fiona (1988) 'Land reform: a failure of neoclassical theorization?', *World Development* **16**(8), 935–946.

Bangladesh Institute of Development Studies (BIDS) (1994) *Draft Report on Sustainability of RDP*, Dhaka: BIDS, mimeo.

Bardhan, Pranab (ed.) (1989) *The Economic Theory of Agrarian Institutions*, Oxford: Oxford University Press.

Bell, Clive (1990) 'Interactions between institutional and informal credit agencies in rural India', *World Bank Economic Review*, **4** (September), 297–329.

Bennett, L. (1993) 'Developing sustainable financial systems for the poor: where subsidies can help and where they can hurt', World Bank Asia Technical Department, unpublished paper.

Berenback, Shari and Diego Guzman (1994) 'The solidarity group experience worldwide', in M. Otero and E. Rhyne, *The New World of Microenterprise Finance*, London: Intermediate Technology Publications, ch. 7.

Besley, Timothy, and Ravi Kanbur (1991) 'The principles of targeting', in V. Balasubramaniam and S. Lall (eds), *Current Issues in Development Economics*, London: Macmillan, ch. 5.

Binswanger, Hans and Donald Sillers (1983) 'Risk aversion and credit constraints in farmers' decision making: a reinterpretation', *Journal of Development Studies* **20**, 5–21.

Blair, H. (1984) 'Agricultural credit, political economy and patronage', in D.W. Adams, D.H. Graham and J.D. von Pischke (eds), *Undermining Rural Development with Cheap Credit*, Boulder, Col.: Westview Press, 183–193.

Bolnick, Bruce R. (1988) 'Evaluating loan collection performance: an Indonesian example', *World Development*, **16**, 501–510.

Boomgard, James J. and Kenneth J. Angell (1994) 'Bank Rakyat Indonesia's unit desa system: achievements and replicability', in M. Otero and E. Rhyne (eds), *The New World of Microenterprise Finance*, London: Intermediate Technology Publications, ch. 11.

Boomgard, James J., James Kern, Richard Patten and William Miller (1992) 'A review of the prospects for rural financial institution development in Bolivia', Gemini Technical Report no. 42, Bethesda, Md: Development Alternatives Inc.

Chambers, R. (1983) *Rural Development: Putting the Last First*, London: Longmans.

Chambers, R. (1995) 'Poverty and livelihoods: whose reality counts?', IDS Discussion Paper no. 347, Brighton: Institute of Development Studies.

Chang, H.-J. (1993) 'The political economy of industrial policy in South Korea', *Cambridge Journal of Economics* **14**, 131–157.

Chipeta, C. and M.L.C. Mkandawire (1992) 'The informal financial sector in Malawi', *African Review of Finance, Money, and Banking* **2**.

Clay, E.J., and B. Schaffer (1984) *Room for Manoeuvre: An Exploration of Public Policy in Agriculture and Rural Development*, London: Heinemann.

Conroy, Anne (1993) *The Economics of Smallholder Maize Production in Malawi with Reference to the Market for Hybrid Seed and Fertilizer*, PhD thesis, University of Manchester.

Copestake, James (1994) 'NGO sponsorship of group lending in rural India: context, theory and a case study', Occasional Paper 02/94, Centre for Development Studies, University of Bath.

Copestake, James (1995) 'IRDP revisited', unpublished paper presented to conference on Finance against Poverty, University of Reading, 27–28 March.

Cornia, G.A. and F. Stewart (1993) 'Two errors of targeting', *Journal of International Development* **5**(5), 459–496.

Darling, Malcolm (1924) *The Punjab Peasant in Prosperity and Debt*, Oxford: Oxford University Press.

David, Cristina C. and Richard L. Meyer (1980) 'Measuring the farm-level impact of agricultural loans', in J. Howell (ed.), *Borrowers and Lenders: Rural Financial Markets and Institutions in Developing Countries*, London: Overseas Development Institute, 201–234.

DeLong, B. and L. Summers (1991) 'Equipment investment and economic growth', *Quarterly Journal of Economics* (May), 445–501.

Demery, L. and T. Addison (1992) 'The impact of macroeconomic adjustment on poverty in the presence of wage rigidities', unpublished paper presented at ESRC Development Economics Study Group Annual Conference, Leicester, April.

Department of Agriculture, Malawi (1988) *National Sample Survey of Agriculture*, Zomba: Government Printer.

Desai, B.M. and John W. Mellor (1993) *Institutional Finance for Agricultural Development: An Analytical Survey of Critical Issues*, Washington, D.C.: IFPRI, Food Policy Review 1.

Devereux, Stephen and Henry Pares (1987) *A Manual of Credit and Savings for the Poor of Developing Countries*, Oxford: OXFAM.

Donald, Gordon (1976) *Credit for Small Farmers in Developing Countries*, Boulder, Col.: Westview Press.

Doyal, L. (1983) 'Poverty and disability in the Third World: the crippling effects of underdevelopment', in O. Shirley (ed.), *A Cry for Health: Poverty and Disability in the Third World*, Frome, Som.: Third World Group for Disabled People.

Doyal, L. and I. Gough (1991) *A Theory of Human Need*, London: Macmillan.

Dreze, J. and A. Sen (1989) *Hunger and Public Action*, Oxford: Oxford University Press.

Dreze, J. and A. Sen (1991) 'Public action for social security: foundations and strategy', in E. Ahmed, J. Dreze, J. Hills and A. Sen (eds), *Social Security in Developing Countries*, Oxford: Oxford University Press.

Due, Jean M., R. Kurwijila, C. Aleke-Dondo and K. Kogo (1991) 'Funding small-scale enterprises for African women: case-studies in Kenya, Malawi and Tanzania', *African Development Review* 58–81.

Edgcomb, Elaine L. and James Cawley (1994) 'The process of institutional development: assisting small enterprise institutions to become more effective', in M. Otero and E. Rhyne (eds), *The New World of Microenterprise Finance*, London: Intermediate Technology Publications, ch. 4.

Edwards, Michael and David Hulme (1992) *Making a Difference: NGOs and Development in a Changing World*, London: Earthscan.

Edwards, Michael and David Hulme (1995) *NGO Performance and Accountability: Beyond the Magic Bullet*, London: Earthscan.

Friedmann, J. (1992) *Empowerment: The Politics of Alternative Development*, Oxford: Basil Blackwell.

Fuglesang, A. and D. Chandler (1986) *Participation as Process: What We Can Learn from Grameen Bank*, Oslo: NORAD.

Fuglesang, A. and D. Chandler (1993) *Participation as Process – Process as Growth*, Dhaka: Grameen Trust.

Gibbons, D. (ed.) (1992) *The Grameen Reader*, Dhaka: Grameen Bank.

Gibbons, D.S. and S. Kasim (1990) *Banking on the Rural Poor*, Center for Policy Research, Universiti Sains Malaysia.

Glosser, Amy J. (1994) 'The creation of BancoSol in Bolivia', in M. Otero and E. Rhyne (eds), *The New World of Microenterprise Finance*, London: Intermediate Technology Publications, ch. 12.

Goetz, A.M. and R.S. Gupta (1994) 'Who takes the credit? Gender, power and control over loan use in rural credit programmes in Bangladesh', IDS Working Paper no. 8, Brighton: Institute of Development Studies at the University of Sussex.

Gonzalez-Vega, Claudio and Rodrigo Chavez (1992) 'Indonesia's rural financial markets', unpublished report for the Financial Institutions Development Project, Colombus, Ohio: Ohio State University.

Grameen Bank (1992) *The Annual Report 1991*, Dhaka: Grameen Bank.

Greeley, M. (1994) 'Measurement of poverty and poverty of measurement', *IDS Bulletin*, 25(2), 50–8.

Hassard, J. (1993) *Sociology and Organisation Theory: Positivism, Paradigms and Postmodernity*, Cambridge: Cambridge University Press.

Hazell, Peter B.R. (1993) 'The appropriate role of agricultural insurance in developing countries', *Journal of International Development* 4(6), 567–582.

Healey, J. and W. Tordoff (1995) *Votes and Budgets: Public Expenditure Management under Different Political Systems*, London: Macmillan.

Heisey, Paul (1993) 'What is a Green Revolution?', Mexico City: Centro International para el Mejoramiento de Maíz y Trigo (CIMMYT), unpublished paper.

Henderson, Dennis and Farida Khambata (1985) 'Financing small-scale industry and agriculture in developing countries: the merits and limitations of "commercial" policies', *Economic Development and Cultural Change* 33, 349–373.

Hoff, Karla and Joseph Stiglitz (1990) 'Imperfect information and rural credit markets: puzzles and policy perspectives', *World Bank Economic Review* 4, 235–251.

Hoff, Karla, Avishay Braverman and Joseph Stiglitz (1993) *The Economics of Rural Organization: Theory, Practice and Policy*, New York: Oxford University Press.

Holt, Sharon (1991) *Women in the BPD and Unit Desa Financial Services Programs: Lessons from Two Impact Studies in Indonesia*, Gemini Technical Report no. 19, Bethesda, Md: Development Alternatives Inc.

Holt, Sharon and Helena Ribe (1991) 'Developing financial institutions for the poor and reducing barriers to access for women', Washington, D.C.: World Bank Discussion Paper no. 117.

Hossain, Mahabub (1984) *Credit for the Rural Poor: The Experience of the Grameen Bank in Bangladesh*, Dhaka: Bangladesh Institute of Development Studies.

Hossain, Mahabub (1988) *Credit for the Alleviation of Rural Poverty: The Grameen Bank in Bangladesh*, Washington, D.C.: IFPRI.

Hulme, David (1991a) 'The international transfer of institutional innovations: replicating the Grameen Bank in other countries', in R. Prendergast and H. Singer (eds), *Development Perspectives for the 1990s*, London: Macmillan, 249–265.

Hulme, David (1991b) 'The Malawi Mudzi Fund: daughter of Grameen', *Journal of International Development* 3(4), 427–432.

Hulme, David (1993) 'Replicating finance programmes in Malawi and Malaysia', *Small Enterprise Development* 4 (October), 4–15.

Hulme, David, N. Sanderatne and E. Cromwell (1994) 'Food subsidy policy and democracy: a comparative study of Sri Lanka and Zambia', *Democratisation* 1 (July), 461–484.

Huppi, Monika and Gershon Feder (1990) 'The role of groups and credit cooperatives in rural lending', *World Bank Research Observer* 5(2), 187–204.

Hussi, P., J. Murphy, O. Lindberg and L. Brenneman (1993) *The Development of Cooperatives and Other Rural Organisations: The Role of the World Bank*, World Bank Technical Paper no. 199, Washington, D.C.: World Bank.

International Development Support Services (IDSS) (1994) *Final Report of Study 1: Alternative Credit Delivery Systems*, Manila: Asian Development Bank.

International Fund for Agricultural Development (IFAD) (1985) *The Role of Special Projects in Reaching the Poor: IFAD's Experience*, IFAD Special Studies Series, Oxford: Tycooly Publishing.

International Labour Organisation (ILO) (1984) *Group-based Savings and Credit for the Rural Poor*, Geneva: International Labour Organisation.

Jodha, N.S. (1988) 'Poverty debate in India: a minority view', *Economic and Political Weekly* (special issue) (November), 2421–2428.

Kanbur, R. (1987) 'Structural adjustment, macroeconomic adjustment and poverty: a methodology for analysis', *World Development* 15, 1515–1526.

Kane, E.J. (1984) 'Political economy of subsidizing agricultural credit in developing countries', in D.W. Adams, D.H. Graham and J.D. von Pischke (eds), *Undermining Rural Development with Cheap Credit*, Boulder, Col.: Westview Press.

Khalily, B. and Richard Meyer (1993) 'Factors influencing the demand for rural deposits in Bangladesh: a test for functional form', *Journal of Developing Areas* 26, 371–382.

Khan, N. and E. Stewart (1992) 'Institution building and development in three women's village organizations: participation, ownership, autonomy', Research and Evaluation Division, Bangladesh Rural Advancement Committee, unpublished paper.

Khandkar, Shahid, B. Khalily and Z. Khan (1993) 'Grameen Bank: what do we know?', Washington, D.C.: World Bank, unpublished paper.

Korten, David (1980) 'Community organisation and rural development: a learning process approach', *Public Administration Review* 40, 480–511.

Krahnen, Jan Pieter and Reinhard H. Schmidt (1995) *Development Finance as*

211

Institution-building: A New Approach to Poverty-oriented Banking, Boulder, Col.: Westview Press.

Lane, Jan-Erik (1993) *The Public Sector: Concepts, Models and Approaches*, London: Sage.

Lele, Uma (1981) 'Cooperatives and the poor: a comparative perspective', *World Development* **9**(1), 55–72.

Lele, Uma and Arthur Goldsmith (1989) 'The development of national research capacity: India's experience with the Rockefeller Foundation and its significance for Africa', *Economic Development and Cultural Change* **37**, 305–343.

Leonard, D. (1991) *African Success: Four Public Managers of Kenyan Rural Development*, Berkeley, Cal.: University of California Press.

Levene, Ross and David Renelt (1992) 'A sensitivity analysis of cross-country growth regressions', *American Economic Review* **79** (September), 942–963.

Lindblom, C.E. (1979) 'Still muddling, not yet through', *Public Administration Review* **39**(6), 517–526.

Lipton, Michael (1988a) *The Poor and the Poorest: Some Interim Findings*, World Bank Occasional Paper no. 25, Washington, D.C.: World Bank.

Lipton, Michael (1988b) 'The place of agricultural research in the development of Sub-Saharan Africa', *World Development* **16**, 1231–1257.

Lipton, Michael and Richard Longhurst (1989) *New Seeds and Poor People*, London: Unwin Hyman.

Lipton, Michael and John Toye (1990) *Does Aid Work in India? A Country Study of the Impact of Official Development Assistance*, London: Routledge.

Lovell, C.H. (1992) *Breaking the Cycle of Poverty: The BRAC Strategy*, West Hartford, Conn.: Kumarian Press.

Mackintosh, M. (1992) 'Introduction', in M. Wuyts, M. Mackintosh and T. Hewitt (eds), *Development Policy and Public Action*, Oxford: Oxford University Press, 1–12.

Magill, John H. (1994) 'Credit unions: a formal-sector alternative for financing micro-enterprise development', in M. Otero and E. Rhyne (eds), *The New World of Microenterprise Finance*, London: Intermediate Technology Publications, ch. 8.

McGregor, J. Allister (1989) 'Towards a better understanding of credit in rural development. The case of Bangladesh: the patron state', *Journal of International Development* **1** (October), 467–486.

Mishra, Pramod (1994) 'The Indian comprehensive crop insurance scheme: an economic analysis', unpublished DPhil thesis, University of Sussex.

Montgomery, Richard (1995) 'Disciplining or protecting the poor? Avoiding the social costs of peer pressure in solidarity group micro-credit schemes', paper presented to conference on Finance against Poverty, University of Reading, 27–28 March.

Montgomery, R.M., D. Bhattacharya and D. Hulme (1994) 'Credit for the poor in Bangladesh', Universities of Manchester and Reading Working Paper on Finance for Low-income Groups, Manchester: Institute for Development Policy and Management.

Moore, Mick (1985) *The State and Peasant Politics in Sri Lanka*, Cambridge: Cambridge University Press.

Moore, Mick (1994) *Institutional Building as a Development Assistance Method: A Review of Literature and Ideas*, a report to SIDA, Brighton: Institute of Development Studies, mimeo.

Mosley, Paul (1987) *Overseas Aid: Its Defence and Reform*, Brighton: Harvester Wheatsheaf.

Mosley, Paul (1994) 'Policy and capital-market obstacles to the African Green

Revolution', in G.A. Cornia and G. Helleiner (eds), *From Adjustment to Development in Africa*, London: Macmillan, Ch. 12.

Mosley, Paul and Rudra Prasad Dahal (1985) 'Credit for the rural poor: a study of two schemes in highland Nepal', *Development Policy Review* 2, 107–119.

Mosley, Paul and Rudra Prasad Dahal (1987) 'Credit for the rural poor: a comparison of policy experiments in Nepal and Bangladesh', *Manchester Papers on Development* 3(2), 45–59.

Mosley, Paul and R. Krishnamurthy (1995) 'Can crop insurance work? The case of India', *Journal of Development Studies* 31 (February), 427–450.

Mosley, P., J. Harrigan and J. Toye (1995) *Aid and Power: The World Bank and Policy-based Lending*, 2nd edn, London: Routledge.

Mudgil, K.K. and Y.S.P. Thorat (1995) 'Restructuring of the Regional Rural Banks', paper presented to conference on Finance against Poverty, University of Reading, 27–28 March.

Myrdal, Gunnar (1967) *Economic Theory and Underdeveloped Regions*, London: Allen & Unwin.

Nattaradol, Pittayapol (1995) 'Lending to small-scale farmers: BAAC's experience', paper presented to conference on Finance against Poverty, University of Reading, 27–28 March.

O'Donnell, G.A. (1975) *Modernization and Bureaucratic Authoritarianism: Studies in South American Politics*, Berkeley, Cal.: Institute of International Studies, University of California.

Osmani, S.R. (1989) 'Limits to the alleviation of poverty through non-farm credit', *Bangladesh Development Studies* 17(4), 1–18.

Osmani, S.R. (1991) 'Social security in South Asia', in E. Ahmad, J. Dreze, J. Hills and A. Sen (eds), *Social Security in Developing Countries*, Oxford: Oxford University Press.

Otero, Maria (1994) 'The evolution of nongovernmental organisations toward financial intermediation', in M. Otero and E. Rhyne (eds), *The New World of Microenterprise Finance*, London: Intermediate Technology Publications, 94–104.

Otero, Maria and Elisabeth Rhyne (eds) (1994) *The New World of Microenterprise Finance*, London: Intermediate Technology Publications.

Panos Institute (1989) *Banking the Unbankable: Bringing Credit to the Poor*, London: Panos Publications.

Patten, Richard H. and Jay Rosengard (1991) *Progress with Profits: The Development of Rural Banking in Indonesia*, San Francisco: International Centre for Economic Growth.

Peters, T.J. and R.H. Waterman (1982) *In Search of Excellence: Lessons from America's Best Run Companies,* New York: Harper & Row.

Pulley, Robert L. (1989) *Making the Poor Creditworthy: A Case Study of the Integrated Rural Development Programme in India*, World Bank Discussion Paper no. 18, Washington, D.C.: World Bank.

Quasem, M.A. (1991) 'Limits to the alleviation of poverty through non-farm credit: a comment', *Bangladesh Development Studies* 19(3), 129–132.

Rahman, H.Z. and M. Hossain (eds) (1992) 'Re-thinking rural poverty: a case for Bangladesh', Analysis of Poverty Trends Project, Dhaka: Bangladesh Institute of Development Studies, draft.

Ravallion, M. (1992) 'Poverty comparisons: a guide to concepts and methods', Living Standards Measurement Study Working Paper no. 88, Washington, D.C.: World Bank.

Remenyi, Joe (1991) *Where Credit is Due: Income-generating Programmes for the Poor in Developing Countries*, London: Intermediate Technology Publications.

Reserve Bank of India (1954) *All-India Credit Survey,* Bombay: Reserve Bank of India.

Rhyne, Elizabeth and Sharon Holt (1994) 'Women in finance and enterprise development', Washington, D.C.: World Bank, unpublished paper.

Robinson, Marguerite (1992) *Rural Financial Intermediation: Lessons from Indonesia,* 3 vols, Cambridge, Mass.: Harvard Institute for International Development.

Robinson, Marguerite (1995) 'Microfinance: the old and new paradigms', paper presented at conference on Finance against Poverty, University of Reading, 27–28 March.

Romer, Paul (1986) 'Increasing returns and economic progress', *Journal of Political Economy* **94**, 1002–1037.

Rothschild, Michael and Joseph Stiglitz (1976) 'Equilibrium in competitive insurance markets: an essay on the economics of imperfect information', *Quarterly Journal of Economics* **86**, 629–649.

Salamon, L. (1993) *The Global Associational Revolution: The Rise of the Third Sector on the World Scene,* Baltimore, Md: Johns Hopkins University, Institute for Policy Studies.

Salloum, Douglas (1993) 'The business of lending to the smallest of the small enterprises', unpublished paper presented to BancoSol Workshop on 'The Commercial Approach to Micro-Credit', 26–28 April, Santa Cruz, Bolivia, Toronto: Calmeadow Foundation.

Sanderatne, N. (1986) 'The political economy of small farmer loan delinquency', *Savings and Development* **10** (October), 343–354.

Schuler, S.R. and S.M. Hashemi (1994) 'Credit programmes, women's empowerment and contraceptive use in rural Bangladesh', *Studies in Family Planning* **25** (April), 65–76.

Seabright, Paul (1991) 'Identifying investment opportunities for the poor: evidence from the livestock market in South India', *Journal of Development Studies* **28**, 53–73.

Sen, A. (1981) *Poverty and Famines,* Oxford: Clarendon Press.

Singh, Inderjit (1990) *The Great Ascent,* Baltimore, Md: Johns Hopkins University Press.

Stiglitz, Joseph and Andrew Weiss (1981) 'Credit rationing in markets with imperfect information', *American Economic Review* **71**, 393–410.

Thillairajah, S. (1994) *Rural Financial Markets in Africa,* Occasional Paper 216, Washington, D.C.: Africa Technical Department.

Townsend, P. (1993) *The International Analysis of Poverty,* London: Harvester-Wheatsheaf.

Toye, J. (1987) *Dilemmas of Development: Reflections on the Counter-revolution in Development Theory and Policy,* Oxford: Basil Blackwell; 2nd edn, 1993.

Udry, Christopher (1990) 'Credit markets in northern Nigeria: credit as insurance in a rural economy', *World Bank Economic Review* **4** (September), 251–271.

United Nations Development Programme (UNDP) (1994) *Human Development Report 1994,* New York: United Nations Development Programme.

United Nations Research Institute for Social Development (UNRISD) (1975) *Rural Cooperatives as Agents of Change: A Research Report and a Debate,* Geneva: UNRISD.

van Koppen, Barbara and Simeen Mahmud (1995) 'Case studies of two BRAC tubewell groups', Dhaka: BRAC, mimeo.

von Pischke, J.D. (1980) 'The political economy of specialised farm credit institutions', in J. Howell (ed.), *Borrowers and Lenders: Rural Financial Markets and Institutions in Developing Countries,* London: Overseas Development Institute.

von Pischke, J.D. (1991) *Finance at the Frontier: Debt Capacity and the Role of Credit in the Private Economy*, Washington, D.C.: Economic Development Institute of the World Bank.

von Pischke, J.D., Dale Adams and Gordon Donald (1983) *Rural Financial Institutions in Developing Countries*, Washington, D.C.: Economic Development Institute of the World Bank.

Wade, R. (1990) *Governing the Market*, Cambridge: Cambridge University Press.

Webster, Leila (1991) 'World Bank lending for small and medium enterprises: fifteen years of experience', *Small Enterprise Development* 2, 1–15.

Weeks, John (1971) 'Uncertainty, risk and wealth and income distribution in peasant agriculture', *Journal of Development Studies* 8, 28–36.

White, S.C. (1991) 'Evaluating the impact of NGOs in rural poverty alleviation', Bangladesh Country Study, ODI Working Paper no. 50, London: Overseas Development Institute.

Wood, G.D. (1994) *Bangladesh: Whose Ideas, Whose Interests?*, Dhaka: University Press.

Wood, G.D. and R. Palmer-Jones (1991) *The Water Sellers: A Cooperative Venture by the Rural Poor*, London: Intermediate Technology Publications.

World Bank (1975) *Agricultural Credit: Sector Policy Paper*, Washington, D.C.: World Bank Agricultural Policies Division.

World Bank (1984) *Agricultural Credit: Sector Policy Paper*, 2nd edn, Washington, D.C.: World Bank.

World Bank (1989a) *World Development Report 1989*, Washington, D.C.: World Bank.

World Bank (1989b) 'Review of Agricultural Credit Review Committee Report, India', Bombay: Reserve Bank of India, unpublished paper.

World Bank (1990) *World Development Report 1990: Poverty*, Washington, D.C.: World Bank.

World Bank (1991) 'The case for a research project on drought insurance', Washington, D.C.: World Bank Agricultural Policies Division, unpublished prospectus.

World Bank (1993a) *A Review of Bank Lending for Agricultural Credit and Rural Finance (1948–1992)*, Report no. 12143, Washington, D.C.: World Bank Operations Evaluation Department.

World Bank (1993b) *Poverty Reduction Handbook*, Washington, D.C.: World Bank.

Yaron, Jacob (1991) *Successful Rural Finance Institutions*, 2 vols, Washington, D.C.: World Bank Agricultural Policies Division.

Yunus, Mohammad (1993) 'Hunger, poverty and the World Bank', speech to World Bank Conference on Overcoming Global Hunger, Washington, D.C., 29 November–1 December.

Zander, R. (1992) 'Financial self-help organization in rural Sri Lanka: responses to political and economic adversity', paper presented at 8th World Congress for Rural Sociology, Pennsylvania State University, 11–16 August.

INDEX

access, by poor borrowers 8, 15
ACCION International, American NGO
    148, 168, 170, 172, 179
Adams, Dale 3
administrative costs of lending institutions
    20, 27, 46–49, 159–164
adverse selection 18, 67
aid, for development 1, 201; *see also* aid
    donors; subsidy
aid donors: relationships with credit
    institutions 153, 175, 177; and gender
    125; 'approval culture' 201; *see also* World
    Bank; USAID: ODA: Asian
    Development Bank; NGOs
Akerlof, George *see* 'lemons model'
altruism 166
Amanah Ikhtiar Malaysia *see* Malaysia
arrears rates 14, 43, 50–54, 59
Asian Development Bank 148–149, 177
authoritarianism 143
autonomy of financial institutions from
    government 143–145, 154

BAAC *see* Bank for Agriculture and
    Agricultural Cooperatives (Thailand)
backwash effects of micro-credit 206
Bali 178
'balloon repayments' 59
BancoSol (Banco Solidario, Bolivia) 9, 13,
    43–46, 50–54, 59, 65, 70, 89, 95, 114,
    121, 147–148, 151, 160–161, 170–171,
    175, 195; *see also* Bolivia
Banda, Hastings Kamuzu 143, 145; *see also*
    Malawi
Bangladesh 91, 109, 113, 125, 143, 155, 167
Bangladesh Rural Advancement Committee
    (BRAC) 9, 13, 50–54, 57, 70, 89,

119–121, 124, 148–149, 151, 153, 160,
    167, 193; *see also* Bangladesh
Bank for Agriculture and Agricultural
    Cooperatives, Thailand (BAAC) 60, 83,
    179
Bank Rakyat Indonesia (BRI) unit desas 9,
    13, 17, 43–46, 50–53, 65, 72, 102–103,
    154, 160–161, 167, 202; *see also*
    KUPEDES; Indonesia
banks: private sector 1, 200; for individual
    banks examined in this book *see under*
    name of bank
Bennett, Lynn xvi, 197
BIMAS 96, 98, 104; *see also* Indonesia
BKK (Badan Kredit Kecamatan, Indonesia)
    17, 37, 43–46, 50–54, 57, 65, 96, 104,
    160–161, 193, 204; *see also* Indonesia
Blair, H. 139–142
Bolivia 59, 91, 144
bonuses: for prompt repayment *see*
    incentives to repay; for bank staff 50–54,
    63–65
Boomgard, James 198
BRAC *see* Bangladesh Rural Advancement
    Committee
'break-even condition' 19; *see also* financial
    sustainability; interest rates
BRI *see* Bank Rakyat Indonesia
bribery 140

Calmeadow Foundation 80
capital deepening 92, 94
capital widening 92
cattle-keeping 119
CGAP (Consultative Group to Assist the
    Poor) *see* World Bank
Chambers, Robert 95, 105, 115, 136
charisma 150; *see also* leadership

217